THE
EVERYTHING®
HARD CIDER
BOOK

All you need to know about making
hard cider at home

Drew Beechum

Adams Media
New York   London   Toronto   Sydney   New Delhi

Adams Media
An Imprint of Simon & Schuster, Inc.
100 Technology Center Drive
Stoughton, MA 02072

An Everything® Series Book.
Everything® and everything.com® are registered trademarks of Simon & Schuster, Inc.

ADAMS MEDIA and colophon are trademarks of Simon and Schuster.

For information about special discounts for bulk purchases, please contact Simon & Schuster Special Sales at 1-866-506-1949 or business@simonandschuster.com.

The Simon & Schuster Speakers Bureau can bring authors to your live event. For more information or to book an event contact the Simon & Schuster Speakers Bureau at 1-866-248-3049 or visit our website at www.simonspeakers.com.

Manufactured in the United States of America

10 2021

Library of Congress Cataloging-in-Publication Data has been applied for.

ISBN 978-1-4405-6618-9
ISBN 978-1-4405-6619-6 (ebook)

Always follow safety and common-sense cooking protocol while using kitchen utensils, operating ovens and stoves, and handling uncooked food. If children are assisting in the preparation of any recipe, they should always be supervised by an adult.

THE
EVERYTHING®
HARD CIDER
BOOK

Dear Reader,

It may seem odd to devote a whole book to the idea of fermented apple and pear juice. You may have even picked up this book with confused wonderment, thinking back to childhood winters with a glass of hot, spicy apple juice. Real cider is something more, something that is simultaneously simple and stupendously complex. Locked inside your friend, the apple, is a whole world that needs your help to blossom. The best part is it's not that hard!

My goal with *The Everything® Hard Cider Book* is to provide you with simple ways to enjoy homemade cider without the need to grow your own orchard of apple trees, hunt out rare varieties, or build complicated equipment (though we'll cover some of that, too!). You can make serious cider even from the juice you find in the grocery store!

From a few simple, well-chosen ingredients and basic equipment you can produce a drink that you're proud to share, and too greedy to want to. If you or someone you know is reducing your gluten intake, cider is naturally gluten free, without packing the alcoholic punch of wine.

I hope this serves as a departure point for you into the world of do-it-yourself fermentation. The same knowledge you gain from making your own cider may also serve you in making other fermented foods—beer, wine, mead, cheese, pickles, and more.

Once you've sampled your cider, I guarantee nothing mass-produced will ever satisfy you in the same way. If you're ready to give it a try, I'm ready to show you what you can do!

Drew Beechum

Welcome to the EVERYTHING® Series!

These handy, accessible books give you all you need to tackle a difficult project, gain a new hobby, comprehend a fascinating topic, prepare for an exam, or even brush up on something you learned back in school but have since forgotten.

You can choose to read an Everything® book from cover to cover or just pick out the information you want from our four useful boxes: e-questions, e-facts, e-alerts, and e-ssentials.

We give you everything you need to know on the subject, but throw in a lot of fun stuff along the way, too.

We now have more than 400 Everything® books in print, spanning such wide-ranging categories as weddings, pregnancy, cooking, music instruction, foreign language, crafts, pets, New Age, and so much more. When you're done reading them all, you can finally say you know Everything®!

QUESTION

Answers to common questions

FACT

Important snippets of information

ALERT

Urgent warnings

ESSENTIAL

Quick handy tips

PUBLISHER Karen Cooper

MANAGING EDITOR, EVERYTHING® SERIES Lisa Laing

COPY CHIEF Casey Ebert

ASSISTANT PRODUCTION EDITOR Alex Guarco

ACQUISITIONS EDITOR Pam Wissman

SENIOR DEVELOPMENT EDITOR Brett Palana-Shanahan

EVERYTHING® SERIES COVER DESIGNER Erin Alexander

Contents

Acknowledgments

I would like to thank the old school John Chapman (Johnny Appleseed) and his modern counterparts in the American cider industry for providing a ton of inspiration while writing this book (mmm . . . cider). The same goes to all those keeping the fermenters roiling at home and keeping the tradition alive.

Cookie the Wonder Dog deserves some credit for her silent vigil at my feet until it was time for bed.

But of course the real acknowledgment goes to Miss Amy, who tolerated many hours of me being here without "being here." Thank you, dear!

Introduction

CIDER IS A BEVERAGE of long world standing that has sadly—in all but the most purist circles—fallen on hard times. Cider was so central and important that laws dictated that American settlers plant apple orchards. But this once-proud tradition faded in the face of a growing population, industry needs, and a shift of palates to beers produced by and for a new wave of immigrants.

Even in the United Kingdom, traditional homeland of hard core cider drinkers, cider has fallen on hard times. Gone are the complex, flavorful products produced by hand by cidermakers closely connected to the orchard where the apples grow. Instead most things labeled as cider are mass-produced sweet alcoholic sodas with a vague thought of things appley.

Put simply, real cider is a traditional form of fruit wine, albeit one made with apples and/or pears (perry). It can be anywhere from desert-dry to dessert-sweet. The carbonation ranges from nonexistent to gushing, like champagne. It may taste clean and simple or challenge your taste buds with acidity and an intense, ancient, and wild character.

So why cider now? Look at American culture over the past sixty years. The 1950s saw the great "blandification" of American tastes. Food became an industrialized commodity with a focus on convenience rather than taste. Periodically, little pockets of rebellion would kick up. The '60s and '70s saw the rise of the American wine industry. In the '80s and '90s, the first craft breweries began from the fevered experiments of homebrewers. As the country hit the turn of the millennium, real cooking became cool again.

The new craft beer and food movements gave rise to an revitalization of the local and traditional. Call it locavorism, if you must, but people have discovered the power of knowing where something is made and who made it. With that, cider is finally seeing its long-predicted renewal as a bright member of the American drinks squad. Serious money and talent is beginning to focus on the apple. Old-school craft brewers are eyeing the field and bring products to market. Farmers are happily following right along since they finally have a market that needs decent and odd apples for a good price.

Another compounding reason for cider's growth is the rise in the interest of low-gluten diets. Low- or no-gluten diets are a response to the increased diagnosis of gluten intolerance like celiac disease. Unfortunately for sufferers, gluten is a combination of two very common proteins, gliadin and glutenin. Together they form gluten, a tough webby mesh that gives things like bread its "chew."

Sadly, this means beer is out if you are gluten intolerant. Sure you can drink wine, but sometimes you want to relax with something bubbly and low-key like beer. You'll notice that cider is being heavily promoted as gluten-free and why not? Cider tastes awesome while gluten-free beer, despite everyone's best efforts, still tastes pretty blah.

No matter the reason you want to explore cider—be it dietary, historical, or just the want for a different taste—there's a way to enjoy and appreciate the gift of the apple tree. It starts in your home. It requires just a few tools, a few ingredients, and a little patience. Put those together and you're on your way to enjoy a great tradition!

CHAPTER 1

A Cider Primer

Cider played an important part in American history, and in many ways it was the country's original drink. Unfortunately, the forces of Prohibition and industrialization conspired to reduce cider from its proud, noble perch to a sad, neglected state. But just as wine and beer enjoyed their own revivals, people who are interested in flavor, tradition, and craft are now rescuing cider.

Cider Apples Versus Culinary Apples

As you read about cider, you'll notice a fair amount of discussion centering on culinary versus cider apples. What does this mean? Culinary apples are the eating or baking apples that you encounter in your supermarket produce section. Think your everyday Red Delicious, Golden Delicious, Fuji, or Granny Smith apples. These apples, even the tart Granny Smith, all contain a high amount of sugar with a restrained bitterness and acid level.

Cider apples used to be the dominant form of apple. The average orchard focused on these mean little hard globes. If you were to grab a traditional cider apple, like a Winesap or a Cox Pippin, and take a bite, you'd be floored by the flood of sharp and bitter flavors.

Instead of a wave of sugary sweetness, the juice is heavily acidic like a Granny Smith. The juice also carries an astringency that, to our modern tastes, rings alarm bells. A good comparison to this level of puckering is the taste of medicine, like aspirin, left on the tongue too long. Ironically, cider apples tend to be as sugar filled, if not more so, than culinary apples; you just can't taste it due to the other sensations.

You may think it strange that for most of history these unpalatable little buggers have been cherished, fostered, and shepherded around the world. The reason should be obvious, given that you are reading a hard cider book! When the juice is extracted and mixed with yeast (naturally occurring or introduced by the cider maker), the previously harsh characters change and begin to meld into a beverage of great character.

Most cider books will now stop and say, "Don't make cider with culinary apples. They can only make bland, insipid, boring cider. Use real cider apples!" This is sound advice; cider apples do make better cider. The problem for most cider makers is the impracticality of procuring enough true cider apples without growing your own. Thankfully, there are a few tricks that you can use to transform bland culinary apple juice into a great-tasting cider.

Cider—Magic Apple Saver

Food spoilage has always been a big problem for humanity. To combat this, mankind developed a number of techniques, including pickling, salting, drying, preserving, and fermenting.

Picture a bag of apples. You store them somewhere cool, maybe your fridge. For a few weeks your apples are just fine—crisp, juicy, sweet. But slowly, imperceptibly at first, the apples lose their crispness. Softness creeps in. The flesh turns mealy. Then faster, brown bruised spots that taste sickly sweet and just a little funky begin to appear. The apple withers and shrinks, the once-taut skin becoming wrinkly and rubbery.

Today, this is a cause for grumbling and a trip to the store to buy some more apples. Back in the day, it could spell disaster for you and your family. Even in the coolness of a proper root cellar, apples will only last for a few months.

The phrase "bottom of the barrel" has multiple origin stories attached to it, one of which relates to the notion that the apples at the bottom of the barrel were the least desirable due to age and bruising from the weight of the apples above.

People turned, as they always do, to the mystical art of fermentation. Why make booze out of something semiedible? You have to remember that fermentation is a natural part of the rotting process. But clever people realized that if they controlled the ferment, they could prevent the ruinous decay and get a bonus buzz out of it. The relaxing hit was a pleasant side effect, and it was a way to preserve calories and nutrition while providing something safe to drink.

While a barrel of apples may last for a few months, a barrel of cider remains consumable for a year. If the cider begins to spoil, you have vinegar, a wonderfully useful substance. Overall, that is a much better fate than a pile of rotten goo.

Think about it this way: Every major alcoholic beverage started life as a foodstuff that needed saving. Barley becomes beer, grapes become wine, corn becomes whiskey, and rice becomes sake.

Making Cider—A General View

To make cider, first you must find a source of apples, preferably cider apple varieties. You then grind (scrat) the apples into a coarse pulp.

The pulp is gathered into loose sieve bags (also known and sold as jelly strainer bags or cheeses). In days of old, the pulp was stacked in layers of straw and wooden platforms. The bags are then placed in a press and allowed to drain and filter through a sieve. As the "free run" juice stops flowing, the press is slowly cranked down until every last drop is extracted. This collected juice is called must. The remaining fruit sludge is referred to as pomace.

ESSENTIAL

It takes about 36 apples to make 1 gallon of apple juice and, after fermentation, cider. This is another reason people loved cider. It takes up much less room!

The juice is placed in a fermenter, typically a bucket. Yeast is introduced, or the cider maker depends on the natural yeast carried in the apples from the orchard, to start fermentation. After a period of fermentation (2 weeks), the now-alcoholic cider is transferred, aged, bottled, and allowed to mature for a month or more before it's ready to drink.

In this book, you'll explore some of the gathering, grinding, and pressing steps, but most of the focus will center on selecting juice, fermentation, bottling, and drinking.

Cider in the United Kingdom

It would be fair to say that no countries on Earth are as closely identified with cider as Great Britain and Ireland. In part, this is because most of the canned and bottled cider found on shelves today are made or distributed by a British (H. P. Bulmer) or Irish (C&C Group) company. These two companies control a majority of the world's cider manufacture.

The first written evidence of cider in the United Kingdom comes from Norfolk, England, in A.D. 1204, as a record of payment. Farms would continue to use cider as payment for workers until the late 1800s, when the British parliament stopped the practice. Everywhere the apple grew, cider became popular. In Britain, the traditional cider lands are the rural counties that make up the West Country and the areas of Kent and East Anglia. In other words, the whole southern coast of England was engaged in growing apples and turning them to drink. The ciders varied regionally based on the types of apples that grew best in the various locales.

Beyond the farm, British pub culture embraced cider. Like the beer of the time, the ciders were served from casks and either pumped into the glass or poured from the barrel directly. The cider was served at cellar temperature, which is around 50°F–55°F; not warm, but definitely not the ice-cold 32°F–38°F preferred by modern lager drinkers.

Cider's current reputation in the United Kingdom is in need of serious rehab. Long gone are the romantic visions of farmers ladling fresh cider from wooden barrels in the barn. Today, cider is something largely produced on the cheap, designed to hug the tax guidelines to pay minimal tax for maximal alcohol.

Hope is rising, though, as people long for a return to authentic, quality cider. The Campaign for Real Ale (CAMRA) is one of the groups leading the way. It is a special and rare treat to walk up to their Real Cider and Perry bar at the annual Great British Beer Festival (and at other festivals) and taste 100 percent artisanal, traditional cider.

Cider in America

When the first Europeans landed in the Americas, they were desperate for a drink. There's a passage in a Pilgrim's diary of the *Mayflower*'s voyage describing how the boat was forced to seek landfall because the beer supplies were running low. But when the Pilgrims hit the shore in 1620, all they found were native species of crab apples. Crab apples are a great spice to add to a cider, but you rarely want to make a fermented beverage wholly from them.

It was a few years later that subsequent waves of immigration finally brought the European apple to Boston. In short order, the first truly American varietals appeared, namely the Roxbury Russet, named for the former town-turned-city of Boston.

Given the rough-and-tumble nature of the American frontier, and the lack of resources available to most colonists, early apple-growing processes revolved around the planting of apple seeds and not grafted apple branches (scions) as are used today. This encouraged a wild flush of genetic diversity, and hundreds of new varieties appeared that were suited to the soils and weather of the Americas. Each subsequent wave of immigration brought new apple varieties and new cider styles to explore.

Just how popular was cider? Just prior to the American Revolution, everyone was drinking cider. It was plentiful, cheap, and more reliable than the local beer. Ironic, since the opposite was true in England. On average, more than 30 gallons were being made per year for each person in the colonies.

FACT

Booze used to play a huge role in American politics with candidates openly offering drinks in exchange for votes. Then as now, image mattered. Today you might see a presidential candidate drinking a tall glass of beer to convince everyone he is the kind of person you'd like to share a beer with. In 1840, William Henry Harrison used hard cider (and a log cabin) to convince voters that he was one of them and not born of a rich Virginia family.

What happened to cider? A few things occurred that, when combined, reduced the popularity and availability of hard cider as America's drink of choice. The first was the titanic population shift from the farm to the city. Take this population movement and factor in waves of beer-loving immigrants (Germans, Austrians, Poles, etc.) and the rise of big breweries that could serve an urban crowd, and it's no wonder that cider began to fall by the wayside. Like in the United Kingdom, the American cider industry couldn't make the transition with the drinkers. Almost everyone who made cider still made it right on their farms for neighbors.

Since reliable sanitation or true pasteurization had yet to be discovered by this time (1840s–1850s), cider had to remain a steadfastly local trade. Shipping cider for any real distance meant a real possibility of a stale or sour glass being poured for a customer more than twenty miles away. In rural times, this was as far as you were likely to ever travel in your life. Like their counterparts in the United Kingdom, cider makers pushed the strength of their alcohol higher and higher with sugar to help their ciders survive the transport. It became a cheap means to get intoxicated.

Prohibition's Effects on Cider

Ultimately, the now supremely boozy reputation of cider put it straight into the firing line of Prohibitionists, who used restricting cider's alcoholic content as an early test for their efforts to ban all alcohol. In fact, it was the temperance movement that transformed the American and Canadian use of the word *cider* to include unfiltered sweet juice in an effort to change drinking habits.

As Prohibition loomed, thousands and thousands of apple trees were destroyed in an attempt to hamper cider making. This was the major death blow for hard cider as a common drink, and it led to the nearly total destruction of the once-startling variety of American apples.

After that point, apple growers focused on a few simple, marketable varieties that could be easily cloned, were hardy, stored well, looked pretty, and tasted sweet. Thanks to refrigeration technology, apples for eating were available to Americans year-round for the first time.

Today, growers are paying a price for the apple monoculture fostered during Prohibition. Apple trees became genetically stagnant, and new diseases have evolved that, unchecked by massive chemical spraying, can tear through a modern apple orchard in no time at all.

Fortunately, a lone Soviet botanist who survived Stalin's purges, and who knew of the origin of the apple in Kazakhstan, caught the attention of American scientists. He showed them the wild groves of Almaty, a city known for its apples. Cuttings and seedlings have been transferred to government research orchards in the United States where they have been studied and bred to find new varieties that meet modern needs.

American Cider Today

Thanks to the growth and interest in artisanal products like bread, cheese, wine, and beer, cider finally seems to be back on the road to becoming a great American tradition.

Remember, the combined effect of Prohibition and agricultural disasters wiped out a good portion of America's cider apple orchards. People's changing drinking habits nearly finished the job as most orchards turned to popular eating apples to survive. However when most orchards around the world produce Red Delicious apples, the price falls precipitously.

The financial pressure of cheap culinary apples has given incentive to orchard growers to explore thousands of lost heirloom varieties. Growers have reported that the prices they can fetch for quality cider apples are many times that of the regular supermarket apple. These pioneers have also been responsible for producing the first wave of "craft" ciders, effectively recovering the lost art and teaching others about quality cider.

Others are finally noticing and getting into the game, and new cideries are opening seemingly every month. John Hall, the founder of Goose Island Brewing, is taking the proceeds of the brewery's sale to Anheuser-Busch InBev and is working with a new cider group in Illinois. Vermont Cider Company, makers of the Woodchuck brand, controls 50 percent of America's cider market but were just bought by the Irish C&C Group. Boston Beer Company, brewers of Sam Adams, launched a cider brand—Angry Orchard. Miller has acquired two cider makers—Crispin and Fox Barrel—to make and sell cider for the company. Even Anheuser-Busch has gotten into the mix with a "light cider" released under their Michelob Ultra brand. Not surprisingly, some of these brands are better than others.

If you haven't yet raced to your local good spirits emporium to try what ciders are available to you, then there's been no better time to do it than now!

CHAPTER 2

Your First Batch

Now that you've got a basic background in cider and apples, it's time to make your first cider! This chapter contains the basic foundation, not just for cider making, but also for all sorts of fermentations—beer, wine, mead, sake, etc. Consider this your fermentation primer. Pay close attention and later you'll see just how easy it is to expand your skills. In a short 4–6 weeks, you'll be enjoying your first homemade cider!

What to Expect

The earliest fermentations happened completely by accident. There were no careful controls, no efforts at sanitation or understanding of contamination. One day, someone discovered that their apples had gone bad in a particularly interesting way. So in that same vein, your job right now is to not stress and overcomplicate your cider's life but rather to pursue simplicity. The basic steps of cider making are these:

THE CIDER-MAKING CHECKLIST

❏ Produce (or buy) your juice
❏ Add sulfite to your juice
❏ Wait 24 hours (optional—don't worry about this until later)
❏ Clean and sanitize your fermenters
❏ Ferment the juice for 2–3 weeks (Congrats, it's officially cider!)
❏ Rack (gently transfer) the cider
❏ Clarify for 2–3 weeks
❏ Package (bottle) the cider
❏ Chill the cider
❏ Drink!

Executing all of these steps may take as long 2–6 months, but the total active time commitment can be measured in a handful of hours. Most of your time as a cider maker is spent letting the juice and yeast work their quiet magic. For the first few days, you'll want to check on the cider daily to track the most active part of the ferment, but that will only be a few minutes per day at most.

The longest time you'll actively spend with your cider is when it comes time to bottle it. If you're making a few gallons, you can expect to spend a couple of hours sanitizing bottles, preparing and transferring the cider, and then getting it sealed into the bottles. There are steps you can take to minimize that time, but that will be discussed in later chapters.

For now, just know that each batch of cider will demand around 4 total hours of your time. Surprisingly, as your batch size grows, the time doesn't multiply. Instead of 4 hours for 1 gallon of cider, 5 gallons will probably only require 5 hours of time (mostly for sanitizing and filling the extra bottles).

Take that into consideration as you start thinking about how much cider you want to make!

What You Need for Your First Batch

Your first task as a cider maker will be to gather up your ingredients and your basic equipment. This first batch is simple and designed to make a little less than a gallon of cider that will be ready to drink in 6 weeks. Don't be surprised if on your first taste you find the cider a little bland. You'll learn later how to take even the dullest cider and make it sing.

For your first batch you will need:

- ❑ 1-gallon glass jug (two if you want a sparkling cider)
- ❑ 4' clear, food-grade polyvinyl tubing ⅜" in diameter
- ❑ 1 gallon fresh, raw, sweet apple cider (preferably from an orchard or a good brand like Trader Joe's Current Crop Gravenstein Apple Juice)
- ❑ 1 packet dry beer or ale yeast (not bread yeast!)
- ❑ ½ teaspoon yeast nutrient (optional)
- ❑ Bleach
- ❑ Aluminum foil
- ❑ 4 (1-liter) soda or sparkling-water bottles with caps

Most of these items can be found at your local grocery store. The jugs, tubing, yeast, and yeast nutrient can be found at your local home-brewing shop or at numerous online retailers. The tubing can be found either at the homebrew store or the hardware store. See Appendix B for more sources.

QUESTION

Can I use a plastic jug for fermentation?
You've no doubt noticed that apple juice tends to come in plastic bottles. Can you make your cider in those same jugs? You'll probably be safe for one batch, but don't trust them beyond that since the plastic in those bottles isn't intended to hold up to the stress of repeated use. In addition, unless the bottle held something sparkling previously, don't use it for bottling!

If you have a friend who brews or makes wine, consider asking him to get involved with your first batch. If he hasn't experimented with cider before, he will probably be grateful for the opportunity to exercise his skills.

Juice

Your primary concern as a cider maker is finding the best juice possible. No matter how skilled you become, the initial quality of your juice drives the ultimate character of your cider. Getting great apple juice involves more than popping off to the supermarket. Fortunately, in this day of artisanal tastes and interest in eating locally produced food, you have many more options than before.

What do you need to look for? Your ideal juice will be sweet but not cloying. It should taste bright and zippy but not sour, and finally earthy and just a touch astringent. The typical American sweet juice probably won't hit all of these notes, but there are ways to adjust your raw juice.

The best juices are the least processed—cloudy, cold, and raw. It sounds odd since modern society is obsessed with clarity, but the more cloudy the juice, the more interesting the cider. Why? Unfiltered juice has at least one fewer step involved in it, and all those proteins and other unfiltered elements can have a flavorful impact on your cider.

ALERT

Read your labels closely! If the juice you're looking at has potassium sorbate or sodium benzoate in it, skip it. Both will prevent a successful ferment and make you a sad cider maker. Remember, the fewer ingredients in your cider, the better!

So where should you go to find your juice? Here are a few options:

- **Orchards.** Honest-to-goodness apple orchards are by far your best choices for finding juice. Get the juice straight from the press and get your cider life started right. Sadly, this option is only really available during the fall and early winter. So if it's not the right time of year, find another option.

- **Farm stands or farmers' markets.** If you can't make it to an orchard, check your area for farm stands or farmers' markets. Every fall, you should see jugs and jugs of fresh, sweet juice available for your cider making. Don't forget to ask if they have a bulk discount!
- **Holistic, cooperative, and organic markets.** Your local organic food market should stock sulfite- and preservative-free unfiltered apple juice. Look around the juice section and you may even find some interesting varietals and flavors to use.
- **Trader Joe's.** This one sounds odd, but if you have a Trader Joe's near you, check for their Current Crop Gravenstein Apple Juice. It's flash pasteurized, relatively inexpensive, and makes an easy and amazing cider. If they don't have the Gravenstein, they'll have another unfiltered juice in plastic jugs.
- **Local grocery store.** Many better stores now stock organic, minimally processed fruit juices in the produce section. Martinelli's juices contain a blend of apples, including the Gravenstein variety available at Trader Joe's.
- **Frozen foods section.** Last (and way down the chain of options) is the gooey, sticky, frozen apple concentrate lurking in the frozen foods section next to the frozen waffles. If you literally cannot find anything else, you can make cider from it, but be prepared for less-than-ideal results.

ESSENTIAL

Pasteurization makes juice stable, but the quick, high-heat exposure destroys delicate flavors and compounds. Remember: Fresh is always best!

Yeast

For this first batch of cider, you'll want to use something simple, clean, and no fuss. To that end, grab a packet of dried ale yeast (preferably something English) from your local homebrew shop. Save the wine yeast, other beer yeast variants, and liquid yeasts for later experiments.

Ask your friendly homebrew store clerks (or online store) for their recommendations for yeast nutrients, like GO-FERM, designed specifically for use with dry yeast. Yeast nutrient isn't always necessary, but as an insurance policy, it never hurts and is relatively cheap. As you ferment more juice, nutrient will be critical to your success.

Cleaning and Sanitizing

You could just let your cider ferment away in whatever you have handy—that's how people used to do it, after all. However, you probably want a cleaner-tasting cider than the dodgy stuff coming out of an old barrel with bits of straw in it, so you'll need to embrace cleaning and sanitizing!

ALERT

You will be using a bunch of different chemicals to clean and sanitize your equipment. While none are inherently dangerous, a few of these chemicals can be harsh on your skin. Consider investing in a pair of thick cleaning gloves if your skin is sensitive!

Cleaning

Cleaning your cider gear is a little more complicated than squeezing dish soap on everything and scrubbing away. For one, you don't want to use regular soap. The squeeze bottle of dishwashing soap sitting in your kitchen is a high-tech marvel of surfactants that are designed to help free organic material from a plate. They work best with the mechanical assistance of a sponge or brush. Look at your tubing. How are you going to scrub that?

For cider making and other fermentation projects, you'll want something a little stronger. Old-school texts will tell you to use the cleaning agent trisodium phosphate (TSP). These days, because of its effects on rivers and lakes, most TSP cleaners are made with TSP substitutes of varying natures. For that reason, it is not recommended to use them. Fortunately, there is a very common cleaner that you know from late-night television—OxiClean. Make sure you only buy the Free variety because it contains no dyes or perfumes. You don't want perfumes and dyes in your cider!

To clean your gear, mix 1 tablespoon of OxiClean with 1 gallon of 120°F–140°F water. Soak your gear in the mixture for 15–30 minutes. Fill your hoses, etc., with the solution. Gently use a bottle brush to loosen any stubborn material. Once free of residue, rinse the gear with hot water until the surface no longer feels soapy slick. And yes, you'll want to wash any new gear!

ALERT

With anything plastic, you have to be gentle when scrubbing. Scratches in a plastic surface provide a protected breeding ground for bacteria. A scratch in any surface will keep sanitizers from reaching the bugs to kill them.

Sanitizing

You're now halfway to having usable gear. The next step is to kill the critters that live on the gear's surfaces. It's a simple fact of the universe that no matter how clean you are, your surfaces are covered in countless germs. For the most part, these germs won't do you any harm. Your cider, on the other hand, could definitely suffer at the hands of bacteria. It could go from a pleasant fruit-filled beverage to tasting like battery acid.

Your cider will eventually contain two things that make microorganisms unhappy—alcohol and acid. When it first starts as juice, though, it lacks those protective elements. Your job is to reduce the amount of bacteria, allowing your yeast time to generate the alcohol and lower the pH to a point where further harmful growth will be minimized. Your job is sanitation.

FACT

Sanitation is not sterilization! It's easy to confuse the two, but sterilization is the elimination of all microorganisms on a surface. Sanitation is the removal of enough organisms to create a safe fermentation environment.

To start your first fermentation off right, you can use common household bleach at the ratio of 1 tablespoon per 1 gallon of water. The chlorine will rupture enough undesirable bacteria, mold, and fungus cell walls after a soaking period of 20 minutes. After the long soak of everything that needs sanitizing, you'll need to rinse the bleach from the container. Rinsing with tap water is convenient, but you're adding microorganisms back with the unsanitary water. The proper technique is to use freshly boiled water that you cover and cool before using. You need to remove all traces of bleach from the gear, unless you want your cider to taste like chlorine. Rinse well, and rinse more than you actually think you need.

After the gear is rinsed, let it hang upside down to drip and air-dry. When everything is perfectly dry, you're sanitized and ready to go. You'll want to do this in as still a room as possible. Your enemy when sanitizing is a breeze that can blow bacteria-laden dust onto your newly sanitary surfaces.

If it seems like a lot of work to sanitize—it is. There are other ways of sanitizing that are more convenient, but they require more expensive, and less commonly available, chemicals. Sanitizing doesn't last forever, but as long as you keep the surfaces from open-air currents, you'll be fine to sanitize an hour ahead of time.

ESSENTIAL

Remember, cleaning and sanitizing are two aspects of the same process. You cannot sanitize something dirty! Don't skimp, and don't cut corners—do the work to make your gear ready so that you don't waste your money or your time.

Your First Cider

This is it: Time to make your first cider! This recipe and its procedure is the standard procedure for making cider (and for that matter, almost every fermented beverage). As you go through this book, you'll notice that most recipes will reuse this same process again and again. The art of cider making lies in finding good juice, managing your ferment, and adjusting or adding other flavors. There are a few other techniques, but you can build a cellar full of great cider with just this one process.

There may seem to be a lot of different steps here, but don't worry about the number of instructions. Take it slow and practice good fermentation, and you'll make fantastic cider. As you explore other types of cider, everything will build on this basic process.

ESSENTIAL

In many of the later recipes in this book, you'll see a designation on the juice specifying that a juice should be "balanced to the sweet" or "acidic" or "bitter." It means the recipe works best when made with a juice that is either sweet (low acid/low tannin), acidic (high acid/low tannin), or bitter (high tannin). If you can't balance your apple blend, simply adjust your favorite juice with acid and tannins to achieve the desired target.

The Standard Cider-Making Procedure

This is the basic process that you'll use for every cider in this book and almost every other fermentation you can think to perform. This recipe will net you 4 large bottles of inexpensive cider. You can enjoy this cider after 4–8 weeks.

INGREDIENTS | 4 (1-LITER) BOTTLES OF GOOD CIDER

1 pint water
Pinch of yeast nutrient
1 packet dried ale yeast, preferably English
1 gallon apple juice, room temperature
1 ounce (by weight) corn sugar (optional—use only if you want sparkling cider)

1. Clean your fermenting vessel with a nonsoap detergent like perfume- and dye-free OxiClean. Rinse well and air-dry. You must rinse the vessel clean. Any trace residue will end up in your cider and cause off flavors!
2. Sanitize your fermentation vessel and 2 foil sheets. If using bleach, mix 1 tablespoon of bleach per 1 gallon of water. Soak for 20 minutes. Rinse thoroughly with boiled, cooled water and air-dry upside down. (For other sanitizers, follow their directions.)
3. Boil 1 pint of water, and let cool to 105°F. Mix in a pinch of yeast nutrient, and sprinkle the yeast over the water. Cover with sanitized aluminum foil, and let sit for 15 minutes.

4. Warm the apple juice to 60°F.
5. Add the juice to the fermenter, and mix in the foamy yeast. Cover with more sanitized foil, and place somewhere dark and cool, preferably around 60°F. An interior closet works for most people.
6. After 2–4 weeks, the yeast should be done fermenting and will have dropped clear with all the yeast and protein settling toward the bottom of the fermenter. If not already somewhere high, gently move the fermenter and allow to resettle. Sanitize your plastic bottles, caps, and tubing.
7. To bottle still cider (without carbonation): Siphon the cider from the fermenter, being careful to avoid the muck at the bottom, into each of your plastic bottles. Fill completely. Stop the flow of cider by pinching the tube before moving the hose to the next bottle. Screw on the caps and chill the cider in your fridge and drink when cool. Serve around 50°F.
8. If bottling sparkling carbonated cider: Dissolve the corn sugar in ½ cup of water and bring to a light boil for 5 minutes. (If the water evaporates, add more water. You want the syrup to be almost as thin as water to blend more easily.) Place the resulting syrup in the bottom of a sanitized bucket or jug. (You need to create this sugar syrup, because adding the sugar dry will cause the cider to foam uncontrollably.)
9. Siphon the cider from the fermenter, being careful to avoid the muck at the bottom, into the container with the syrup. The flow of the cider should mix the sugar syrup evenly, but if you want to be sure, grab a whisk, sanitize it, and gently swirl the cider for a minute. Siphon the now sweetened cider into the bottles, leave approximately two fingers width of airspace in the bottle, screw on the tops, and wait 2 weeks before chilling. You'll know you're ready when the plastic bottles become stiff and unyielding to the touch.
10. When cold, usually around an hour, just pop the top and carefully decant (pour without disturbing the sediment) your cider into your favorite glass to enjoy! The still cider won't have the full spritely carbonation of a sparkling cider. It may be what the French term *pétillant*, or just having a light prickly carbonation level that teases your tongue.

Keep a notebook and take copious notes while making your cider. Record the type of juice, the recipe, how the juice tastes, what the fermentation looked like, and even what the temperature was like. These notes will come in handy later when you want to figure out what went right and wrong in your cider experiments. You can find a handy tracking sheet in Appendix D or on *www.drewbeechum.com*.

Racking and Siphoning—Critical Skills

Racking, or gently moving your cider from one vessel to another, is a skill you need to master. Learning how to make a siphon is critical to racking your cider and leaving behind fermentation detritus. Your goal is to move your cider as gently as possible, avoiding stirring oxygen into your cider and without disturbing the settle.

The principles behind siphons have been documented as far back as the Egyptians. If you don't set up your siphon correctly, you'll suffer a lot of heartache. However, if you mess this up, don't be discouraged! Getting a siphon to run properly is one of those skills that requires a little practice before you can do it perfectly. If you want to practice, try siphoning water around until you think you've got the feel for it.

Siphoning takes advantage of atmospheric pressure and gravity in order to function. When you lower one end of the tube, the fluid flow creates a partial vacuum in the hose, and the atmospheric pressure pushes the liquid from your higher vessel up into the tube, causing the flow to continue unabated until you break the column of liquid.

ALERT

Lots of old timers say, "Start a siphon by sucking on the hose." Don't! Your mouth is filled with things that would love nothing better than to infect your cider. Skip this advice, and potential infections, by following the fill-and-drop method explained here.

The Fill-and-Drop Siphon Process

1. Put your fermentation vessel somewhere higher than your target vessel or bottles. Do this a few days before you want to transfer. You want all the apple parts, yeast cells, and other goodies to have time to settle firmly to the bottom and not transfer over to your next vessel.
2. Make sure everything is sanitized, then position a receiving vessel and a waste container below your source.
3. Fill your transfer hose (and racking cane if using, see Chapter 4) with sanitizer (or freshly boiled water). When you remove the hose from the sanitizer, hold both ends facing up. Basically make a *U* out of your hose to keep the fluid in there.
4. Pinch off one end of the tube. Put the other end in your starting container (your fermenter), quickly lower the other end, and point it at your waste receptacle. Unpinch and watch the flow start!
5. Once the sanitizer is out of the hose, pinch the hose and open it up in the receiving vessel. Don't worry about losing some cider when you start the siphon, your loss will be minimal.
6. If at any point in time you lose your siphon (i.e., the liquid stops flowing), just repeat the process again. Don't forget to respect the need for sanitation even in a hurry. Be careful about disturbing your source cider!

Once you get the hang of siphoning, this will become second nature to you. There are a few gadgets out there, like an auto-siphon (see Chapter 4), that are designed to help make siphon starting super easy, but it's better (and less expensive) to learn how to properly siphon.

CHAPTER 3

The Core Ingredient

What makes an apple an apple? Think you've seen every apple out there? Bet you didn't know that apples are part of the Pome family! The world of pomes (fleshy fruits such as apples, pears, and quinces) is wide and varied, and most can be used in making ciders of astonishing characters. While you learned some basics in Chapter 1 now it's time to get your advanced degree in Apple-ology. Only by knowing your ingredients can you master your fermentation!

Join the Pome Family

Apples have a large and surprisingly twisty family tree. To start, the apple's great-granddad is the rose. Roses and apples are both members of the Rosaceae family. The rose family is a large and varied family of more than 2,800 different species of flowering bushes and trees. It includes many fruits that you may know and enjoy, including stone fruits like apricots, cherries, plums, peaches, and, interestingly, the almond. All of these are members of the *Prunus* genus and are considered drupes. A drupe is a fruit consisting of skin (exocarp) and flesh (mesocarp) surrounding a seed with a hardened shell.

FACT

Prunus is a direct sister to the *Malus* genus, also known as the apple. Both are part of the subfamily Amygdaloideae. *Malus* itself contains only about fifty distinct species of trees. Remember that from a scientific point of view, most apples you enjoy are varieties of the same species—*Malus domestica*. Different types of wild crab apple make up most of the remaining species of the *Malus* genus.

The Apple Itself

What people normally think of as an apple is actually an overprotected ovary. Most apples, like many fruits, are not self-pollinating. In other words, pollen must be mechanically transferred from one flower to another to cause reproduction. Insects, such as butterflies or bees, usually accomplish this.

These insects land on the apple blossoms and pick up protein-packed pollen during their quest for sweet flower nectar. When they visit another flower, some of the pollen they carry transfers to the new flower in an act known as pollination.

Some flowering plants require that pollination occur from the same variant of plant. Apples, however, freely cross-pollinate with other varieties that are blooming at the same time. Many growers plant varieties that bloom at the same time near each other, or they'll use strategically placed bunches of flowering crab apple branches to provide the necessary pollen.

Following pollination, two cells of plant sperm are transferred into the ovary from the stigma (the female sex organ of a flower) via the pistil. This is called double pollination. Once in the ovary, one sperm fertilizes the egg cell and forms the basis for the seed interior, while the other sperm triggers the production of the endosperm or seed coat. The delicious sweet flesh of the apple forms around five carpels holding fertilized seeds from both the ovary and the hypanthium (the fleshy bit at the bottom of an apple blossom that holds the flower together).

FACT

Most apples are diploid, that is, they have two sets of chromosomes. Several apples throw that standard for a loop by being triploids, with three sets of chromosomes. This means they're basically sterile and require extra care to pollinate.

The end result of all this blooming and growing is the apple fruit you know and love. You've been trained by years of shopping to expect a big globe- or heart-shaped fruit with a bright solid or striped skin. It will surprise you then to see the endless shapes, sizes, and colors that apples take. You can find wonderful-tasting fruit hidden inside squat flat disks with mottled skin.

That mottled, slightly wrinkled skin is referred to as a "russet." The skin is usually rough and the color usually is spotted with highlights of yellow and green flecked over a brownish skin. Sadly, with the importance of appearance to today's consumer, a number of delightfully nutty, complex apples have fallen by the wayside in favor of the pretty and bland. This includes a number of important apples, including America's first native apple, the Roxbury Russet.

ESSENTIAL

One characteristic that is definitely not good for growers is the tendency for some trees to produce biennial yields (every other year). Either by quirk of genetics or dint of growing conditions, a plant may switch to producing a good yield only every other year. This can be devastating for a commercial producer.

One of the aspects of apples that is a boon to the farmer is their variable harvest times. Each variety harvests and blooms at different times of the year. Smart farmers plant rows of varieties that have different cycles so as to spread their work out over the course of months rather than having to harvest all their orchards at the same time.

Grafting

The apple's easy hybridization and cross-pollination characteristics make it possible to create endless new varieties. Each fruit contains seeds that harbor a different sort of apple tree than its parents. Plant the seeds and discover something new! This is great if you always want a different experience, but not if you're a commercial farmer looking to sell a particular variety of apple.

In order to create an orchard of trees producing nearly identical fruit, farmers turn to grafting. In grafting, growers cut a sample, called a scion, from a branch of a tree that produces fruit they want replicated. The cut end of the branch is shaped into a flat wedge. They take another tree with characteristics that they enjoy—like hardiness, size, shape, and growth—and "top" it, or cut off the fruiting portion, leaving just the rootstock. This grounded stub of the rootstock is notched to match the cutting, and then the two halves are joined together.

The farmers tape them together, and within a few weeks the two trees are joined and act as one. The tree grows like the rootstock, with fruit from the scion. You can even do this so that you have multiple varieties of fruit growing from the tree by grafting different scions to the rootstock. This grafting process explains how you can grow tons of nearly identical fruit despite the tree's proclivity to genetic change.

Apple Breeding

The breeding of new apple varieties used to be a haphazard exercise of trial and error. In 1875, the United States opened its first government-sponsored agricultural research station in Connecticut, attached to Wesleyan University. The station proved to be such a success that the federal government stepped in to authorize money for research stations in every state to be directed by a land-grant college.

These research stations, as well as others around the globe run by governments and private enterprises, have revolutionized the discovery of new varieties of apples and other produce. The goals of these institutions are usually to find new versions of staple crops that are hardier, more disease resistant, and better yielding. You may notice flavor is not in that list. That's because more flavorful varieties are usually more finicky and harder to grow.

To find new varieties, breeders and research stations grow a number of seeds. Remember, each seed could be a potential different type of apple. The trees are grown, nurtured, and examined for characteristics. As trees display their characteristics, trees that fail the selection criteria are winnowed out.

ALERT

If you're buying apples from a non-farm-associated retailer, consider buying organic. Conventionally grown apples continually top lists of produce grown with the most chemical treatment. If you do buy conventional apples, make sure to give them a thorough scrubbing before using!

Others are selectively bred to emphasize desired traits. Eventually, after hundreds or thousands of trees are grown, evaluated, and bred, comes the one tree that carries everything the breeder wants. From there the tree is cloned, tested, and then eventually, maybe, put on the market. Each modern apple you eat was the result of this sort of process!

The Pear

Also in the Amygdaloideae subfamily is the genus *Pyrus*, also known as the pear. Like the apple, the pear is believed to have originated in the area of the Tien Shan Mountains, though in the region that is now China. There are more than twenty distinct species, and, like the apple, virtually every pear you've encountered is the same species, *Pyrus communis*, the common European pear.

One thing that stands out about pears over their cousins is the grittiness of the flesh from sclereids, or stone cells. These little nuggets of cellulose and lignin would, in full fiber form, support the vertical growth of the fruit. In a pear they provide texture, where in an apple they provide the walls encasing the seeds. Another common characteristic of pears is the presence of sorbitol, a natural sugar alcohol made from glucose. Dieters use sorbitol as a sugar substitute, and it can be found most commonly in sugar-free gum. Because sorbitol is not a sugar, yeast can't ferment it, so it remains behind and lends a sweet taste to pear cider.

It is estimated that at one point there were over 120 varieties of perry pears (pears grown for cider) in the United Kingdom, largely around the Gloucestershire area, as well as in the Normandy area of France. Sadly, like the strange, less-edible creature that is the cider apple, perry pears were ripped out of the ground as demand fell and people shifted to other drinks. Of the old varieties still to be found, the Blakeney Red pear, named for the village of Blakeney, is the most commonly grown in the United Kingdom.

ESSENTIAL

In the United States, there was never a strong pear cider (perry) tradition, so specific pear cider varietals are hard to find. For the true perry experience, try growing your own. Your local orchards might be able to supply perry tree whips or check the online retailers listed in Appendix B.

Fortunately, like the hardy apple, long-neglected stands of perry trees still remain. With the recent revival of interest in real perry, explorers have been rooting around in the old orchards and rediscovering varietals once thought to be lost.

Other Pomes

The pome family is comprised of more than just the apple and pear, and most are good for use in fruit wines and ciders as flavor enhancers. Mankind has used three other main pome fruits in the past to make fruited beverages.

The first of these is the loquat, also known as the Japanese plum. It is believed to be Chinese in origin despite being grown in Japan for a millennia. The evergreen tree bears little yellow fruits maxing out at about 2" by ¾". There are many different varieties adapted to climates all over the globe. The flesh itself is usually white to orange with a few large seeds. Its unripe fruit is incredibly acidic, while the ripe fruit is supremely sweet.

The hawthorn, despite its Celtic name, originated in China before aggressively spreading out to Europe. In the southern United States, you may have heard of the mayhaw, which is the same species. The small berry-sized fruits are used largely in jams and jellies, but they are no strangers to the brew pot and fermentation cycle. Usually the fruit is used as flavoring, an accent to add to another beverage.

Last of the commonly used pomes is the quince (*Cydonia oblonga*). At one point this fruit, which looks like a cross between a lemon and an apple, was so common in the Middle East that many of the biblical fruit references are to it and not the apple. In a change of pace from the other major pomes, quinces don't come into their own until they're cooked. Raw, most varieties are incredibly sour and hard. To use them, you take ripe quinces and grate them. The pulp is then boiled in water to free the good stuff. Is it worth the effort? Quinces have such a distinct aroma and flavor that you'll have to try one and see for yourself.

ALERT

Some fruits, including pomes like rowan, require extra care before they can be eaten. Unlike quinces, which require cooking to reach maximum sweetness, rowan contains parasorbic acid, which can damage your kidneys. The parasorbic acid in rowan becomes scorbic acid. Add potassium to it, and it becomes a cider maker's friend, potassium sorbate.

The Crabby Apple

An important category of apples that you'll hear of is the crab apple. This is a catchall term for the other plants of the *Malus* genus. A good number of them are decorative only. The members of *Malus baccata* (Siberian crab apple), *Malus sylvestris* (European crab apple), and *Malus coronaria* (North American sweet crab apple) are used commonly in jams and jellies because they contain a large amount of pectin.

Crab apples are usually shunned due to their high acidity and tannic nature. You can take advantage of this fact by crushing and juicing a few raw crab apples. Add the juice to your cider blend and watch it come alive.

You can find crab apples at most orchards and in grocery stores during the late fall.

▼ **GREAT GROCERY STORE CIDER: COMPARING DIFFERENT JUICE AND SUGAR CONTENT (BRIX AND SPECIFIC GRAVITY)**

Type	Notes	Sugar Content (Brix)	Sugar Content (Specific Gravity)
Fuji	Culinary apple	13.0B	1.052
Granny Smith	Culinary apple	11.0B	1.044
Golden Delicious	Culinary apple	14.25B	1.058
Arkansas Black	Cider/cooking apple	15B	1.061
Crimson Gold	Hybrid crab apple	17B	1.070
Kingston Black	Cider apple	14.75B	1.060
Apricot	Apricot	14.3B	1.058
Black cherry	Cherry	15.6B	1.064
Merlot	Grape	22B	1.092
Orange	Citrus	11.8B	1.048
White peach	Peach	8.5B	1.034
Bartlett pear	Pear	14B	1.057

Commercial Apples

Those bright, shiny grocery store apples you buy year round have likely been stored since the last harvest in specially prepared, controlled atmosphere (CA) storage facilities. These apples are pretreated with carbon dioxide to flush out oxygen held in the apple. They are then placed into special cooled rooms that are sealed and evacuated of most of the room's oxygen. Special scrubbers remove the ethylene gas that's released from the apples to avoid premature ripening or rotting.

These CA vaults are then opened throughout the year as needed to meet consumer demand. Between these storage techniques and the global trade in apples, you are able to have "fresh" apples year round.

The Red Delicious, a monster-sized softball of an apple with a hardy skin and a bland, almost starchy flavor, typifies the modern culinary apple. It wasn't always so. The original Delicious apple came from a chance seedling that won contests in 1880s Iowa. That apple was crisp and sweet and was shortly joined by a sister variety, the Golden Delicious. Over the years, farmers have bred the Delicious until finding today's bulletproof, bland supermodel. Twenty years ago, it accounted for 75 percent of Washington's apple harvest. Today, the Red Delicious portion of the crop has fallen drastically in favor of newer varieties like America's number two apple, the Gala.

AMERICA'S TOP TEN APPLES (U.S. APPLE ASSOCIATION)

1. Red Delicious: The American classic that defines the look of a red apple
2. Gala: Developed in New Zealand, this grainy, sweet apple has been growing in popularity since 1974
3. Golden Delicious: Very sweet, delicate, yellow-green apple
4. Granny Smith: From Australia, this green apple defines tartness for most apple eaters
5. Fuji: A Japanese variety that is extraordinarily popular in Asia—dense, sweet, and firm fleshed
6. McIntosh: Tender and tart, makes excellent pink applesauce and sweet cider
7. Rome: America's premier cooking apple, subtle
8. Empire: Hardy and resilient with a firm crunch
9. Honeycrisp: A newish variety that has become popular—sweet and firm
10. Idared: Tart, juicy red apple

Apple Varieties

Given the bewildering variety of apples available, there is a simple classification system that British cider makers use to help guide the picking of varieties. Apples are categorized by their sweetness (sweet), acidity (sharp), and tannic astringency (bitter). This results in four possible styles of apples.

APPLE FLAVOR CATEGORIES

- **Sweet:** Low in both acid and tannin, these apples provide big sugar and classic apple flavor. Virtually any apple with the name "Sweet" in it, like Sweet Coppin, falls under this category. Sweet types usually have lousy storage characteristics.

- **Sharp:** Sharp apples are high in acid but still low in tannin. These provide crispness to a cider. The most common sharp apple would be the Granny Smith, but in terms of true cider apples, you'll want an apple like the classic British Brown's Apple or the American Baldwin.
- **Bittersweet:** These apples contain a fair amount of tannin but fairly low acid levels. The effect is that of a sustained mouth experience as the astringency works to cut the natural sweetness of the cider. Examples are Bulmer's Norman from France or Dabinett from the United Kingdom.
- **Bittersharp:** Containing both high levels of acid and tannin, these provide much of the needed character for a classic English-style cider on their own. Many varieties went extinct because the apples are generally dreadful when eaten. The archetype is the Kingston Black, but "Jersey" in the name is a safe indication of bitterness.

QUESTION

Why is the Kingston Black so beloved amongst cider makers?
It's one of the few apple varieties that can make a pure varietal cider that's considered great. In each apple resides a near-perfect balance of sugar, acid, and earthy tannin bite to yield a cider that needs very little, if any, adjustment.

Cider Apples

Cider makers look at apples with a different eye than the regular consumer. They don't care so much about the perfect appearance, the mottled skin, and the planetoid-sized body. What they care about is the taste of the juice.

▼ **IMPORTANT CIDER APPLE VARIETIES**

Name	Notes
Ashmead's Kernel	Old-fashioned, dense russet with aspects of sweet pear and other fruits
Ashton Brown Jersey	Classic bittersweet that can provide rich, pleasant cider
Baldwin	One of America's old standbys—provides sweetness with just enough acid to balance. Definitely a good base for cider
Bulmer's Norman	Originally from France, it produces sweet and astringent juice that ferments to a mildly bittersweet cider

Name	Notes
Chisel Jersey	Like the Bulmer's Norman, only amped up. The Chisel produces a full, bittersweet cider from its forceful juice
Cortland	A McIntosh derivative that is best fresh with a balance of sweet and acid. Produces plenty of juice
Cox's Orange Pippin	Striking, red-orange apple that comes from the United Kingdom. Enthusiasts describe the flavor as unparalleled. Subtle fruity tones mixed with a bright acid
Crispin or Mutsu	Japanese apple that is large, with a crisp, spicy, sweet-tart juice when fresh pressed
Dabinett	A smallish apple with a big flavor. The juice is rich, flavorful, and bittersweet. Makes a wonderful partner in a blend
Empire	Popular East Coast apple with firm, white flesh and sweet, crisp juice
Foxwhelp	Classic bittersharp apple that is strictly a cider apple; it produces a deeply aromatic and earthy cider
Golden Delicious	Exceedingly popular apple with a number of desired characteristics. The juice is rich and sweet when the fruit is allowed to ripen on the tree
Golden Russet	Another New York apple with a russet skin. Very similar to the Ashmead's Kernel
Gravenstein	A small commercial variety that has issues with disease, but the apple produces a sweet, nutty juice
Harrison	The great American New Jersey apple once lost to history but recently recovered. Lots of color and intense flavor
Jonathan	Old-school American apple, with a bracing dose of acid over a sweet juice
Kingston Black	One of the few apples to perfectly balance sweetness, acid, and tannin so that you can make a great varietal cider. Finicky to grow
Medaille d'Or	As the name indicates, the apple has a French origin. It is a brown russet with an incredibly high sugar content with just a little astringency
McIntosh	The staple crop of the eastern United States and the forefather of a number of apples. The juice is both aromatic and spicy while retaining the simplicity needed for broad appeal
Newtown Pippin	The apple with a presidential stamp of approval from Thomas Jefferson. Needs storage before the apple reaches its peak with a piquant sweet juice
Northern Spy	Hardy winter apple with enough acid and sweetness to make a good cider when given a tannin boost
Roxbury Russet	The original American apple; sugary with a moderate acid that combines to make a pleasing cider
Stayman	Winesap derivative; still popular on the East Coast, the flavor contains notes of raisins and grapes
Sweet Coppin	Classic English cider apple with very low tannin; the juice is sweet and without acid or tannin, makes a bland cider

Name	Notes
Virginia Crab	North American crab apple first described in 1717. Low nutrients make for a slow ferment, but the resulting cider is very flavorful.
Wickson Crab	A Northern Californian crab apple that produces an intensely sharp juice with a bracing tannin. Wandering Aegnus Ciderworks makes a 100 percent Wickson "apple wine" (8.2% ABV) that is shocking in its character.
Winesap	Associated with Virginia; produces lots of juice with vinous characters on top of a strong yet balanced sweetness and acid; too potent for solo usage, so blend with something softer.
Yarlington Mill	Vintage English apple with a sweet, lightly tannic juice.

Practical Apples

In an ideal world, you would have access to all of those great cider varieties. But for most amateur cidermakers, there's no corner store or farm stand you can bop to and fill your cart with a blend of Pippin, Kingston Black, and Virginia Crabs. Instead, the great megamarts of today are filled with a plethora of varieties, but most make lousy cider. Here then are arguably the most important varieties you can find at the store or farm stand.

PRACTICAL APPLES FOR THE CIDER MAKER

- **Gravenstein:** This American apple variety has never caught on commercially, but the juice is an excellent base for your cider.
- **Fuji:** Developed in Japan from a pair of American apples, the Fuji is mostly sweet, with a bright, taut skin.
- **Arkansas Black:** An old American apple that has a reputation as a good storage apple that when treated right is juicy, acidic, and slightly bitter.
- **Granny Smith:** For the average home cider maker, the Granny Smith can be a major source of bright acidity.
- **Jonagold:** A cross between the old-school Jonathan and a Golden Delicious, it provides a huge amount of juice, sugar, and acid. Very well balanced.
- **Empire:** A bright red apple from New York, it is best fresh, when it contains a profound earthy fruitiness to go along with its sweetness.

- **Winesap:** Old-school Virginian apple that is popular with orchards for sweet juice production, so it will probably be in any fresh juice you buy. It can provide a good sugar base, but needs extra help to round out the cider.
- **Crab Apples:** You won't get much choice in the grocery store for crab apple varieties, but any variety you can find should provide that missing bite your cider needs.

CHAPTER 4

Additives, Chemicals, and Gear

Now that you've made your first batch of cider, it's time to talk expansion. You'll need to know about the chemicals that will enhance your next batches of cider. There are just a few and they are perfectly safe and provide great benefits to your cider. In addition to that, it's time to expand your selection of gear! Having the right gear can greatly simplify your cidermaking life. Make good choices now and you'll never have to buy better gear!

Additives and Chemicals

Additives may make you think of the strange and weird chemicals on the ingredients list of processed foodstuffs. But have no fear—not all additives are the stuff of fearful mutation. In cider making, there are a few key chemicals that can make your ciders much more stable and better tasting.

These chemicals fall in a few categories. Some are meant to clean, some are used to sanitize and kill bad things, and others are meant to preserve your cider.

Preservatives and Antioxidants

Fermentation is a natural process. It is part of the cycle of life and death and the return to life again. Most preservatives are all about preventing fermentation from happening, but don't think these are an all-powerful force to stop rotting. Fermentation doesn't always happen at the hands of yeast. Other spoilage mechanisms exist that can rot your juice. This is why you have to take care sanitizing your gear!

Here are some common preservatives:

- **Sodium benzoate ($NaC_6H_5CO_2$; E211).** A salt formed from benzoic acid. When added to an acidic environment, like apple juice, it acts as a reproduction disruption agent for both bacteria and fungi. In other words, when yeast cells encounter sodium benzoate, they absorb it and cannot reproduce. This inhibits yeast cells from successfully reaching the fermentation stage of their growth cycle. You can buy sodium benzoate online, but most cider makers don't use it. Some argue that it is more stable and carries less of a flavor impact than potassium sorbate, but it does require the use of campden to ensure complete fermentation blockage. Mostly, you need to know sodium benzoate to avoid juice that contains it!
- **Potassium sorbate/sorbistat K ($C_6H_7KO_2$; E202).** This salt is from sorbic acid, which was originally derived from the rowan tree. When dissolved in water, the salt disassociates back into sorbic acid. Unlike sodium benzoate, it is not acidity dependent. Like sodium benzoate, sorbistat prevents yeast from reproducing. Unlike sodium benzoate, it will not stop an active fermentation. Do not expect to keep a cider

sweet by adding a dose during fermentation. However, adding it post fermentation will prevent the yeast from restarting and eating the sweetness you've added.

- **Ascorbic acid ($C_6H_8O_6$; E300).** One of the many chemicals the human body uses as vitamin C. Ascorbic acid is a powerful antioxidant, an oxygen-reducing agent that can chemically neutralize potentially dangerous free-radical molecules. It does not have microbial effects, meaning it will not stop yeast or bacteria. When combined with sulfur dioxide (SO_2), ascorbic acid causes the compound to be far more effective in stunning yeast and bacteria. According to researchers, ascorbic acid aids cider makers in two ways: It prevents the juice from browning, and it preserves a brighter fruit character. Added before bottling, ascorbic acid will protect your cider from many aging defects.

FACT

The E number system used when talking about food additives is a European system of labeling common chemicals used in food manufacturing. As a cider maker, you should be concerned about E numbers in the E200–E299 range, which is reserved for preservatives. Not all preservatives will prevent you from fermenting juice into delicious cider!

Cleaners and Sanitizers

When you made your first batch in the earlier chapter, you learned an easy method to clean and sanitize your gear. But there are a few more options that you should know about. Remember that cleaning and sanitizing are the one-two punch in the world of fermentation. Any residue allowed to remain on the surface of your fermenter is a likely hiding spot for spoilage organisms.

ESSENTIAL

While cleaning and sanitizing chemicals are mostly safe, a smart cider maker will make sure to wear safety equipment, especially gloves!

Cleaners

Your first instinct will be to grab whatever soap is available to you. Please don't! Most household soaps have questionable qualities, like rinse resistant residues, that make them less than desirable. Instead, focus on a few simple cleaners that can break down organic matter with minimal effort on your part. Remember that warmer temperatures are better (100°F–140°F are best) as there is more energy available to the cleaning compounds. A good bottle or carboy brush never hurts, and if you must scrub, scrub with a surface that is nonstick safe!

ALERT

Always add a strong chemical (cleaner, acid, sanitizer) to water, not the other way around. Not only can you splash dangerously concentrated chemicals around when adding water, but some chemicals can generate strong reactions with only a limited amount of water, which raises the danger factor!

Here are some commonly available cleaners:

- **Bleach.** If you have the old-fashioned, regular-dilution, unscented sort of bleach, you can use it. A few capfuls of bleach in hot water will dissolve a bunch of organic material over time. Just make sure to rinse extremely well. It can pull double duty as a sanitizer as well, but use a fresh batch!
- **OxiClean.** The infomercial-advertised sodium percarbonate cleaner turned household item. Relatively cheap and available, OxiClean, and related knockoffs, are potent oxygen-based cleaners. Sodium percarbonate is referred to as a solid form of hydrogen peroxide. Make sure you use products free of any dyes or fragrances. Also, rinse really well. If you feel any slickness, rinse some more.
- **Powdered brewery wash (PBW).** Available at homebrew stores, this a specially formulated percarbonate cleaner mixed with metasilicate and other goodies that are especially effective at cleaning fermentation residue.

- **Caustic—potash or sodium hydroxide.** It is strongly recommended that you do not use caustic unless you really have no other choice. This stuff can burn you and strip skin. It's mentioned here because what it will do to your skin is precisely what it will do to anything stuck to the walls of your gear.

FACT

The sodium-percarbonate-based cleaners have a limited amount of time to be effective, since much of their action is due to oxygen bleaching. Don't try and reuse old PBW or OxiClean solutions.

Sanitizers

There are a few different means of sanitizing your surfaces. The first group, the sulfites, is super traditional and comes from the wine world. The second group involves newer chemicals like phosphoric acid and iodine, and are used heavily in brewing. Both groups have their advantages and disadvantages. For instance, the sulfites have the disadvantage of releasing sulfur into your cider, while bleach can add a pervasive note of "pool chlorine" to your drink.

THE BISULFITE FAMILY OF SANITIZERS (THE WINE WAY)

- **Metabisulfite: potassium metabisulfite ($K_2S_2O_5$) and sodium metabisulfite ($Na_2S_2O_5$).** Both are sulfur salts called disulfites because of the presence of S_2O_5. When added to an acidic solution, the molecule disassociates into three molecules, including the critical component sulfur dioxide (SO_2). Many vintners use potassium metabisulfite (k-meta) to avoid adding sodium.
- **Sulfur dioxide (SO_2).** Usually introduced to the must by additions of metabisulfite powder, sulfur dioxide exists in solution in a few states: bound, combined with phenol compounds in the fresh juice (aka must); or free, either as a solid bisulfite ion or as a dissolved gas. The dissolved gas is what does the actual antimicrobial work. When the must is lower in pH, the ratio of the free molecule tilts toward the active gas form. This is why an acidic must uses smaller doses.

OTHER SANITIZERS (THE BEER WAY)

- **Bleach.** The old standby, bleach, or sodium hypochlorite (NaClO), is an effective, cheap, and potent sanitizer. As you know if you've ever used it, the smell is atrocious and lingering. Bleach has a long contact time (about 20 minutes) and requires a thorough sanitized water rinse and air-dry before using—unless you like your cider to smell like an old hospital, that is. It is recommended that you employ other less-intrusive means for sanitizing.

- **Iodophor.** A combination of the very effective sanitizer iodine, plus surfactants and other chemicals that help increase the solution's ability to reach all the surfaces of your vessels. If used in a properly diluted amount, it is absolutely no-rinse, safe, and has zero flavor impact. Above the recommended dilution, you'll notice it because your plastic parts will stain and your cider will taste like medicine. If you're near farms, check with them. A lot of farms use iodophor as a sanitizer—just make sure it doesn't have lanolin in it like the iodophor solutions used to sanitize the nozzles that milk a cow.

- **Isopropyl/ethanol alcohol.** It's the sting that means you're clean, right? Alcohols are commonly available and cheap, but surprisingly not very effective. To start, the alcohol level must be above 70 percent to have a real effect. It also has a long contact time—about 30 minutes. It's handy to keep on hand in a spray bottle to use around airlocks and the mouths of carboys.

- **Star San/Saniclean.** These are modern acid-based sanitizers and are a mixture of phosphoric acid and more surfactants, and in Star San, foaming agents. Mixed with water, these sanitizers work quickly with quoted contact times of 30 seconds. The foam is designed to help the acid penetrate every surface because it clings and wets surfaces. The best part about Star San is that it's incredibly safe and has no effect on your cider's flavor. You may get sticker shock at first, since it's the most expensive sanitizer, but a little goes a long way, and when mixed with distilled water, it lasts for months. Don't want to soak? Mix Star San in a spray bottle with distilled water and spray your surfaces thoroughly.

Clarifiers and Fining

Somewhere along the way, people decided they liked drinking things they could see through. It probably happened in the 1800s, when clear glasses became affordable for everyone! This process of making cider (or any liquid) clearer is called fining.

Of these clarifying agents, one requires use at the prefermentation stage. All of the others you'll use by adding to already fermented cider. The idea is to pull out the particles still floating in your cider that make it cloudy.

ESSENTIAL

Some people may consider these clarifiers cheating, unnatural, or the sign of an impatient cider maker, but what do they know? The one part to take away from that attitude, though: Time and cold will usually help clarify everything.

Here are some common clarifying agents:

- **Pectinase.** Technically this should only be needed if your juice is heated and not treated by the press. Pectinase is an enzyme that will break down pectin, a protein structure that when exposed to heat, acid, and sugar forms a gel. In a cider it gums up the mouthfeel and makes the cider hazy. Follow the instructions on your pectinase and use before the ferment to watch it chop up the pectin and allow it to settle out.
- **Bentonite.** A claylike mix of silica, aluminum, and salt, bentonite has been used for centuries in winemaking to pull together protein chains and yeast and get them to settle out. Follow the instructions on the package to use.
- **Gelatin.** Easily available from the grocery store. Collagen from the bones of animals attracts negatively charged haze particles. It requires rehydration in cold water first before being heated and mixed thoroughly into the cider.
- **Isinglass.** Used traditionally in beer, made from the swim bladders of fish. Used all over the British Isles and requires 2 weeks to firmly settle things out.

- **Polyclar.** Looks like plastic shavings because that's what it is. Blenderize Polyclar with a little cider or cold water, and allow it to work over a week or so.
- **Sparkolloid.** Part diatomaceous earth, part complex starch and protein chains. Sparkolloid requires very little agent mixed into the cider to pull out negatively charged, haze-causing proteins. Requires boiling to be made ready
- **Super-Kleer.** A very powerful one-two punch of chitosan and kieselsol. Chitosan is a polysaccharide found in the shells of shrimp. Kieselsol is a silica gel. When added in sequence, the two combine to pull everything out of solution. Works remarkably quickly, needing only a few days.

With all of these clarifying agents, it's important to understand that they aren't destroying the particles. They're forcing them to settle out. What this means for you is that you must be careful not to stir the sediment back up into the cider when you rack off the newly cleared cider. If you do pull any muck or stir things up, your cider will now be gritty, which is far worse than not being pretty.

Gear—What to Buy and How to Clean

There are endless amounts of things that people are willing to sell the home cider maker. Don't fret too much about the high-end fancy stuff. Most of the expensive gear are things you will rarely need at the home level. Remember that cider making is something nature wants to happen. Your job is to nudge it along and make sure it happens according to your whims.

While the following items are handy to have, never forget all you need to make basic cider is:

❑ Juice
❑ A clean, sanitized container to store the juice while it ferments
❑ A piece of tubing
❑ A clean, sanitized container to store the cider before you drink it

Everything else is icing on the cake that helps you make your cider better, more interesting, and more consistent.

Glass Carboys

Until recently, the water cooler that workers gathered around was heavy-duty glass. Usually 5 gallons in size, these glass carboys ruled the office space until the advent of the plastic water cooler bottle.

The main advantage of a glass carboy is why scientists still use them to this day. Glass is extraordinarily nonreactive and nonporous. Acid can safely be stored in glass, and oxygen cannot travel across its walls. This imperviousness means that it can be cleaned with the toughest of chemicals, sanitized easily, and used to store cider for long terms without worrying about picking up staling levels of oxygen.

The huge disadvantage of the glass carboy is the breakable nature of glass. You must be really careful handling your carboys. A short fall, even an inch or two, may be enough to cause the carboy to shatter into thousands of pieces. It is not uncommon in home-brewing circles to hear of brewers ending up with lacerations and stitches from trying to catch a falling carboy.

FACT

Another problem is that, until recently, relatively cheap carboys were being produced in Mexico and imported, quite affordably, into the United States. That factory closed, leaving the nearest carboy manufacturer in Italy.

To clean your carboys, time is your best friend. Load up the vessel with your cleaner of choice and let it get to work. Homebrew shops sell a special curved brush designed to help clean off the shoulders of the carboy. Take a lesson from others and bend the brush to fit better.

Additionally, save yourself a lot of heartache. When you finish using a carboy, immediately rinse it out and knock off most of the gunk. You'll be thankful that you did.

The Plastic Bucket

The common HDPE (high-density polyethylene) bucket is cheap and widely available, and it makes primary fermentation safe from the effects of gravity-induced breakage. Virtually shatterproof, the bucket remains a popular choice for experimenting with fermentation. With its handle, lid, and a wide-open mouth that means you can reach in and clean to your heart's content, the plastic bucket seems a perfect choice.

As long as you buy new buckets or buckets that previously held food, you can be reasonably assured that your HDPE bucket is food safe. Not sure if a bucket is HDPE? Check for the recycle code. Inside the little recycle triangle there is a number—if it's 2, then you have HDPE and are safe to go.

You can get used buckets from restaurants, but given that a new 5-gallon bucket costs about $2–$4 at the hardware store, you can probably skip the leftovers. If a bucket previously held something vinegary, like pickles, you'll have a devil of a time getting rid of the smell. So unless you want to make pickle cider, skip it.

FACT

Your local homebrew shop will also carry larger buckets, 6.5–7 gallons, that are suitable to fully ferment 5 gallons with room to spare for an active fermentation. These also come with lids that are ported for airlocks. If you want to make massive amounts of cider, look for 20-gallon white food-grade trash cans or ask your homebrew shop to let you buy their used malt syrup drums.

If buckets are light and shatterproof, then what's not to love? Their lightness comes at a dual cost. Where glass was impervious to chemicals and oxygen, plastic is not. Also, the amount of oxygen absorbed through the walls of the bucket is astonishing. It tops even that of the old wooden barrel. This means the bucket is great for primary fermentation, but it's absolutely dreadful for any sort of long-term storage.

A useful variation on the bucket is the bottling bucket, which is a 5-gallon bucket with a spigot and a hose designed for filling bottles. It makes it very easy to add sugar syrups, then rack the cider on top of the syrup to allow it to mix naturally before filling the bottles with a tube.

Plastic's shatterproof nature comes from its ability to flex and bend and deform without breaking. Sadly, this same suppleness allows scratches to form very easily, and scratches mean death to a bucket. Be very gentle when cleaning because even the slightest scrape can provide creepy crawlies a place to hide, and that will make for very sad cider.

ESSENTIAL

There has been a lot of concern recently about the amount of bisphenol A (BPA) found in common plastic items. This has led to manufacturers searching out new formulas that don't use the controversial chemical. Rest assured that food-grade HDPE contains no BPA.

The Better Bottle/Plastic Carboy

With safety concerns over glass carboys and the issues with plastics, it was inevitable that someone would step into the market and aim for the middle ground—something with the oxygen imperviousness of glass and the shatter resistance and light weight of plastic.

That something is the Better Bottle. These look very similar to that water bottle floating around the office but are different in a few ways. They're stiffer, clear, and, though you can't see it to the naked eye, they don't let oxygen through nearly as much as the water bottle or bucket.

These are still new compared to other technologies, but they've seen fast adoption by concerned brewers. Just remember these are still plastic and the scratching rules still apply. A downside to the water bottle shape is now you have more spaces to brush, as with a glass carboy.

Stainless Steel

If you can get your hands on a few kegs or kettles with good lids, either homebrew-sized or commercial, these can make great fermenters. Stainless steel is the ultimate in imperviousness to oxygen, chemicals, and gravity. The only problem is it doesn't come cheap!

Plenty of folks use the standard ½-barrel keg as a 15-gallon fermenter. Before you begin messing with a keg, make sure it is depressurized. Bad things happen when you suddenly release a lot of stored pressure!

Some winemaking supply companies now offer 14- and 28-gallon stainless steel storage tanks for $100–$200, and these make great short-term fermenters. If you have more money than you know what to do with or have an orchard's worth of apples to deal with, take a look at variable volume tanks. Primarily targeted to the wine industry, these are stainless steel tanks that contain a special bladder that you can inflate to fill any airspace between the lid and the top of the liquid. These are highly priced, but for the truly serious cider maker they provide an easy way to enjoy to your harvest.

Cleaning a stainless steel surface requires no special precautions. Just go for it! But remember, no bleach! If you're using kegs, make sure you disassemble and clean them well (for more on kegs, see Chapter 8).

ALERT

Don't use aluminum for fermentation. Aluminum reacts poorly to acidic liquids like cider and will leach foul-tasting oxides and metal into your cider.

Racking Canes and Hoses

Racking simply means moving the cider from one vessel to another. Cider makers have it a little easier than beer makers in the racking department. Brewers have to worry about heat and moving hot things around, whereas cider makers actively avoid heat.

You'll want to use basic clear vinyl hoses to move your cider around. You'll need to decide whether you want to use ⅜" inner diameter tubing or ½". Parts are available in both sizes. The ⅜" size is more common, but the transfer is slower. Don't be shy about replacing your hoses, as they will get dirty despite cleaning. The hoses are cheap, and it's not worth damaging your cider for a dollar's worth of hose.

To help pull the cider up and over the side of the fermenter, many use a racking cane, which is just a stiff tube with a crook in it like a shepherd's staff. You slide the hose onto the crooked short end and use the stiff longer side to hold steady in the cider.

A great, cheap way to soak all your hoses and racking canes is to use a couple of cheap plastic wallpaper paste trays layered together. Stack them up to gain stiffness, and then fill with your cleaner/sanitizer of choice and let the parts soak in the liquid.

If you've decided that siphoning is not for you, consider an auto-siphon, which has a pump built into a racking cane. You use the same hose, just stick the cane into the cider, give it a few pumps, and let gravity take over. But beware: Some auto-siphons are notoriously fragile.

If you have a massive amount of postfermentation cider to move around, consider buying a pump. For cider, as with wine, it is recommended that you use a gentler diaphragm pump after fermentation to avoid aerating and damaging it.

CHAPTER 5

Fermentation

Fermentation is a magical time in the life of young juice. It marks the actual transformation from sugary sweet kids' beverage to the harder, sharper drink of the adult. Having a good handle on how fermentation transforms your apple juice into apple cider is critical. Don't you want to know how yeast lives when you introduce it to the cider and what it's actually doing? Oh and don't think that "yeast" is a monolithic thing. There are myriad varieties all waiting to grant your cider a different flavor!

Yeast: An Introduction

It may seem dramatic to say, but society would be radically different without the impact of a unicellular microbe that occurs naturally. Yeast makes it possible for us to have beer, wine, cider, sake, and much more. The botanical name for culinary yeast is *Saccharomyces cerevisiae* (which translates to "sugar mold of beer"). This little microbe made it possible for humanity to unlock a world of nutrition that was otherwise unavailable to us. Because of its importance and simplicity, scientists have delved hard into the study of this fungus.

Yeast's natural food is sugar, and the simpler the better. They love the sugars found in fruits and will happily munch away on the more complex sugars pulled from grains. This process of consumption is known as fermentation, and it allows yeast to store energy while excreting two things we care about greatly: ethanol and carbon dioxide.

When they're not fermenting, yeast live a quiet, dormant life waiting for more food. When introduced to an abundant supply of sugar, they'll immediately begin gobbling up oxygen and nutrients to replicate themselves before they send the whole legion after the sugar. They reproduce asexually by "budding." This entails a small growth (a daughter cell) growing from its mother's cell walls and eventually breaking off. If they survive dinner, the yeast will go back to sleep, waiting for the next batch of food to arrive. Cells grown in undernourished conditions or forced to excessively reproduce because not enough cells were pitched into the wort will die, fall to the bottom and emit flavors and aromas that are less than pleasant.

The Fermentation Cycle

There are several stages yeast cells go through when it's time to ferment. Yeast may not look like much, but each yeast cell is a whirling dervish and goes through distinct phases of activity.

THE STAGES OF FERMENTATION

1. **Lag phase:** Just after adding your yeast, what brewers/vinters call "pitching," the yeast is in what is called the lag phase. This is the period of time when yeast cells begin taking up nutrients and oxygen found in the

juice. The yeast use this time to build strong cell walls that will help deal with the osmotic pressure of the dissolved sugar, the toxicity of alcohol, and the stress of reproduction.

2. **Accelerating growth phase:** Within an hour or two of being in its new home, the yeast will have finished its vitamins and begin reproducing. During this time they're generating and storing energy.

3. **Exponential reproduction:** Approximately six hours after pitching, the yeast begin reproducing exponentially. It is during this reproductive period that most of the yeast-generated flavors are created. If the yeast is too hot, too old, or lacks nutrients, this is when most off-flavors and stressor chemicals will appear. As the yeast saturates the must (the juice pressed from the apples), you'll begin to see little islands of foam, and that's your sign you're about to hit the next phase.

4. **Decelerating growth (high krausen):** There's nothing slow about this phase. While the yeast has stopped growing, it is actively fermenting. It's during this phase that yeast cells are going to town on the simple sugars found in a cider must, and when the magic happens that marks the transition from apple juice to apple cider. Sit back and enjoy the burbling sound of a happy ferment. You'll want to make sure that the temperature is under control before this point since fermentation gives off a lot of heat.

5. **Stationary phase:** After three to four days, the yeast begins running out of sugar to consume. The krausen falls, and the yeast begins to settle. What remains in suspension continues polishing off the last of the nutrients and sugar, then the hardy yeasts sweep up the messy chemical byproducts like acetaldehyde, diacetyl, and sulfur. After that, the remaining yeast will settle with their task complete. All you need to do is wait for the cider to age.

Things to Do Before You Ferment

There are a few things to consider when you're getting ready to ferment your juice. First, you need to decide whether you want to reduce or inhibit any wild yeast in your juice. The second is how to deal with the nutrient level in your juice. Also, don't forget that from the time you bought or made your juice to the time you pitch the yeast, you'll want to keep everything—juice and yeast—cold, or the cider might just ferment on its own and your yeast will die.

Sulfites

The next time you pick up a bottle of wine, you may notice that there's a warning on the label: "Contains sulfites." What are sulfites, and what do they have to do with cider making? When vintners or dried fruit manufacturers talk sulfites, they usually mean sulfur dioxide (SO_2).

ESSENTIAL

Sulfites are only "necessary" when using fresh-pressed cider that has not been pasteurized in any fashion. Even then, the need for sulfites is hotly debated. If you're planning to hit the cider with a lot of yeast or if you want a little "funk" taste, you'll be fine not adding sulfite to the juice.

Looking behind the scientific nomenclature, sulfur dioxide provides both a preservative and antibiotic effect in wine and cider making. Fruit comes in from the orchard with heavy amounts of naturally occurring yeast and bacteria on the skins and in the apple. Left unchecked, those wild yeast cells will tear right into the newly freed juice, leading to some intensely strange characters. Some forms of ciders rely on wild yeast, but if you don't want to, you can take a lesson from winemakers and use a small dose of SO_2 to give your cultured yeast an opportunity to grab hold.

Despite sulfite's use as a wine sanitizer, it's more correct to think of it as a yeast and bacterial stunner. When you treat your cider, you provide a brief window for your yeast to establish a dominating population that prevents wild yeasts from consuming enough resources to affect the cider's character.

Lots of traditionalists argue for sulfite because that's how they were taught to do it. It's a classic winemaker's trick that stuck with cider makers. In the days before you could get reliable yeast, it made perfect sense, too. These days, you can simply overwhelm the skin-borne yeast and bacteria with a large dose of yeast.

Many people, particularly those with respiratory conditions like asthma, are sensitive and allergic to sulfites. Sulfites can trigger temporary breathing issues. You can use brewing sanitizers like iodophor and Star San to keep equipment clean and large initial yeast pitches to overwhelm wild yeast, but you'll miss sulfite's natural preservative effects.

To add sulfite, you need to know your must's pH. The pH scale measures how acidic or basic a substance is. For more on pH, see Chapter 6. Sulfur dioxide becomes more effective as the cider becomes more acidic. As the environment becomes more acidic, more SO_2 remains unbound and able to act. Musts above a pH of 3.8 should be acidified to at least 3.8, to avoid overly aggressive sulfite additions. A must made from regular culinary apples will almost certainly require acidification.

Unless you're planning to be a full-time assayer of fermentations, skip the gadget temptation of a pH meter in favor of pH range-specific testing papers. They're cheaper, just as accurate, and require less care to keep stored properly. Check a wine- or beer-making store for these papers.

Acidify via small additions of a food-grade acid like malic, lactic, or citric acid. Start with 1 gram per 1 quart of must. Stir thoroughly and retest. Like salt, it's easier to add more acid but difficult to remove once added, so take it slow!

Adding acid by weight is critical. Get (or borrow) an inexpensive scale to learn the weight of your acid and other chemicals, like sulfites. Adding by volume can lead to trouble.

Once you've got your pH at 3.8 or lower, you can add sulfite in the form of potassium metabisulfite or sodium metabisulfite. Campden tablets, which come in either form, are a convenient way to do this (though powders are more flexible). Use potassium metabisulfite, if you can, since the potassium ion that remains has less of a flavor impact than the sodium from sodium metabisulfite.

▼ SULFITE DOSING BY pH PER GALLON

pH Range	SO_2 Target (ppm)	Metabisulfite (grams/teaspoon)	Campden Tablets
3.0–3.3	50	0.38 / 0.25	1
3.3–3.5	100	0.75 / 0.5	2
3.5–3.8	150	1.14 / 0.75	3

Anything below a pH of 3 requires no sulfite; anything above 3.8 should be acidified before sulfite additions.

A ¼ teaspoon of potassium metabisulfite contains approximately 1.5 grams of powder.

After dosing and stirring your sulfite into your must, wait 24 hours for the SO_2 levels to drop and then pitch your yeast as normal. This is critical; if you pitch too soon after adding sulfite, you will just render your yeast useless.

Yeast Nutrient

Yeast cells need nutrients to thrive. Sadly, a cider must is the equivalent of an all-you-can-eat fast-food buffet for yeast. Everything about the juice is simple sugars and minimal proteins, but yeast cells need complex minerals to cleanly power through the juice.

Is adding yeast nutrient 100 percent necessary? No, there are at least two circumstances in which skipping it is a smart plan. One, if you want the stressor flavors in your ciders. Some of these can add interesting effects to the cider. Diacetyl, for instance, which has a buttery flavor, adds slickness to the mouthfeel.

The other case, and more likely, is that by depriving the yeast of nutrients, you can also force it to stop fermenting short of completion. In other words, you can leave the cider naturally sweet, without resorting to chemical tricks. The French take it a step further with a process called keeving (discussed further in Chapter 16) that removes much of the already poor nutrition from the must (the liquid extracted from the apple-mashing process during cider making).

ALERT

If you try and bottle a sweet cider without sorbate, you run the risk of the ferment starting again and exploding your bottles. You can always keep the bottles cold!

Preparing and Using Yeast

Once you decide that you're going to skip a wild fermentation and use a store-bought, pure, cultured yeast strain on your cider, you'll be faced with a set of choices and steps you'll need to follow to ensure success. This may seem overwhelming at first, but you'll get the hang of it in no time.

Which Yeast to Use

Your first choice is going to be a hard one. There are over 100 different strains of yeast on the market available for you to use, and 100 different strains mean 100 different flavors from the same juice. Just like apples belong to the same species, despite their variation, the same is true for yeasts—hundreds of variations on the same species.

Here is a quick look at your options:

YEAST STRAIN CHARACTERISTICS

- **Cider strains:** There are yeasts that are sold as cider strains, and all of them appear to be wine yeasts repurposed for making cider. Since a cider is really just a low-alcohol fruit wine, there is nothing wrong with that at all. (Recommendations: White Labs WLP775 English Cider Yeast)
- **Wine strains:** There are a wide variety of wine strains available. For ciders, most people choose strains associated with white wines, like Côte des Blancs or Epernay (two favorites) wine yeast. Wine yeasts will tear through a cider, leaving it bone dry with some fruity tones. Also note that most wine strains are so-called "killer" strains that will

prevent beer or cider yeasts from working. (Recommendations: Red Star Côte des Blancs, Red Star Premier Cuvée, Lalvin EC-1118 Prise de Mousse)

- **Beer strains:** Here's where the massive variety factor kicks in. To beer, yeast is a central component of the flavor and aroma. You can take the exact same beer, only fermented with two different strains of yeast, and end up with final products miles and miles apart. Generally speaking, American strains tend to be very "clean" with few fruit esters. German strains, with the exception of the banana-bread-tasting hefeweizen yeast strains, are very straight-laced and restrained. British beer strains tend to leave things a little sweeter with fruity cherry and apple tones as well. Finally, the Belgian beer scene is distinctively complex, which is reflected in their spicy yeast strains. Each strain does something radically different. (Recommendations: White Labs WLP001 California Ale Yeast, Wyeast 1275 Thames Valley Ale, White Labs WLP565 Belgian Saison I Yeast, Wyeast 3787 Trappist High Gravity)

One funny thing about using beer strains in cider: Since they don't have the same nutrient profile available to them, they tend to have a different impact on ciders than beer. This is not to say that they produce banana instead of cinnamon aromas. The difference tends to be one of power. All of the beer strains' characteristics tend to be softer when fermented in cider, not beer. This is probably due to missing chemical precursors that the yeast needs to make flavor compounds.

Yeast Forms

These days the yeasts available to home experimenters come in two primary forms: dry and liquid. If you've baked at home, you'll instantly recognize the dry yeast form factor. The stuff is convenient, stable, and easy. You can store it in the fridge or the freezer for years until you need it. It does come with a limitation, though: The variety of dry yeast strains is limited. Oddly, almost all wine yeasts are sold in the dry format.

Older texts may tell you that dried yeasts have contamination issues. If you examined dried yeast under a microscope, you'd find plenty of creepy crawlies that shouldn't be there. Since the 1980s, though, yeast companies have improved the sterility of their drying techniques.

The other common format is liquid yeast. This is primarily what brewers who utilize a diverse supply of strains use. This is probably influenced by the frequency of beer production as opposed to wine and cider, which are seasonal. Today, there are two primary companies supplying the home cider maker with yeast: Wyeast and White Labs. Wyeast sells their yeast in foil pouches, and White Labs sells theirs in test tubes. Yeast from either company works great, and you'll find a whole smorgasbord of flavors to pick and choose from.

Liquid yeast requires more care since it's alive and more fragile. It must stay refrigerated, but not frozen, and it expires quickly. So why use it? Because the range of flavors you can get from liquid yeast is bewildering.

ALERT

If you're trying to produce a gluten-free beverage, be careful with liquid yeasts. Unless they're otherwise marked, the liquid growth media may contain gluten and may cause issues for gluten-intolerant folks. The major dry yeast brands (Lalvin, Red Star, Fermentis) are gluten free, both wine and beer strains.

The Proof Is in the Pudding

When you bake bread, the instructions always call for you to "proof" your yeast by soaking it in hot water. You do the same thing with your dried yeast before you throw it into cider. If you're using dry yeast, sprinkle the yeast over a bowl of freshly boiled water that has a small pinch of a yeast nutrient, like GO-FERM. This will help promote stronger cell walls. If you try to pitch your dry yeast directly in the cider, you'll lose 70 percent of the population instantly from shock.

Liquid yeasts may need a little "preferment" to get a jump-start on the fermentation. Simply take a little bit of juice (a pint or quart) and place it in a sanitized container. Add the liquid yeast and cover with foil. Give it a shake every day for a day or two. This is called a "yeast starter," and it will get your yeast raring to go.

Temperature Control

To ensure the best flavor for your cider, you want to control the temperature of the fermenting juice. If you live somewhere with fall weather in the

50°F–60°F range you're fine, but any warmer and you'll need to keep the ferment from getting too hot.

If you have a spare fridge that you can dial in at 60°F, then you're good. Set the fermenter in the fridge and let the magic happen. If you have the spare fridge, but can't set it, look for an override thermostat. It is an electronic device with a temperature probe. The controller keeps the temperature of the probe around what you set it by turning the refrigerator/freezer on and off.

No spare fridge? If you have a large trashcan, or a party tub, just fill it with cold water. Set the fermenter in there and chuck fresh ice in the tub when the thermometer shows that it's too warm. Even better, freeze water in a couple of two-liter soda bottles and rotate those into the tub or the freezer to control the temperature.

If that requires too much space or gear, you can use an old T-shirt and a fan to cool your cider. Stick the fermenter in a shallow pan of water. Cover the fermenter with a T-shirt. Let the shirt fall in the water and begin wicking moisture up the sides of the fermenter. Point a desk fan at the shirt and watch the fermenter stay cool.

Secondary Fermentation

The term *secondary fermentation* is used to mean that time after primary fermentation is completed and you've racked the cider to another vessel. There is really no fermentation going on during that period. It should be called a conditioning phase. You're waiting for two things to happen to the cider: get clear and mellow out.

Over time, various flavor compounds will slowly change, drop below sensory thresholds, or merge with other flavors. This is good, but it takes time and there's no way to rush it. So just let it sit there, check on it periodically, and let the cider tell you when it's ready to drink.

Your one job during this conditioning period is to keep the conditioning vessel topped up. What this means is replacing any cider lost to evaporation or sampling. You need to keep the open airspace to a minimum to prevent staling and mold growth. Top up with fresh cider or a previous batch, or even some commercial cider.

This is also the time to bust out the airlock and stopper you got from your local homebrew shop. (You didn't get one? Now's the time.) Keep the airlock filled with cheap vodka to avoid contamination.

ALERT

Be careful when you're messing with CO_2. In small quantities, that nasal burn is harmless, but in larger quantities it can be dangerous, causing you to pass out or suffocate. CO_2 is heavier than air and will pool in places like basements, refrigerators, and chest freezers. Make sure the area is well ventilated, and if you "smell" that nasal burn, move out of the area.

Cider Saison

Belgian Saison is a strange beer style with distinctive yeast that originally hails from the farms of Wallonia. The beer is made with whatever ingredients are on hand and its aim is to slake the field hands' thirst. Who's to say that one Wallonian farmer didn't just have a mess of apples on hand?

INGREDIENTS | YIELDS 1 GALLON

1 gallon fresh, unpasteurized apple juice
½ teaspoon yeast nutrient
1 package White Labs 565 Belgian Saison I Yeast

1. Mix the juice and nutrient in your fermenter. Use the Standard Cider-Making Procedure described in Chapter 2. Skip the usual temperature controls. This yeast loves to run hot.
2. Lower the temperature on the cider to 36°F to settle any remaining yeast.
3. Package sparkling to 3.0 volumes of CO_2. (See Chapter 8 for how to package for sparkling.)

Saison Nature
This will be softer than a saison beer (Belgian farmhouse beer), but you should still detect a wonderful earthiness, topped by notes of cinnamon and nutmeg. The beer version already comes out very dry, so this cider should feel naturally right.

The Dreaded Autolysis

Cider making is such a leisurely and slow-paced activity that it is tempting to walk away from the cider after the primary ferment ceases being raucously active. In fact, it's so easy to do that you'd assume it's just natural to leave the cider in place until you're ready to bottle.

There is, however, one problem—the yeast. Yeast cells, as they lay dormant, will burn through their glycogen stores built during a properly nutritious ferment. When this happens, some cells will stop functioning and automatically "lyse."

Autolysis happens because, without energy, the cells' lysosomes will no longer contain their digestive enzymes. These enzymes flood the cell and proceed to chemically destroy the cell walls. When the walls are breached, the guts of the cell leak into the cider. As you can imagine, this can add deeply weird flavors to your cider, often described as meaty, plastic, smoky, and rubbery.

If you want to avoid this, the solution is simple. Get the cider off the lees (spent yeast) before the yeast cells lyse. You should be safe as long as you transfer the cider out of your primary fermenter within a month. Like all things fermentation-wise, autolysis is hotly debated with some objecting to the flavor descriptions, others denying that it's a problem, and, in some traditional cases, others claiming the flavors are a hallmark of a certain style. The classic example is champagne. Producers use that meaty, bready, yeasty flavor as a backbone for the wine.

Cider au Naturel

After all the talk of yeast and fermentation control, this recipe will seem redundant, but you should definitely try this at least once to get a sense for a natural cider flavor. And yes, your juice needs to be fresh and unpasteurized.

INGREDIENTS | YIELDS 1 GALLON

1 gallon fresh, unpasteurized apple juice
1 package dried yeast or liquid cider yeast (optional, see note)

1. Place the fresh juice in a sanitized fermenter and cover with foil. Within 2–3 days you should see activity and smell fermentation. Don't be scared if it smells bad—it should get better! (There are no sure things with 100 percent wild ferments.)
2. Wait until fermentation subsides completely, about 2 months. Transfer to a secondary fermenter and let the cider age for 3–4 months before bottling and tasting.

Helping Nature

If you don't want to do a 100 percent natural ferment, then use the yeast. Just let the cider sit for 2–4 days in the fermenter at fermentation temperatures. This will give the wild, native yeast time to get started and impact the flavor before you shut them out with the packaged yeast. Incidentally, this is a great way to add complexity to your regular ciders!

CHAPTER 6

Technical Matters

Time to break out some lab coats and get scientific. There are a few simple measurements, tests, and calculations that will prove useful to your cider efforts. Are these absolutely necessary for the home cider maker? Not necessarily, but they will help you understand what is going on with your cider.

Why Test and Measure

In the world of home-fermentation enthusiasts, there's a bit of resistance to the notion of testing and measuring. But knowing the numbers can help you know how things are going, where they're going, and even how they got there. When you discover flavors that you like, the numbers can help you get other batches to that same area without guesswork.

Almost all of the fundamental characteristics that you care about—levels of sugar, alcohol, acid, and sulfite—are measurable at home. The one thing that isn't easily measured is the level of astringent tannins your juice and cider contain. For that, you'll have to rely on your palate (or, if you are really comfortable with chemistry, you can check out the Lowenthal permanganate titration method as described by Andrew Lea in his cidermaking book and website; see Appendix B).

Finally, don't be fooled by fairy tales of cider makers lovingly tending to crops that magically yield wonderfully complex flavors naturally without any assistance. Anyone making cider to sell tests and tracks these numbers. After all, romance can't pay the bills when a batch of cider falls flat.

Getting the Gravity of the Situation

One of the questions you will be asked about your cider is, "How much alcohol does this have in it?" To legitimately know, beyond a measure of doubt, how much ethanol your cider contains requires expensive lab equipment. However, you can get a ballpark figure with two simple measurements and a little math, but first you've got to know the gravity.

Gravity is a measure of the amount of dissolved solids in a liquid. In juice and cider, the vast majority of those dissolved solids are the various forms of sugar from the fruit. A very tiny part of it belongs to proteins and other bits.

There are multiple ways of measuring and expressing this, but the primary one used by home fermenters is "specific gravity." It is a ratio that compares the density of the sample fluid to a target reference. In the case of fermenting beverages, you are comparing the gravity of your juice/cider to distilled water. It is read in a scale that centers on 1.000 as water and climbs with sugar content. Raw juice tends to fall in the range of 1.040–1.080. To simplify, you can use a system called "gravity points," which simply uses the numbers to the right of the decimal. For example, raw juice tends to fall into the range of 40–80 gravity points.

FACT

Knowing the specific gravity of your juice can help you plan any sugar additions that you want to make to the cider. All you need to remember is that most forms of solid sugar will add, per pound, about 47 specific gravity points to a gallon of liquid. In other words if your juice came in anemically at 1.040, adding a pound of sugar to a gallon would raise the gravity to 1.087.

Before you begin your ferment, you can measure the amount of sugar you have from the raw juice and any other ingredients you add (fruit, sugar, honey, syrups, etc.). This prefermentation measurement is called the "original gravity." It is important because you'll use this to determine when your ferment is done, among other things.

As the fermentation proceeds, gravity measurements will reveal that the density of your proto-cider is rapidly approaching 1.0000, equal to water (because the yeast is eating the sugar). The fermentation can be safely considered done when the gravity doesn't change after three to four days. If your gravity is too high, say above 1.020, then you'll need to fix the "stalled ferment" by rousing, or adding more yeast.

With the simple sugars found in your cider you'll even notice that as fermentation wraps up, the specific gravity may fall below 1.000 into something like 0.995. This is because alcohol is less dense than water, so it's perfectly normal and nothing has gone wrong with your measuring gear. The final gravity measurement taken before you package is called the cider's "final gravity" or in some literature "terminal gravity."

Something important to realize—the measure of sugar in your cider tells you very little about how sweet you perceive the juice/cider to be. Things like acidity, tannins, carbonation, and ethanol all impact and shift your perception of sugar. A very tannic cider, for instance, with a residual gravity of 1.020, may feel less sweet than cider that finishes at 1.000.

Measuring Gravity

There are two main tools to measure the gravity of your liquids. One (the hydrometer) is very cheap and works directly on juice and cider, but in a limited temperature range and requires a larger sample. The other (the refractometer) is less temperature dependent and requires far less juice, but most versions use a different scale and it costs ten times as much.

The Hydrometer

The hydrometer is an ancient measuring tool dating back to A.D. 400. It is based on the principle of displacement with the measurement scales being based on the amount of force needed to float a known weight.

Technically speaking the hydrometer you use for your cider is called a "saccharometer," that is, it's a hydrometer for measuring sugar densities. If you've ever measured your radiator fluid for proper mixture of water to anti-freeze, you've used another form of hydrometer.

Your saccharometer is relatively easy to use. Put a sample of your juice/cider in a narrow jar. Most hydrometers come in a plastic tube that is completely usable for this. They also sell footed hydrometer jars that are steadier. Fill the tube with your sample juice, drop the hydrometer, weighted-side down, into the liquid and give it a spin. Let it settle so that it's not touching the sides of the jar. Look at the scale at the point of the liquid's surface. Don't read the scale at the point where the liquid crawls up the scale, but level with the surface of the cider. Make sure you read the specific gravity units and not potential alcohol.

ALERT

The spinning helps release any bubbles that cling to the hydrometer that could affect the reading. When measuring fermented cider, it is important to degas the sample by vigorously pouring it between two glasses to avoid an artificially high reading caused by CO_2 bubbles lifting the hydrometer.

Done? Nope! You also need to know the temperature of the liquid. The reason is that the apparent density of most aqueous solutions goes up as the liquid is colder and down as it is warmer. Your hydrometer will be calibrated for a specific temperature. This is usually 60°F or 68°F and is marked on the scale itself. If your sample is reasonably close, you can correct it with the table, but remember that the further you have to correct, the less reliable your measurement is.

Lastly, once you're done measuring the juice/cider—drink the sample. There are two good reasons to do this: One, you should know how your beverage tastes at the various stages of production. Two, you don't want to return the now dust-contaminated sample to the remaining cider, which could lead to ugly infections.

▼ HYDROMETER TEMPERATURE CORRECTION

Cider Temperature (°F)	Correction Factor
54	-0.002
62	-0.001
68	0
74	0.001
79	0.002
84	0.003

Example: If your juice reads 1.060 at 79°F, the corrected gravity is 1.062. If your 1.060 juice instead was read at 62°F, the juice gravity is 1.059.

Refractometer

The other method of measuring density is to use a refractometer. It is a small device with an eyepiece that you look through to obtain your reading. It uses a tiny amount of juice to read the gravity, and this is why it is the preferred tool of vintners measuring the sugar level of their grapes in the fields. The magic gizmo works on the principle that light refracts based on the change in density of the solution. The denser the solution, the more it bends.

Many refractometers measure in a system called Brix, which is another means of quantifying the sugar in a solution and is, in fact, the preferred methodology for vintners. (Another scale, Plato, is preferred by professional brewers.) It is easy to find refractometers that read sugar in specific gravity.

Since it uses so little juice, you don't have to worry about the temperature that much. Just place a few drops on the sample glass, close the lid, smooth out any bubbles, and wait a minute. Then look through the eyepiece with the sample tray pointed at bright light. Your gravity is right where the dark blue stops.

FACT

If you want a quick gut check on the gravity and all you have is Plato or Brix reading, multiply the Plato/Brix reading by 4 and that will put you reasonably in the area of your specific gravity for most "normal" gravities.

Sounds easy, right? It turns out that hydrometers are much, much cheaper, and they don't require math to use when the juice has started fermenting. Remember that alcohol lowers the density of your liquid, but, perversely enough, alcohol raises the index of refraction. In other words, as the amount of ethanol increases, as the fermentation gets closer and closer to the end, the reading will become more and more off.

It is possible to correct for this change with a gnarly regression equation. For that reason, it is recommended that you find an online calculator or spreadsheet such as *www.morebeer.com/public/beer/refractbeer.xls* to perform the correction for you.

To give you a feel for how off the readings can be, if you have a cider that started life at 1.060 (15 Brix) and your fermentation reading is 10 Brix, your cider is actually around 1.027 and not 1.040 if the reading was right. If the reading is 6 Brix, the corrected reading puts it at 1.002, not 1.024! That's a difference between being nearly done with fermentation as opposed to having real problems with it!

Calculating Gravity from Additions

Every addition that you make to your cider has an impact on the gravity. You just need to know how many gravity points your addition has, and how much volume it adds. For ease of calculation, use gravity points instead of the full three-decimal-point gravity measure. The formula looks like this:

Original Gravity Points = Starting Gravity Units × Starting Volume
Addition Gravity Points = Addition Gravity Units × Addition Amount

$$Adjusted\ OG\ Points = \frac{(Original\ Gravity\ Points + Addition\ Gravity\ Points)}{(Starting\ Volume + Addition\ Volume)}$$

Say you add 2 pounds of sugar (47 points per pound) to 5 gallons of cider that starts at 1.050.

Original Gravity Points = 50 × 5 = 250
Addition Gravity Points = 47 × 2 = 94
$$Adjusted\ OG\ Points = \frac{(250 + 94)}{(5.0 + 0)}$$
Adjusted OG Points = 68.8
Your cider is now at 1.069, with rounding.

Notice that the sugar points are calculated by the pound, but it has a zero volume addition. That's because sugar is almost completely mixable in water. When you mix it, the sugar molecules effectively disappear into the empty spaces between water molecules, and they don't change the volume.

For a more liquid case, let's say you add 2 quarts of sour cherry juice that measures 1.070 to a juice that again starts at 1.050.

Original Gravity Points = 50 × 5 = 250
Addition Gravity Points = 70 × 0.5 = 35
$$Adjusted\ OG\ Points = \frac{(250 + 35)}{(5.0 + 0.5)}$$
Adjusted OG Points = 51.8
Your cider barely moves and is now at 1.052, with rounding.

Also note in this case, we changed the 2 quarts into 0.5 gallons. You want to keep your units the same when doing these calculations.

Predicting Alcohol

Here's why you take those notes at the beginning. This is the way to answer your friends' questions without spending a ton of money. To roughly estimate your alcohol levels, you simply subtract your gravities and multiply the differences by 131. You'll find different factors for calculating this online, and it has to do with respecting the sugar that remains behind in your beverage. The multiplication factor 131 is used by vintners and cider makers because grape wine and cider finishes fermenting with virtually nothing left behind. Mathematically speaking, all of that looks like this:

Alcohol by Volume (ABV) = (Original Gravity – Finishing Gravity) × 131

So how much booze is in a hypothetical cider that starts with an OG of 1.053 and ends at 1.000?

ABV = (1.053 – 1.000) × 131
ABV = 0.053 × 131
ABV = 6.98% ABV

Acidity

Acidity is a concept that confuses many people. Most people think of pH when they think of acid. Scientists at the Carlsberg Laboratory (founded by J. C. Jacobsen, the founder of the Carlsberg Brewery in Denmark) developed the measure of pH (power of hydrogen) in the 1900s. It is primarily a measure of the concentration of the hydrogen ions in a solution and therefore how strongly acidic or basic (alkaline) a solution is. It ranges on a scale from 0 (very acidic) to 14 (very basic) with 7 being purely neutral.

In cider making, a pH measurement is used to determine the effectiveness of sulfite additions. It is critical to determine the effectiveness of the chemical reaction.

What pH is not good for is determining how acidic the cider tastes, because pH is a strength measurement that is affected by the types of acid (some taste stronger than others) and other compounds (potassium, for instance). For the sheer amount, the percentage by weight, you need to know the "total acidity" of your cider. This measure gives you the best correlation to the acidic taste of your cider.

Measuring pH

There are two primary ways for the home brewer to determine the pH of a solution. There are pH testing papers or pH meters. The papers come in a variety of different ranges, but the idea is always the same: Grab a sample, dip the paper in the sample, discard the remaining sample, and wait for the paper to turn a color. Compare that color to the range indicators on the box, and you know your pH. For cider-making purposes, you'll want to use the pH papers made for wines, as your pH will usually be in the 3–4 range, like a wine. You'll want to toss the sample you test unless you really want to add some of the testing paper's strange chemical compounds to your cider.

If looking at a color and estimating what the pH is isn't your thing, then you'll want to get a pH meter. These portable little electronic gadgets will take a sample, measure an electrical reaction, and give you a numerical readout with a precision that will make you feel comforted. However, pH meters are best suited to those who will use them often. They're semidelicate creatures that need care and maintenance with special chemical compounds, storing the electrodes wet, calibrating, etc. For most purposes, it is highly recommended that you use the papers, which store for a long time if kept dry.

Measuring Acid

To know the total amount of acidity in your cider, you are going to have to act like a scientist and use a process called titration to determine the acid. Most of the kits for testing total acidity or titratable acid are made for vintners, but that's fine. You can treat your cider as a white wine and follow the same instructions.

To titrate a solution, you will take a measured quantity of your test liquid (cider), modify it with some indicating chemical, and then slowly add another chemical until you observe a change in the color of the indicating chemical. The amount of the second chemical then gives you a way to find out how much of your target chemical exists in the sample solution. In the case of cider, you want to find out how much acid is in it.

Most wine titration kits involve these generic steps.

1. Draw X ml of cider/wine.
2. Dilute by a specified amount with distilled water in a test vial.

3. Add Y drops of phenolphthalein to the diluted solution.
4. Add a fixed amount of sodium hydroxide (caustic) solution and shake.
5. The cider will turn magenta and then slowly fade. When it takes a fixed period of time to fade, you're done. Record the amount of reagent you added.
6. Your kit will then contain a conversion factor between the amount of reagent and both the percent TA (total acid, or how much of your cider's weight is acidity) and the grams/liter (g/l) your cider contains.

Most kits will also include instructions on how to use a pH meter to more accurately determine the reaction rather than color observation. For cider-making purposes, you'll want your cider in the 0.6–0.8 percent TA range. But use this range as a guide to compare the ciders that feel right to you and know what your preference is!

Measuring Sulfite

Knowing how much free sulfite remains in your cider is important to understand the long-term protection against oxidation, or shelf life, that you have. There are two primary types of wine SO_2 kits on the market that you can use. One test kit, called Titrets, is very easy to use. Just crack open the test vial, use the included bulb to measure out small amounts of the chemical inside, and watch a color change. The scale will then tell you the amount of SO_2 that you have. Unfortunately, these simple kits are susceptible to bad reads in the presence of ascorbic acid. If you get a read above 40 ppm, you'll want to check with the second kit.

The second and more expensive kit, the Accuvin Free SO_2 Test Kit, is even easier to use. Just grab a sample in the provided apparatus, squeeze into the sample jar, and shake and read. It is also twice as expensive as the Titrets test kit.

The amount of sulfite in your cider will vary with the pH, time, fermentation, and packaging. If you want to take advantage of the stabilizing properties of sulfite, you'll want your ready-to-package cider to be no greater than 30 ppm of sulfite. This is enough to stabilize your cider while having minimal impact on the taste.

Testing for Clarity, Fermentability, and Stability

There are a few other things you should know how do scientifically as a cider maker. These are simple tests you can perform at home to see how your procedures are, what's going right, and what's possibly going to go wrong.

Testing Clarity

This one is simplicity itself. To test clarity, and your dissolved solids, you just need to pour your cider into a tall, conical glass, then let it settle, covered, overnight in the fridge. Ideally, you would use a special glass called an Imhoff Cone with a rack, but it's not an absolute requirement to spend $30 on this glass and rack that will probably have your friends and family questioning your sanity.

Look at the settled particulate matter in the morning. The creamy brown stuff is yeast, which should naturally fall out of solution over time. Look for other bits—is there a bunch of crackly dark brown material? What about anything jellylike? This will tell you if you need to fine (see Chapter 4) your cider or add pectinase.

The second half of the test is even easier. Let the cider warm up. If the cider is hazy while cold (adjusting for the condensation on the glass), but it clears up as the cider warms, you have a polyphenol haze called chill haze. Extending settling time at cold temperatures will allow these complexes to form and settle out, or you can speed it up by hitting the chilled cider with a fining agent after the chill haze has formed visibly.

Testing Fermentability

Fermentability is not usually a problem for ciders since the sugars present are readily available for the yeast to chow, but you can have problems due to the yeast's health or nutrition, or unknown preservatives. It is nice to know precisely where your cider can ferment to in order to provide a baseline. For this purpose, there is a test called the forced ferment test (FFT).

To conduct an FFT, take a pint of your cider just after pitching the yeast (or taken straight if you are going to perform a natural ferment). Set it aside in a sanitized clear glass container, cover, and place somewhere warm (around 75°F). Swirl it regularly throughout the test. If you have a magnetic stir plate (a number of brewers do, for instance), use the stirrer and stir bar to continuously agitate the cider. Once the signs of fermentation are done (roughly two days), grab a sample and measure the gravity. This should be the lowest gravity you will achieve with your yeast and nutrition rates.

If the FFT falls abnormally high (1.015+), you probably need to add some yeast nutrient to the cider. Boil the nutrient in some water and add. If your cider stops 5+ points from the FFT result, something went wrong with your yeast. Swirl them and warm them up or repitch.

Don't rely on the taste of the FFT to indicate what your cider will taste like. The FFT purposely pushes for maximum fermentation, not best flavor production.

Testing Stability

Lastly, you want to know how stable your juice is and how clean your ferment is. Simply take your sulfited or pasteurized juice from your fermenter prior to pitching. Store it with foil tightly covering a sanitized jar. If your cider was stunned of all wild yeasts, and your fermenters are appropriately clean and sanitary, the cider should stay sweet and clean for five days before the wild yeasts recover enough to begin fermenting.

CHAPTER 7

Troubleshooting and Adjusting

So far you've been making cider from straight-up juice. While this can make perfectly reasonable cider, it's bound to be less than perfect. But you have the technology to rebuild and make your cider even better! All it takes are a few simple tools and ingredients, and you can make even the dullest of apples sing.

Why Adjust Your Cider?

Why do you have to adjust your cider? For one, apples are an agricultural product that varies from season to season. Some years your apples may be extra sharp or bitter. Sometimes there may be an abundance of sugar, or in wet years the juice can be diluted. So because of this you need to be on your toes and learn to give your apples the help they need. Also, because of this variability, it's impossible to say what your apples need and how much of it to add.

Before you can adjust anything you have to figure out what's gone off. The only way to do that is to start tasting early in the process. Taste your juice before you use it. Take notes on what you taste. It will take time, but you'll eventually be able to predict with reasonable certainty what your cider will taste like after it ferments.

But no matter how certain you are—leave your adjustments for after fermentation! The only preferment addition that you make should be acid adjustments necessary to bring your juice's pH in line for sulfite treatment. Why? Fermentation is a complex process with a wide range of effects and impacts on the flavor, and despite your best efforts you'll never quite predict things right. So wait to make changes based on reality and not your suppositions.

But adjustments should be made before you bottle or keg your cider. Yes, you could open every bottle, add your adjustments, and close each bottle, but that's tricky business. You have to duplicate your exact measures on each bottle, which is hard without precise measurement gear.

ESSENTIAL

Don't freak out if you've tasted your newly made cider and discover it tastes strange and funky with sulfurous or other disagreeable odors and aromas. All that means is your cider is still "green" and needs more aging time. If your older cider tastes off, well . . . that's something completely different. The rule to live by: Time heals a lot.

Plus, never forget—every time you manipulate your cider, that's another chance to mess it up. Opening bottles can expose your cider to additional oxygen, leading to faster stalling. Bacteria-laden dust can land in the bottle, and so on. Many pitfalls await the cider maker who has to crack open a whole batch of bottles.

How to Adjust

When you first start making cider, you won't have a good sense of how little additions of acid and tannin can affect the flavor. Instead of risking the whole batch, try adjusting in smaller quantities.

The following technique is one that even seasoned cider makers should follow. Doing this will take the guesswork out of the process and allow you to hit your target every time. It works for more than just the adjustments outlined here; it's for any flavor changes and additions you want to make to your ciders.

SURE-FIRE ADJUSTMENT PROCESS

1. Grab an easily measured sample of your cider.
2. Add a measured amount of your flavoring/chemical. Stir. Record the amount of the addition. Take a small sip and decide if the change was enough or if you need more.
3. Continue adjusting and taking notes until you've reached the desired taste.
4. Look at your final amounts and then multiply the amounts by the number of samples that would make your total volume of remaining cider. Add the multiplied amounts of your additions to your full batch of cider, stir, and proceed.

Example: You pull 1 pint of cider from a 5-gallon batch to check for acid and decide that you need to acidify. Add ⅛ teaspoon of acid blend. Stir, taste, and decide whether you need another ⅛ teaspoon (for a total of ¼ teaspoon per pint). Your 5-gallon batch has 40 pints in it, so you need 10 teaspoons of acid blend for the full batch (or 9¾ teaspoons to make up for the missing pint).

Mixing It Up

Learning to adjust your cider isn't just about correcting errors. It's about learning, having a little fun, and avoiding palate boredom. The Sure-Fire Adjustment Process is a great learning exercise. Who says you have to only use it to plan adjustments? Have a cider-tasting party where you pour and flavor different glasses of cider from the same batch! Start with the regular cider and then add changes to subsequent glasses so that you and your friends can learn how acid and tannin affect a cider. Prepare a bunch of different flavor extracts—cinnamon, ginger, lemon, raspberry, etc.—and add those to glasses. Have fun with it!

You can even do this same technique with bottled cider that you're planning to store. Take the same base cider, divide it into smaller quantities, and then flavor each one. Take careful notes and label the bottles so you know which is which.

What to Do When

If you are currently experiencing the dread of what to do with an off-tasting cider, here's a quick primer on what to do when things go horribly wrong.

▼ **COMMON FLAWS AND THEIR SOLUTIONS**

Flaw	Cause	Possible Fixes
Too acidic	Too much acid in relation to remaining sugar	Add sugar, dilute with new juice
Lacking body	Lack of protein or tannin	Add tannin, add lactose
Color is darkening	Oxidation	Add sulfites or ascorbic acid
Hazy	Yeast in suspension	Crash the fermenter temperature to 32°F for one week

Flaw	Cause	Possible Fixes
Particulates in suspension	Excess yeast, protein	Fine the cider (see Chapter 4)
Jelly-like particles	Pectin, a naturally occurring enzyme, created a gel in the cider	Dose the cider with pectinase, wait 2–3 weeks, and carefully rack (don't heat the juice!)
Moldy/fuzzy growth on surface	Mold/wild yeast/bacteria	Dose the cider with sulfites, taste, verify if the taste is okay, proceed with caution, destroy plastic gear
Not sweet enough	Overfermentation	Back-sweeten (see Chapter 7)
Long, ropy strands	*Pediococcus* infection/wild yeast	Wait out the ropes (they will dissipate), check the flavor, destroy the plastic gear
Too astringent/bitter	Too much tannin in relation to sugar	Add sugar; fine with Polyclar
Too sweet	Underattenuation, sugars remaining in solution	Restart fermentation, add acid to balance

Acid

Acid can lend a sense of zip and freshness to your food. In the wine world, they talk about the tightness of a wine, which is the perceived acid level. If you want to be scientific about your acid additions, then you need to get your hands on an acid testing kit. Why? As explained in Chapter 6, there is a difference between pH and total acidity. The pH measures the strength of the acid as buffered by the solution. Total acidity, on the other hand, deals with the total by weight of acid in the wine. The difference is important. While the strength of different acids by weight may vary, the acids that you use as a cider maker are all similar enough that their weight means more than the pH.

COMMON FOOD-GRADE ACIDS

- **Ascorbic acid ($C_6H_8O_6$):** You know this as vitamin C. While you can use vitamin C pills, your local homebrew/wine shop should have powdered ascorbic acid. Since you don't know what is binding the pills, use the powder or citric acid.

- **Citric acid ($C_6H_8O_7$):** The name of this acid comes from the acid's natural source, citrus fruit. This is the most commonly used acid for beverages, and your brain will pick up lemon/lime notes from it.
- **Lactic acid ($C_3H_6O_3$):** This is milk acid. It is a byproduct of common *Lactobacillus* bacterial fermentation. You experience it every time you eat yogurt or sourdough bread. Food-grade lactic acid is very common at homebrew shops and is fairly neutral.
- **Malic acid ($C_4H_6O_5$):** This is literally "apple" acid, as in it was first isolated from apples. In reality, it is found in a number of foods. This is the acid that you associate with the flavor of green apple. Winemakers consider the flavor very sharp, and they use a process called malolactic fermentation to convert it to the less-aggressive lactic acid.
- **Mead acid blend:** A blend of malic, citric, and tartaric acid that is used heavily by mead makers to try and get a good balanced approach to the tartness of their mead.
- **Phosphoric acid (H_3PO_4):** This is an inorganic acid (notice the lack of carbon in the formula). If you drink soda, then you consume phosphoric acid. Soda manufacturers use it because it is cheaper than other acids. The old soda fountain name for a drink, "phosphate," comes from this acid. It is very potent and should be used several drops at a time.
- **Tartaric acid ($C_4H_6O_6$):** These white crystals are in theory the leftover remains of wine fermentation. If you look at the bottom of an old wine cork (or wine barrel), you may see tartaric acid attached to the surface.
- **Vinegar, or acetic acid ($C_2H_4O_2$):** This is only included here to prevent temptation. Vinegar, also known as acetic acid, is very common and super tart, but the aroma and flavor is very distinctive, and it makes people think, "rotten." Another worry is that if you're using good vinegar with live cultures, the acetobacter on board will take root and convert your cider into distressingly expensive cider vinegar!

It's unusual, but not completely unheard of, to be faced with a cider with too much acidity. The telltale signs are that it's overly sharp and harsh and provides your tongue with the feeling of being freshly shaved. The solution here is one of two choices: dilute the acid with additional sweet cider or juice, or back-sweeten the cider (see the Back-Sweetening Process section later in this chapter) and use the extra sugar to balance the extra zip.

Tannin

Many people think of apples in terms of sweet and sour. On the sweet side you have the Red Delicious apple acting like a big sugar bomb, and on the other side is the pleasingly piquant Granny Smith. People usually forget the other important flavor dimension—astringency. In beer, the astringent bite comes from the bitterness of hops. In wine, the grapes and the oak provide tannin. In traditional cider, the apples provide tannin.

What is tannin? It is any one of a number of bitter polyphenols originally found in plants and now synthesized from a number of sources. Like starches, which are long chains of sugars, a polyphenol is a large molecule constructed of various phenol groups (compounds that provide spicy aromas and flavors). The name comes from the old process of using the bark of trees to prepare animal hides, also known as tanning.

ESSENTIAL

Tannins are powerful compounds with an outsized flavor impact. Go easy with your tannin additions until you know how much you need. Too much tannin will make a cider that is difficult to drink.

Why would you ever want something that can be described as "mouth puckering" in your cider? They have no direct taste or aroma, but they impart dimensionality to the mouthfeel of the cider. The drying finish also accelerates the desire for the next sip by removing any lingering sweetness. Lastly, tannins are antioxidants that slowly age in an oxidative process, and it's believed that this aging process protects the cider from suffering oxidation damage, thus extending the lifespan of the cider.

If you're using culinary apples or regular juice to make your cider, you'll definitely be lacking in tannins. The local homebrew shop will have winemaking supplies on hand to help you fix this problem, and there are other options that you can find in your grocery store.

- **Crab apples.** Once discarded as useless, people are rediscovering the crab apple's tartness and depth. Grab a bunch from your favorite market or forgotten tree and juice them. (A kitchen juicer works great.) Add the juice in parts to find the balance.
- **Grape tannin (powdered or liquid).** Made from the skins of grapes, this is potent. In powdered form, it may take as little as ¼ teaspoon per 5 gallons of cider to give it the right bite. A dose of the liquid tannin starts as low as a teaspoon.
- **Oak.** You can buy oak chips or cubes from the store and give them a quick boil. You can either use the boiled chips or the "tea" you've made to adjust the cider.
- **Tea.** Strong black tea contains a healthy dose of tannin. To avoid adding too much tea flavor, make a cup that is two or three times stronger than normal. Add this in small doses to find the right sensation.

Regardless of the form you choose, add the tannin and wait a week for it to settle before you get the final taste and proceed to packaging.

Too Much Tannin

If your cider is actually too tannic, you have several options to deal with it. First, you could wait it out, but as is the case with red wine, this might be a considerable waiting period. Secondly, you could sweeten or dilute the cider. Sugar distracts from the bitterness, so you could back-sweeten. Lastly, you can try using a fining method like Polyclar (also known as PVPP, see Chapter 4) to remove the tannin compounds. Follow the package instructions to prepare the Polyclar. Add it, then wait one to two weeks for it to settle out.

More Sweetness

Because of the simple sugar nature of apple juice, the biggest worry for most home cider makers is that the cider has too little residual sugar, making a very dry beverage. Some folks find fault with this and would prefer to have a sweeter cider. You can attempt to arrest your ferment by adding sulfite and rapidly crashing the temperature of the cider to near freezing, but you won't be able to carbonate the cider naturally. Remember sulfite and sorbates prevent the yeast from reproducing and fermenting which you need for the yeast to produce carbonation.

If you are unable to manipulate the cider by making it incredibly strong (enough to kill the yeast naturally—see Chapter 10 on sugar additions) or reduce the nutrient levels to naturally stall the ferment (see Chapter 16 for information on keeving), then you'll need to back-sweeten the cider (see following text).

The first choice to make is: Does the cider have to be sparkling? If the answer is yes and you don't have a way to force-carbonate (see Chapter 8) the cider, you need to keep the yeast population active so it can ferment in the bottle and carbonate naturally. Since you can't kill the yeast, you have to sweeten with something that it can't ferment. This will allow you to have sweetness and still be able to add sugar for yeast to use in carbonating. There are several options available in varying degrees of both sweetness and "naturalness."

COMMON NONFERMENTABLE SWEETENERS

- **Aspartame (sold as NutraSweet).** Created in the 1960s, this is the most popular artificial sweetener in the United States. The one thing to be careful of is that aspartame breaks down when heated, losing its sweetness. If you plan on pasteurizing the cider, don't use it.
- **Lactose.** Milk sugar is a common additive in traditional British milk stouts for its body-enhancing qualities. It is many times less sweet than regular sugar, but it does not ferment. If all you need is a little boost, consider using 1 pound of lactose in 5 gallons of cider and see if that doesn't move the needle enough.
- **Saccharin.** Brought to market in the late 1800s, saccharin was one of the first artificial sweeteners to be successful. It is now the third-most popular sweetener in America and is used in Europe in a number of ciders, perry, and sour beers. In the United States, the most common brand is Sweet'N Low.

- **Sorbitol.** A sugar alcohol that is processed by the body very slowly. It is naturally found in pears. It also has a naturally mild laxative effect.
- **Stevia.** A naturally occurring sweetener that is derived from the leaves of the stevia plant. It is aggressively sweet and stable and will not ferment. Sold in the United States as Truvia Natural Sweetener and Pure Via.
- **Sucralose.** A British invention, sucralose consists of sucrose that's had three hydroxyl groups (HO) replaced with atoms of chlorine. The end result is a molecule that is safe, stable, and 600 times sweeter than sugar. You will get some fermentation with Splenda, which is sucralose cut with the food additive maltodextrin (which makes it measurable to the average home user).
- **Xylitol.** Also known as "wood sugar." This sugar alcohol was first created in the late 1800s. Very common in sugar-free gum since it was discovered to have positive effects for fighting cavities. Dangerous in large quantities to dogs.

If the answer to the sparkling question is either no or "Hey, I have kegs," then you can avoid the nonfermentable route and use sugar, syrups, and other things to get your sweetness. Some common fermentable sweeteners include:

- **Apple juice concentrate.** A very common trick is to use a can or two of frozen apple juice concentrate per 5 gallons of cider in a sulfite stunned and sorbated cider.
- **Honey.** Mankind's most commonly available sweetener for millenia. Can have a great impact on aroma, but it is incredibly fermentable. If you hope to preserve the sweetness, you need to sorbate or kill the yeast.
- **Maple syrup.** Smoky, sweet, and not cheap, but it provides a natural New England additive to cider.
- **Sugar.** No matter the form, all sugars will ferment unless the yeast is somehow disabled either via high alcohol levels, filtration, or the use of sorbate.

If you use a fermentable sweetener, you must prevent the yeast from restarting and consuming the newly added sugars. For that, you'll need your old friends metabisulfite and potassium sorbate. Here is the standard back-sweetening process:

BACK-SWEETENING PROCESS

1. After fermentation is complete, rack the cider to a secondary fermenter and add enough sulfite to reach 50 ppm. Stir in the sulfite and let it sit for 24 hours.
2. Add ½ teaspoon of potassium sorbate per gallon. Stir and let settle for 24 hours.
3. Add sweetener to taste and package the cider. If your cider is to remain flat, you're done. If you want sparkling cider, package in a keg and force-carbonate (see Chapter 8).

QUESTION

Do I have to use sulfites when back-sweetening?
No. But it is a safe idea to add sulfite to prevent any still-active yeast cells from consuming their share of sugar and to keep any opportunistic bacteria at bay. Remember, sorbate doesn't prevent yeast from fermenting, just reproducing. It also has a limited effect on other microorganisms.

Less Sweet

A less common flaw is too much sugar remaining in your cider. More than likely this is from a less-than-stellar ferment. Not pitching enough yeast, or using unhealthy yeast from old or improperly stored packs, can cause a stalled ferment. If you sprinkled dry yeast onto your cider without rehydrating properly, then you instantly killed a large part of your yeast population. To fix this, just grab some more yeast and rehydrate it properly. Add to the cider and gently swirl. Consider boiling a dose of yeast nutrient for 10 minutes and adding for some extra yeast help.

If your ferment got too cold, an easy fix is to bring the cider someplace warmer. Let the cider warm up to around 70°F and then rouse the yeast by gently rocking the fermenter, causing the yeast to swirl back into suspension. Between the heat and the gentle swirling, the yeast should get right back to work. Keep an eye out for activity, and then regulate the temperature.

If you added a bunch of sugar to make an apfelwein, you could simply have just too much sugar, and too much alcohol, for the yeast to handle. Some strains do not tolerate more than 10 percent alcohol levels (alcohol by volume). At this point, you must either re-pitch with a new, more alcohol-tolerant strain, or you need to accept that your cider is just not going to get any less sweet. If the latter, use an acid addition to sharpen the cider and make it less cloying.

Dealing with Off Cider

Sometimes you need to deal with a cider where the adjustment isn't a matter of too much/too little acid, tannin, or sugar. Sometimes, something else has gone wrong. Maybe a variety of apple you're using has a disagreeable flavor. Maybe the yeast ran too hot and the flavor is off, or worse, maybe something bacterial got into the cider and now it smells and tastes awful.

So what can you do? It is times like these when the fine art of covering up comes in handy. If the flaw isn't hideously awful, the simple thing to do is distract the palate with another strong flavor. A good example of this is using a strong sweet liqueur. Simply add the liqueur to the cider, let the sugar ferment down, and then bottle it. A favorite for this is raspberry schnapps. The big, bright fruit flavor, the candy tones, and the extra ethanol will baffle and mislead the palate from the offending flavors. Here's the best part: When you serve your cider to guests, you say "Oh this is my raspberry cider. I hope you enjoy it." They never need to know that it smelled like a dirty sock before you added the raspberry flavoring.

On the other front, if the cider is too far gone to take the distraction treatment, you should consider turning your cider into applejack or cooking with it. Those don't appeal to you? Well, then your drains will handle the cider just fine, and you've learned a lesson for the next batch.

Preventing Future Flaws

To prevent future mishaps of a nonagricultural variety (fermentation, bacterial), here are some quick tips. Prevent fermentation flaws by pitching a large amount of healthy and properly prepared yeast. Make sure the yeast has plenty of nutrition, and control the fermentation temperatures. If you don't want "hot" cider, don't let it ferment hot! You're always going to be better off fermenting your cider cool.

On the bacterial front, you need to review your cleaning and sanitation protocols. Check every nook and cranny for gunk, dirt, and crud. Get rid of it all, anything filmy, etc. Then sanitize everything properly with the appropriate rates and times. It is also recommended that you replace any soft plastic parts that come into contact with infected ciders. That means all your tubes, plastic buckets, gaskets, etc. Bacteria love to hide in soft, squishy places that can provide safe haven. So off it goes! Much better to spend the few extra dollars on new gear than to deal with the expense and heartache of wasted batches of cider!

CHAPTER 8

Packaging and Carbonating Your Cider

Unless you're completely attached to the romantic notion of dipping a glass of cider from the barrel, at some point you're going to want to store your cider in something other than your fermenter. After all, you want to drink your cider and use your fermenters for your next cider project.

Things to Consider When Packaging

Packaging isn't a very romantic term. It sounds like you're getting ready to move or ship Christmas presents to far-flung family members, but there's more to it than just choosing between a bucket or a bottle when it comes to storing your cider—hence the industry term *packaging*.

There are a number of things to consider when deciding how to package your cider. Each packaging type involves tradeoffs. Some are simple and relatively cheap but involve a lot of labor to pull off; others require a fair amount of capital investment before you can have a drink.

A universal rule for any packaging is that it should be clean and sanitized before you add your cider to it. You've just spent oodles of cash and countless hours shepherding your cider from the orchard—you want it to survive its slumber before you drink it! Don't risk wasting that time by throwing your cider in dirty, unsanitary packages. Take the extra time to inspect every bottle, bag, keg, etc. A few more minutes cleaning can stave off disappointment.

Aging and Oxygen

A major consideration for you as you prepare your cider for drinking is just how long you want to keep it around. If your answer is "not very long," then you're set because any sort of packaging will work for you. Heck, just grab a bucket with a spigot, sanitize it, fill it with cider, and dispense your cider from the spigot (this will stay good for 3–5 days).

On the other hand, if you want to hold on to your cider for a few months or a few years, you'll want to consider something like glass or a keg, largely because of their key ability to slow down the introduction of oxygen.

Oxygen, in addition to being life supporting, is also a great fuel for all sorts of chemical reactions. This includes reactions that will spoil your cider. Certain types of bacteria and mold will only grow in the presence of oxygen. Staling reactions occur when oxygen is around. You need to do as much as possible to reduce these effects when you package your cider.

The easiest way is to purge everything with a blanket of carbon dioxide (CO_2). A little squirt in every bottle will do wonders to delay the problem. Cider makers also take a cue from the wine world and add metabisulfite to battle oxygen (great for still ciders). If you're using bags, squeeze them out and fill with nothing but cider. If you're capping or corking, make sure your bottles are sealed absolutely properly!

Carbonation

What sort of carbonation are you looking for in your cider? Do you want a wine-like stillness? Do you want a little prickling sensation? Beer-like carbonation? Do you want a full champagne-style blast of bubbles?

Carbonation matters, because carbon dioxide (CO_2) does several things to your cider. When CO_2 dissolves into an aqueous solution it forms carbonic acid (H_2CO_3), a weak acid that provides a bit of extra zip on your palate. Additionally, CO_2 fluffs up and enriches the body and the gas as it evolves from a solution, volatilizing esters and other chemicals to more effectively reach your nose and affect your perception.

On the negative side, excess carbonation can completely overwhelm the more delicate aromas and flavors of your cider. Inhaling large quantities of carbon dioxide literally numbs and burns your nose. This effect is from the combination of CO_2 and water in your nasal cavity turning into carbonic acid. The prickling sensation you feel in your mouth has another side effect as well: It prevents you from tasting other flavors.

If you have a fruity or spicy cider whose flavors you want to sing, then you'll want to explode those aromas from the glass with lots of carbonation. If, on the other hand, you have softer, subtler essences to explore, still or pétillant carbonations are the way to go.

FACT

According to researchers from Britain's National Health Service and the University of California, San Diego, that prickling sensation you get from carbonated beverages is not from bubbles bursting on your tongue! Instead, it's the carbonic acid reacting with an enzyme attached to the sour-sensing taste buds. The message to your brain gets interpreted as that familiar "pop!"

When beverage makers talk about carbonation, they usually talk about it in terms of volumes of CO_2. This measures the amount of carbon dioxide dissolved in the liquid relative to the volume of liquid. In other words, a cider carbonated to 1 volume means there is 1 gallon of carbon dioxide dissolved in every 1 gallon of cider. Since the amount of gas that dissolves in a liquid can vary based on the temperature of the liquid, when people talk about or calculate their volume targets, they do so against a reference temperature of 68°F (20°C).

Traditional Carbonation Levels

There are three or four different levels of carbonation generally recognized for cider. Since cider is a low-alcohol apple wine, these are closely based on the wine world's view of carbonation. Remember, for the most part the only thing needed to make a cider more carbonated is more sugar. So as you increase the carbonation levels, you'll require more sugar and a package that's capable of holding more pressure.

Still: 0 Volumes

Until humanity figured out how to make a pressure-safe enclosure, this was how we drank all of our aged beverages, including cider. Of course, this is where apple juice starts its life before you let it ferment.

Still cider requires a little time and a little work. Let your cider sit for a month at room temperature covered with a breathable bung or foil, and most carbonation will naturally come out of solution. Alternatively, if you bottle with regular wine corks, just wait a few weeks and then cork it. Carbonation will naturally leak out of the bottle. Just make sure you're really done fermenting first!

If you want a truly degassed cider, take a tip from vintners and buy a degassing wand. A few quick twists of the wand will knock out any carbonation, even from the most seemingly flat beverages.

Still cider is enjoying a resurgence, but it requires absolute tiptop apples to successfully pull off. Without the carbonation to liven up the party, the only thing that matters is the fruit and other flavors you may add. Keep an eye out for still ciders! They will shock you with a wine-like intensity of character.

Pétillant: 0.5–1.5 Volumes

Pétillant sounds fancy, but it is a French wine term for a very lightly sparkling beverage. This is actually the natural state for a freshly fermented beverage. As the yeast ferments, secretes ethanol, and emits CO_2, not all of the carbon dioxide goes flying into the atmosphere. Depending upon the temperature you're letting your ferment go at, you can have nearly a full volume of CO_2 dissolved into solution.

To be clear on what a pétillant cider should feel and look like, if you poured a beer that was pétillant, you would be tempted to call it flat. A pétillant cider should have just enough dissolved carbon dioxide to make a few bubbles in the glass and a bit of fizz on the tongue. Lots of bubbles flying out of the glass means you're well above pétillant and more likely medium or sparkling.

Going straight from the fermenter into a bottle (glass or PET) should put you in the low pétillant range (0.8–1.0), as long as your ferment was in the 60°F–68°F range. If you've allowed your cider to warm up above that at all, you'll be lower! This trick only works if you're close to your final gravity. If your cider has a way to go, you'll end up overshooting pétillant and hitting medium or sparkling levels.

Why go pétillant? By taking a step up from a still approach, you imbue your cider with just a little more life, and a little more acid that may be lacking based on your apples. Maybe you have a spice character that you want to drive more, but too much carbonation would make it tongue scraping. Maybe that extra bit of fizz takes your too-sweet cider and pulls it into line.

FACT

Incidentally, British beers conditioned and served traditionally have very low levels of carbonation, sometimes falling in the pétillant range of carbonation. If you get a chance to try "real ale" or "cask ale," you'll now know that it's not flat, it's pétillant!

Medium: 2.0–3.0 Volumes

Stepping up the chain, your next stop is medium carbonation. The easy way to visualize this level of carbonation is to go crack open your favorite type of craft beer. Most craft beer (other than wheat beers) are bottled between 2 and 3 volumes.

Sparkling: 3.0+ Volumes

This is the New Year's Eve of popping bottles, filling the air with flying corks and bubbles. This is also the one time you'll see your cider possibly have a frothy head for a while! Don't count on it lasting, though. Cider, like champagne, doesn't contain enough foam-positive proteins to hold bubbles for very long like a beer does.

FACT

What causes a beautiful head in a beer that is missing from cider and wine? It's the same protein that makes it possible to whip egg whites into a soufflé or meringue—albumin. Since apples don't contribute any albumin to the finished cider, the head fizzes out quickly!

Making a sparkling cider can be a lot of fun, but it comes with danger! Highly sparkling cider (3.5+ volumes) can generate enough pressure to blow up a regular 12-ounce beer bottle. If you want a heavily effervescent cider, take a tip from the champagne producers of the world and use a heavy-bottom champagne bottle. They're designed to hold a lot of pressure, but avoid going over 5 volumes for safety's sake.

One other consideration with sparkling cider is that you need to make sure it is ice cold before you crack it open. If popped while warm, the dissolved carbonation will explode out of the bottle and all over you, your ceiling, and your countertop.

If you're bottle conditioning, or aging, the cider, remember that the amount of yeast settling in the bottom of the bottle is a direct function of how much carbonation you're aiming for. To keep the bottles clear of yeast, consider treating your highly sparkling bottles like champagne and use the classic *méthode champenoise* (see Chapter 16).

Adding Carbonation: A Priming Primer

There are several ways to add carbonation to your cider. They mostly involve taking advantage of the fact that when in the fermentation process, yeast cells convert sugar partially into CO_2. If you want that CO_2 to stay with your cider until you're ready to drink it, then you'll have to trap it and allow it to dissolve into the cider naturally. This takes time, usually around 2 weeks. This is also the last time to easily affect your final cider flavor.

Adding carbonation means adding sugar, a process known as priming. The amount of sweetener or sugar you'll need to add to achieve your target carbonation level can be found in Appendix C. Keep in mind that the precise amounts will vary based on temperatures and fermentation health, but the table should get you in the ballpark.

ESSENTIAL

Don't forget, if you've added anything like potassium sorbate to your cider, you will not be able to naturally carbonate it, because the yeast will not be able to ferment your extra sugars!

Timed Ferment

If you can accurately gauge how much gravity is remaining before your fermentation is going to halt, and get your actively fermenting cider into bottles, then you have no need for external sugar sources and can rely instead on your already supplied sugar. This is tricky and requires a firm grasp on the behavior of your yeast and the makeup of your juice, or else you run the risk of your bottles exploding!

For instance, the average medium-carbonated cider requires about 3 points of gravity to ferment and carbonate at 2.7 volumes. If you know your cider stops fermenting around 1.003, you can bottle the cider when it's at 1.006 to achieve your carbonation.

Juice and Frozen Concentrate

For the purist at heart, there can be no better way to carbonate and add a little extra oomph than to use fresh juice or frozen apple concentrate. The theory is that the extra apple content will help add dimension to your finished cider. How much you need to use is going to depend completely on your juice's sugar levels.

If your fresh juice is 1.050 OG, and you want that medium-carbonation target, you'll need to figure out how many points per ounce you get from the juice (50/128 = 0.39), and then how many ounces yield 3 points (3/.39 = 7.6 ounces). In other words, it takes nearly 1 cup per gallon to make your cider sparkle.

The story is the same for frozen concentrate, except the totals are a lot less. Undiluted concentrate is an astounding 1.350 OG. For our same 3 points, you'll need only about 1 ounce per gallon.

QUESTION

Can I add dry ice to my cider to carbonate it?
No! There are two great reasons not to do this. First, the CO_2 will sublimate from solid to gas more rapidly than the cider can absorb it, leading to dangerously high pressure in the headspace. Second, dry ice isn't necessarily food grade, so it may contain industrial lubricants and other nasty chemicals!

Sugar

Sugar is arguably the easiest way to get the oomph into your cider. It's also provides an opportunity to slap some extra character in your cider. Sure, you can use plain old white sugar that you buy in the supermarket, but you can have a lot of fun with different unrefined sugars, like turbinado, or even a dark molasses brown sugar. At the very least, try and use the dextrose sugar found in your local home-brewing store, since it will be easier for the yeast to consume.

When you add sugar to your cider for bottling, remember to boil it first in some water to make a syrup. If you attempt to add raw sugar to a carboy (a large, globular bottle with a narrow neck) of fermented pétillant cider, the sugar crystals will act as nucleation sites for CO_2 to escape the solution and erupt from the fermenter.

Force Carbonation

This is only available to folks putting their cider into kegs, but it is simple (though derided by purists as cheating). Once your cider is in the keg, you simply dial in your desired pressure and let it sit for 2 weeks, or shake for 10 minutes. The CO_2 from your tank will dissolve into the solution and provide the fizz without the extra wait. It also allows you to make fizzy, back-sweetened ciders!

Bottles

The bottle is quite arguably the easiest and most versatile way of storing your cider. It is also probably the cheapest. When you bottle, you'll have several options to choose from. Do you use plastic PET bottles like those used for soda and sparkling water? Do you use traditional glass bottles? If so, what type and what enclosure?

ESSENTIAL

Play it safe and keep conditioning cider stored safely in a box. If the bottles should explode, you'll at least contain any potential shrapnel.

Glass Bottles

Available in many shapes and sizes, the glass bottle is one of humanity's key inventions. Taking the silica found in sand, melting it, and shaping it allowed for the storage of substances that couldn't be safely stored in clay jars. Here are some of the pros and cons of using glass:

FACT

From about 100 B.C. until A.D. 1904, bottles were a handmade, hand-blown affair. But in 1904, Michael Owens patented the first automatic bottle-making machine, which turned out 240 bottles per minute! His name lives on to this day with his companies Owens-Illinois and Owens Corning.

GLASS PROS

- Glass bottles are very portable. Anyone's fridge can handle a six-pack, and a proper bottle can make a great gift for anyone.
- The glass bottle—like the 12-ounce brown, longneck beer bottle—is cheap and common. You can buy a case of new virgin bottles for relatively cheap, or you can go the recycling route and drink yourself into some empties.
- There are lots of different bottle and enclosure types out there with different colors. Not only can you splurge and make a real statement with your bottle choices, but glass bottles will also handle a wide variety of cider types.
- Glass is incredibly impervious to most chemical substances. It can hold acids and caustics without flinching. It also won't let oxygen permeate your cider as long you seal the top properly.
- Glass excels at being green. Much of the glass you use as a consumer has been recycled from previously used glass because it takes less energy than creating glass from scratch.

GLASS CONS

- Glass is most definitely not shatter resistant.
- That little brown bottle may not seem like it, but it's heavy for its size. Put together a case of them filled with cider, and you're talking 30 pounds!
- You've got to find a place to store those bottles.

Sealing Your Bottles

How you seal a bottle all depends on the type of bottle you choose, which in turn is affected by the cider you're looking to bottle.

Wine Bottles

If you're making still cider, you can go the vintner's route and use classic 750 ml wine bottles. Starting simple, you can simply stopper the bottle with a push cork, sometimes called a T stopper.

Stepping up, you can use regular straight corks. Most cork users give their seals a brief dunk in metabisulfate solution. To insert the corks, you need a corker, a tool that compresses and slides the cork into the bottle. There are simple handheld models that have varying degrees of effectiveness.

ESSENTIAL

The best solution for any seriously corker is a floor or countertop corker, but they are at least five times as expensive as hand corkers. Check with your local winemaking shop; they may let you rent a floor corker for as little as $10.

Beer Bottles

The 12-ounce American longneck is the one bottle you are guaranteed to find right around the corner from home. The crown-capped bottle is, in many ways, the pinnacle of bottling technology. It is engineered to use precisely the least amount of glass needed to safely handle the stresses of a beery life. Safe to around 3.5 volumes, the longneck, and its 22-ounce "bomber" cousin, are good for bottling still, pétillant, medium, and lightly sparkling ciders.

The standard crown cap contains a few feats of engineering in its own right. Each cap is lined with a plastic liner designed to make a tight seal around the bottle top. If you're planning on storing your cider for any period of time, consider the extra investment in oxygen-absorbing caps. The liner in an oxy cap will help absorb some of the excess oxygen in the bottle's headspace that can shorten the cider's lifespan.

To cap a bottle, you'll need a bottle capper. There are a number of models for sale, and most of them are perfectly serviceable, including the venerable wing-style hand capper. Whatever you do, don't go super retro old-school and use a hammer capper. Those are a recipe for heartache and broken bottles.

Don't want to deal with traditional crown caps? Get your hands on flip-top bottles, sometimes referred to as Grolsch bottles, after the Dutch beer that famously comes in flip-top bottles. These bottles are thicker than cap bottles, and they carry their own lid clipped to the bottle. They cost more, but some folks prefer the convenience of them. Make sure your lid seals are in good shape before using. To procure enough bottles, either buy enough Grolsch (Fisher Amber is another common one), or check with your local homebrew supplier.

Champagne Bottle

If you want to aim for stupendously sparkling cider, then you're going to need incredibly sturdy bottles, and there's no form better than the classic champagne bottle. Super thick and shaped to hold incredible volumes of CO_2, the champagne bottle will let you run to around 8–9 volumes, far higher than you'd want to go. American champagne bottles accept an American-sized crown cap, and you can cork and cage them. Save yourself the hassle and avoid the real champagne corks. Pick up the "hammer-in" style of plastic corks and use those. Just twist on the cage with a pair of pliers to ensure the cork won't fly out prematurely.

Filling Glass Bottles

Prime your cider according to your desires, using sugar, juice, or concentrate. Fill your sanitized bottles. If you're making still cider, fill the bottle up to minimize headspace. If you're making cider with carbonation, leave two fingers of empty space. The empty space gives room for gas production. Seal the bottle with your chosen closure and set it aside. Carbonation will take 2–4 weeks before being fully absorbed and ready to drink. Still cider, on the other hand, you can drink immediately.

PET Bottles

Polyethylene terephthalate (PET) bottles, plastic bottles like those used for soda or sparkling water, are amazingly versatile, cheap, and easy to deal with. PET is a near-universal material used as a lightweight-barrier film, which can be molded and shaped into almost any rigid or semirigid shape. Hence its use by the beverage industry.

You can buy new, virgin, brown 500 ml PET bottles from many home-brew shops or online. Alternatively, go to your local grocery store and buy a bunch of soda or soda water. Cider and sparkling soda water make a wonderfully low-alcohol, refreshing spritzer.

Some things to consider when you think about a PET bottle over a traditional bottle:

PET PROS

- They are lightweight. The average PET bottle weighs less than 20 grams. The average glass bottle weighs about 200 grams, or ten times as much!
- They resist shattering.
- When they do finally break, it's much less dramatic. Usually a plastic bottle will burst around a seam, relieving the pressure without shattering into a million pieces.
- You can easily monitor carbonation with them. When you fill the bottles, they will be floppy at first, but as the carbonation builds, the bottle will stiffen. That lets you know the cider is ready for drinking!

PET CONS

- Long-term storage concerns. PET has great gas-barrier properties, but PET bottles allow more oxygen to diffuse into the cider than glass will. In the short term of a few months, this doesn't pose a problem. Longer than that, oxygen becomes a real issue as it begins to oxidize and destroy the flavors you worked hard to create.
- Plasticizers. In recent years, you may have heard stories about BPA (bisphenol A, a chemical found in plastics) and watched bottle manufacturers create BPA-free bottles. Bisphenol A is a complex chemical that allows easier creation of certain types of plastic. It also acts as an estrogen replacement when consumed. Some are really concerned about this and other plasticizers leaking into the food chain while others think it's an overblown fear. Ultimately, the decision is yours.

Using PET Bottles

Prime your cider according to your desires, using sugar, juice, or concentrate. Most soda is carbonated in the 3.5–4.5 volume range, so you'll want to stay below that level. Fill your sanitized bottles, leaving a couple of fingers of empty space. Lightly screw down the cap and gently squeeze the bottle until you've nearly pushed the cider out of the top. Without releasing the squeeze, tighten the cap all the way and put the bottle away for 2 weeks. You do this to eliminate the extra oxygen in the headspace.

ALERT

If the PET bottles start bulging from too much pressure, chill your cider and carefully open the tops to allow the excess pressure to release. This should prevent bottle explosions. Keep the bottles cool, and enjoy!

As the cider carbonates, the pressure from the CO_2 will push the bottle walls out again. Your cider is ready to drink a few days after the bottles become completely rigid. You may notice that a static charge on the plastic bottle walls has caused yeast to settle on the bottle sides. If you want, pick the bottles up, give them a flip, and allow them to settle again.

Kegs—The Stainless Steel Wonder

Kegging your cider means a few great things for the home cider maker. To start with, kegging involves much less cleaning and sanitizing since instead of washing, rinsing, and sanitizing a couple of cases of bottles, you're washing, rinsing, and sanitizing one big bottle. Packaging is much faster. Instead of filling a bottle, pausing, filling another bottle, pausing, etc., you just have to rack from your fermenter to the keg and then close everything up once you're done. Once you've kegged and carbonated your cider, you now have the freedom and flexibility to pour as much or as little as you want (try that with a bottle). Finally, kegs offer you the ultimate freedom to adjust your cider. Do you want to start with still cider, and then try it carbonated? You can. Cider needs more acid or tannin? Pop the top and add more! Want to change the flavor or add more juice? Go for it!

ESSENTIAL

Kegging also makes producing sweet, sparkling cider simple. You just add sorbate to your finished cider, back-sweeten it with sugar or concentrate, and force-carbonate.

It goes without saying that there are a few cons to the myriad pros listed above. First, kegs are the most expensive option available for packaging. There's a fair amount of equipment that you need to procure, including a CO_2 tank, a regulator, serving hoses, and the kegs themselves. All told, before you can enjoy a glass of draft, you'll spend about $200 for a 3- or 5-gallon keg and parts. Subsequent kegs are much cheaper. That doesn't include the fridge you'll need to keep your cider cold.

Space is another issue. Compared to a couple of boxes of bottles, a keg system does require a bit more room and is hard to squirrel away in random corners of your house. There's also the issue of portability. It's easy to take a few bottles from the stash to a friend's house, but it's awkward to do the same with a full keg. Despite some of these hassles, it's safe to say that as a serious practitioner of the fermentation arts, you'll find kegs to be incredibly convenient.

The Corny Keg

The standard keg used at home isn't like one of the huge, hulking 15½-gallon kegs you've seen at parties or bars. Instead, it is a 5-gallon stainless container called a Cornelius, or corny, keg.

The supply of used kegs has dwindled, but new kegs are available along with full draft systems at most homebrew supply shops. At first blush, a corny keg may appear a bit intimidating, but once you learn the parts, you'll see that they're simple and effective.

VITAL CORNY KEG PARTS

- **Keg body:** This is where you put the good stuff. There is usually a rubber foot to make the keg nonskid and nonmarking.
- **Keg lid:** Look for kegs with oval lids and a pressure relief valve. Check the handle to make sure it secures the lid. The big O-ring gasket is what keeps the pressure and liquid in the keg.
- **Gas "in" post:** A steel post that fits CO_2 connectors and seals onto a post on the keg top.
- **Liquid "out" post:** A steel post that fits draft line connectors and seals onto a post on the keg top.
- **Gas dip tube:** A short tube located under the gas post.
- **Liquid dip tube:** A long tube that reaches to the bottom of the keg. The liquid travels through here and out the liquid post and into your glass.
- **Gaskets:** Five in total: one on the lid, one on each post, and one on each dip tube.

OTHER VITAL DRAFT PARTS

- **CO_2 tank:** Usually a 5-pound metal tank that dispenses CO_2 through a valve; you can get this refilled at your local beverage gas provider or welding store.
- **CO_2 regulator:** Attaches to the tank and has at least one gauge reading the PSI being served. In the middle is a setscrew or knob that allows you to raise or lower the pressure. Just below the screw will be a shutoff lever to turn the gas on and off. Finally, there is a nipple that you

hook tubing to to deliver gas. Also check the nut that attaches the regulator to the tank. If there's no plastic gasket affixed inside, ask your gas supplier for one, and use it, unless you like leaking all your CO_2.

- **Gas connector:** A gray plastic connector that attaches to the gas hose and fits over the gas post.
- **Liquid connector:** A black plastic connector that attaches to a serving hose and fits over the liquid post.
- **Serving hose and picnic faucet:** A hose that ends in a black plastic faucet, alternatively called a cobra tap for its shape.

ESSENTIAL

Kegging also makes producing sweet, sparkling cider simple. You just add sorbate to your finished cider, back-sweeten it with sugar or concentrate, and force-carbonate.

Disassembling and Cleaning Kegs

The first thing you'll want to do when you buy a new keg is to verify it's been cleaned. Then, despite the verification, take it apart and replace all the gaskets. If the keg was last used for soda, it's guaranteed it will make your cider taste like soda. Unless you want that, buy a $5 kit of replacement gaskets for each keg.

Start cleaning by releasing the pressure from the keg via the pressure relief valve. If your keg lacks a relief valve, use a screwdriver to push in the center post on the gas post and listen to the lovely hiss. Lift the basket handle on the lid and remove it from the keg. Pull the big O-ring from the lid and toss it. Put the lid in cleaning solution and soak.

Meanwhile, take a ⅞" or ¹¹⁄₁₆" box wrench (or adjustable crescent wrench), and loosen the posts. Remove a post and pop the center post (also know as the poppet). Using a flathead screwdriver or knife, carefully remove the O-ring from the post and replace it. Place each post in a separate container of cleaner. Remove the gas dip tube and push off the gasket. Slide a new gasket in place and soak with the gas post. Remove the liquid dip tube and replace its gasket. Slide the tube back into position in the keg. Fill the keg with cleaner and soak.

Take a deep breath and wait for your soak to finish. Dump the cleaner (or better yet, use it to clean another keg). Rinse the keg and liquid tube well. Rinse each post and reassemble them on the keg. Fill the keg with a no-rinse sanitizer and soak with the lid hanging in the solution.

When done, close the lid and put CO_2 on the gas post. Using a draft hose or a hose with another liquid fitting on it, push the sanitizer from the keg. Once empty, allow the keg to pressurize and store. You're ready to go!

After reading that, you're probably ready to skip the idea of using a keg, ever! Don't worry, you only need to disassemble the keg every year or so. In the meantime, just fill the keg with cleaner, soak, rinse, fill with sanitizer, and purge. Ready to go!

ALERT

Remember! Don't leave any chlorine- or bleach-based solutions in contact with stainless steel for long. The chlorine will pit and weaken the steel. In most gear, this is unfortunate. In a pressure vessel, like a keg, it can allow the keg to burst like a bomb!

Using a Keg

Fortunately, using a keg is much simpler than cleaning a keg. To use, simply rack your cleared cider into the tank and close the lid. Add at least 10 PSI (pounds per square inch) of pressure to the keg, seal, and then chill it down. If you want still cider, you're done! If you want carbonated cider, look at the carbonation table in Appendix C and set the tank to the indicated pressure. Shake the keg for 10 minutes, and set aside to settle for a few hours.

To serve, attach the CO_2 to the keg's gas post, attach your serving hose to the keg's liquid fitting, and squeeze the tap fully open. Dispense into your favorite glass or pitcher and enjoy. At the end of a night's drinking, detach both fittings and spray off the posts and fittings with sanitizer.

Bag in a Box

The British cider industry has picked up on the bag-in-a-box trend and is producing bag-in-a-box cider for both home and pub consumption as a replacement for traditional cask service. Imagine walking into a pub seeing the bartender pouring your pint from tap in a little box! Odds are, though, it'll still be the best cider you've ever had. A few of the bigger American cider companies are getting into the mix as well, selling 3-liter boxes for your fridge.

There are a few factors to consider about bag-in-a-box packaging. The first is the restriction on carbonation. Bag-in-a-box products are designed solely for still beverages. Carbonation may cause the bag to bust, so make sure to degas your cider thoroughly. There are bag-in-keg systems that allow for carbonated beverages. There are also bags (*www.beerpouch.com*) available for home use.

The second consideration is the relative cost. To hold and serve 5 liters (1.3 gallons) of cider, you'll need special barrier bags that cost about $2–$3 per bag, and the special service box, which is about $4–$5. Total cost is about $6–$8. At first glance, it seems a bit expensive for a single container of cider, but compare that cost to a case of 12-ounce bottles (two bottles shy of the bag's capacity), which runs $10–14. As long as you keep the boxes in good shape, you only need to buy new bags for each batch, and some folks have successfully recycled their bags from batch to batch.

Lastly, aging in a plastic bag, even a barrier bag, presents the same problems associated with PET bottles. Studies at the University of California, Davis, America's premier wine university, show that wine aged in barrier bags does not fare as well against oxidation as traditionally bottled wine. Those same studies also found that keeping the wine cool helped prevent issues. Take a lesson and do the same for your cider. Anything that you'll want to store for a while, age it cool!

You can find the bags and boxes for use at some homebrew shops that cater to wine makers. These are still a specialty item, but if you look online, you'll find them available for delivery in short order.

Using a Bag-in-a-Box System

There are several systems on the market, but the most common ones involve a barrier bag with either an attached valve or port for later tapping. To use, degas your cider completely using a degassing wand to avoid extra aeration. Then follow the bag's instructions and remove the valve/port. Sanitize the needed pouches and store the caps/valves in sanitizer. Gently fill the pouch, lightly attach the closure, and squeeze out any air bubbles before tightening the closure.

Place the now-closed bag into a box, pop it in the fridge, chill to serving temperature, and tap! You now have draft cider for a fraction of the cost of a kegging setup. Cellar the other bags in a cool, dark place and chill as needed.

Pasteurization

While working on ways to stabilize beer for longer storage, French scientist Louis Pasteur discovered that a process of rapidly heating and cooling killed off enough microbiological organisms to make beer, wine, and other liquids much more stable. This discovery went a long way in making our modern world safe from spoiled food and drinks.

FACT

While most people credit Pasteur for inventing the pasteurization process, it turns out to be much older. As with all things technological, the Chinese got there first by heating their wines. Pasteur's innovation was cooling the product immediately to limit heat damage.

However, the process comes at a cost. The same heat that kills most of the pathogens also damages the product being pasteurized. For the cider maker, that means that the delicate flavors of your cider, the proteins that can give your cider body, may be destroyed.

By introducing heat to your juice, you also trigger a potential clarity problem. Remember that apples are rich in pectin, a polysaccharide complex that when heated in the presence of sugar and acid creates jelly. For your breakfast English muffin, this is great. A coagulated mess floating in your cider is definitely not desirable. If you add pectinase before you ferment, or keep your cider below 170°F, you won't have to worry about pectin.

Why bother pasteurizing? The main reason is stability. By pasteurizing, you are preventing leftover yeast and wild critters from altering the nature of your cider. It also gives you a way to fix the sweetness level of your cider, and a way to avoid a wild cider that explodes bottles everywhere from excess fermentation pressure.

When pasteurizing sealed bottles, be very careful! Remember, these are under pressure and could potentially explode. Keep a lid on your pot or use a large pressure cooker without the pressure weight. Either of these should contain any bottle breakage.

Here is how to pasteurize your cider.

PASTEURIZING

- ❏ Place room-temperature bottles in a large pot with a riser in the bottom, to keep the glass off the pot's bottom. Fill with water to halfway up the bottles.
- ❏ Heat water to 155°F in a large, covered pot (use a thermometer).
- ❏ Turn off the heat and rest 10 minutes.
- ❏ Remove bottles and place in a room-temperature bath (not ice cold).
- ❏ After 20 minutes, transfer the bottles to a cold-water bath.

Alternatively, if you have a pot with a spigot, you can drain the water from the kettle and leave the bottles in place. Be very gentle when changing the water! Another trick some cider makers have used is placing their cider bottles in a dishwasher and letting it run during the hottest cycle.

If you want to bulk pasteurize your cider, you can simply heat the whole mass in a pot to 155°F for 6 seconds, then crash cool it via ice bottles. This cider can then be bottled still, or it can be put in a keg and carbonated with CO_2. If your cider is already kegged, you can try dunking the whole keg in heated water, but that requires a big pot, as well as care to avoid melting the rubber keg foot!

CHAPTER 9

Tasting and Evaluating

Have you ever stopped to think about how you taste something? On the rare occasions that something becomes "transcendent," sure, but on a day-to-day basis? There's a whole art and vocabulary to actively, consciously tasting things like your cider. What does it mean when someone describes a cider as "earthy"? Time to make like a wine critic and learn how to taste and how to serve your cider!

Tasting a Cider

This may seem like an odd question, but have you ever really tasted anything? You've probably had a glass or two in your time, but have you ever stopped to register what you smell, taste, and feel? It's easy to stop at the level of "Well, this tastes pretty good" without going further.

Now that you're in the cider-making business, it's not overthinking, or pretentious, to try to pinpoint exactly what you taste and smell when you sample your product. It doesn't take a degree, certificate, or class to find out what your cider offers. All it takes is a little practice and soon you'll be holding your own with the most experienced tasters.

Taste Basics

A problem facing tasters is the assumption that the tongue is really doing the "heavy lifting." In reality, the nose handles most of the work. Your brain takes the chemical compounds detected by your nose (part of the olfactory system) and integrates those signals with the signals coming from the tongue (part of the gustatory system) to determine what you taste. Part of the reason food is so bland and unappetizing when you're sick is because the brain can't get aroma data from a clogged nose.

The tongue senses things by way of your taste buds. Your mouth contains somewhere between 2,000–8,000 of these little sensory receptors. You can think of them as little locks that send a signal to the brain whenever the right flavor momentarily unlocks the sensor. The combination of all the stimuli response on the tongue adds up to the flavor you get. There are five basic tastes the human tongue can sense:

FACT

Ever gone back to eat something you loved as a kid only to find you can't stand it anymore? You're experiencing the palate shift that kids undergo when they mature. Children prefer things that are sweet, whereas adults are more attuned to bitter and salty. Evolutionary biologists argue this gives kids priority for high-calorie sugar sources.

- **Sweet.** Sugar! This is a powerful impulse sensation, due to sugar's calorie content.
- **Sour.** The zippy pep that makes foods seem alive. The important vitamin C is found in sour fruits, like citrus.
- **Salty.** Before the advent of modern salt mining, salt was a precious commodity and it remains so in the culinary world because salt boosts the flavor of everything, but in too large a quantity, it makes everything taste like the sea.
- **Bitter.** The most sensitive of all the flavor receptors, bitterness is important because many plant toxins are alkaloids, which are bitter.
- **Umami.** The most recently discovered taste sensation, umami is described as that deep, satisfying, meaty earthiness that comes from protein sources like steak or mushrooms.

In the nose, there are olfactory sensors that are much like the taste buds. They are extraordinarily sensitive and protected behind a bony plate at the top of the nose. Like the locks of the taste buds, the olfactory receptors react to chemical stimulus. Unlike the taste buds, the nose's nerves react to very specific chemicals. This is why the olfactory system provides the finer details of what you sense.

ESSENTIAL

Not everyone can smell the same things! Sometimes this can have deadly consequences. For example, only 20–40 percent of humanity can detect the distinct bitter-almond smell of cyanide! All tasters and testers have different sensitivities to components and therefore will perceive some genuine differences.

Take Notes!

The first rule of tasting is to use your tongue, nose, and brain to figure out what you taste. The second rule of tasting is to take notes! Grab a pen, a paper, your laptop, or iPad. However you feel most comfortable—take notes.

Write down your impressions, and revisit them whenever you have another glass. See what's different and changed with age. Use these notes in conjunction with your recipe and fermentation notes to see what impacted your cider.

How to Serve Your Cider

The first lesson you must learn is the proper service of your cider. Doesn't serving just entail popping open a bottle and pouring it? Not exactly. Although you can worry about every little detail, just focus on these particulars: a properly chilled cider, a clean glass, and a willingness to engage with the cider in front of you.

Temperature

What is the proper temperature for a glass of cider? It depends. The optimum temperature varies with a number of cider factors. Is your cider sparkling? Is it still? Is it astringent? Acidic? Alcoholic? Sweet? Dry? Here are a few basic rules, but remember that these guidelines are affected by personal preference. If you like your cider a few degrees warmer than ice cubes, then drink it that way.

▼ SERVICE TEMPERATURE CHARACTERISTICS

Name	Approximate Temperature (Fahrenheit)	Best For	Notes
Freezing	32°F–36°F	None	Traditional American beer service temperature. The cold numbs your taste buds, masking all flavor. Perfect if you want something that tastes wet and cold, not so great if you want something you can actually taste.
Chilled	38°F–45°F	Sparkling	This is a fine balancing act, where your cider is cold but not frosty. You can still taste the characters of your cider, but the cold lends special emphasis to matters of mouthfeel and texture, like carbonation.

Name	Approximate Temperature (Fahrenheit)	Best For	Notes
Cellar	50°F–55°F	Still, sweet, or traditional ciders	If you want the full-on, proper British cider experience, then this is the temperature you need to have your ciders at. This will make lightly carbonated or still ciders sing as the warmth allows more fruit and spice aromas to drift into your nose while the light chill remains pleasantly refreshing.
Room	65°F–70°F	Dessert ciders	With a sweet, intense cider, it's best to have it at a temperature where everything can shout. Chilling a sweet apfelwein (10–14 percent) is a little like restricting an opera diva to singing "Mary Had a Little Lamb." Don't do it!
Warm/hot	130°F–140°F	Spicy ciders	This is for those cold winter nights, when you need to warm up thoroughly. The heat allows warm spices like cinnamon and nutmeg to suffuse the room and provides you with a glowing warmth.

FACT

Cellar temperature is a poorly understood term in the United States. Americans tend to think of things as cold, room temperature, or hot. Cellar temperature in Europe, especially the United Kingdom, exists in the cool but not freezing 50°F–55°F range. Traditional British ales were served at cellar temperature, which led visiting American soldiers to label the beer as warm, since it wasn't at traditional, icy American beer temps.

When in doubt, it is best to serve cider on the cooler side. If you taste the cider and it feels off, you can let it sit for a few minutes in the glass. Cup it in your hands to bring up the temperature a few degrees. You only rarely want to heat cider (à la mulled cider) because the excess heat will speedily volatize your aroma compounds and soon leave you with a dull glass.

Temperature Taste Test

If you want to experiment to prove to yourself that serving temperature does indeed make a difference, take four bottles of your cider, all chilled to nearly freezing. Pull all the bottles from the fridge at the same time. Crack open the first bottle and sample it while ice cold. Write down your impressions of the flavor and aroma. After a few minutes, sample the next one and take more notes; it should be in the chilled range at this point. A few minutes later, sample another bottle; it should be nearer to cellar temperature. Repeat the opening and note taking. Finally, sample the last bottle. Make sure it's around room temperature, and give it a taste and take more notes.

What differences did you note? In general, the colder versions of your cider should have felt sharper, spicier, and more acidic—the big notes of apples and other fruits would be suppressed. As the cider samples warmed up, more aromas and flavors should have become more evident. Sugar becomes more noticeable, perceived acid levels drop (because the sugar is up), and suddenly there are more fruity aromas reaching your nose.

At some point, your cider may have become too warm, leading to an unpleasant, insipid sweetness and a cider that lays flat and dead on your tongue. If the cider has degassed (lost its carbonation), you'll particularly notice this effect.

QUESTION

Why do cold liquids taste sharper and less fruity?
As the cold liquid hits your tongue, it will temporarily numb your taste buds. This slows down your detection of various sweet and sour tastes. To further ice the sensations, cold slows down the volatilization of the phenols and esters that your nose interprets as fruity or spicy.

The Glassware

Another factor that affects how you taste is the nature of the glass you drink from. Yes, you can drink your cider from anything that holds liquids, but the shape of the glass does affect your experience.

The main effect from a glass is how it shapes your perception of aromas. Look at a modern pint glass. It's a slightly tapered cylinder with a wide opening designed to breathe. It lets aromas escape. Compare that with the narrow opening of a brandy snifter. It restricts the escaping of aromas. The big bowl gives plenty of room for esters to bloom from the liquor into the glass's atmosphere.

You want to hold onto that aroma, right? Maybe you just use big brandy snifters. However, cider contains something that a spirit like brandy lacks, namely, carbon dioxide. Too much carbon dioxide in an enclosed environment causes an unpleasant burning in your nose; definitely not something that you want to experience when you're drinking a cider!

Here are some standard glass types and the benefits of each:

- **Cheater pint:** This is the standard American bar glass. It features slightly tapered walls on a 14-ounce glass. Perfectly fine for your standard cider. The wide mouth tends to blow off a lot of your aroma.
- **English nonic pint:** The English Imperial pint glass features a wider cylinder, with less of a taper than the cheater. Has a flared ring at the top. Like the cheater, it's a good everyday glass with a tendency to push a lot of aroma early.
- **English dimple mug:** These are hard to find, but this is the true traditional English glass. It's a wide glass mug with dimpled windows and a sturdy handle. The wide mouth lets the carbon dioxide fly, but the mug encourages your nose to fall right on top of the liquid as you're drinking.
- **Belgian chalice:** This looks like a classic, rounded saucer elevated on a fine stem. The Belgian chalice is a favorite with very strongly scented Belgian ales and will work fine for stronger ciders.
- **Belgian tulip:** The first glass that focuses the aroma. The bowl and narrowing shape pull the cider and create a bubble when you tip the glass to drink. Your nose fits right in the flared top segment to catch the aromas floating from the bubble.
- **Red wine glass:** The big, balloon-style red wine glass provides acres of space for both your nose and your cider's aroma. Wine drinkers go for these massive glasses for their potent rich reds. Try a traditional still cider in a glass like this and you won't be disappointed.
- **Brandy snifter:** The snifter provides the ultimate air of sophistication as you swirl this glass with its massive teardrop airspace. Brandy drinkers use these glasses to provide a big nose hit from their intense spirit. For the cider drinker, a fortified cider, an apfelwein, or even applejack will shine in this space.

- **Champagne flute:** When you want to have the air of daintiness and class, it's hard to go wrong with a glass that shows off the texture of your bubbles and the beautiful color of the cider. You won't get as much aroma from the glass, but it will help preserve the fizz as you sip a fiercely carbonated cider from it.

Make sure to clean your glasses thoroughly, and rinse them well. Serious beverage folk will admonish you to avoid the dishwasher for your service ware. While you want the glass completely clean and clear—free of spots, free of grease, the remains of lipstick, etc.—you don't want any soap residue or rinsing agents from the dishwasher. Consider buying a simple bottle or glass brush, and hand-wash and dry your glass.

FACT

How important is the glass to some folks? Very! The Boston Beer Company, brewers of Samuel Adams beer and Angry Orchard cider, spent years and several million dollars developing a special glass that accentuates the characters of their beverages. You can order a set of four glasses online.

Serving

Have your cider resting and chilling, either in the fridge or an ice bath, for 20–30 minutes or until you get it to the temperature you want. Pick your glass, give it a quick water rinse, and shake most of the water out. This little rinse not only ensures the glass is free of any particles, but it also acts to help settle the pour and prevent disastrous foam explosions as you pour.

Take your bottle of cider and open it gently. This is not the time for banging it on the counter or using your teeth. All proper home fermentation experimenters are within mere feet of their preferred opening technologies (bottle opener, corkscrew) at all times.

Tilt the glass to a 45° angle, and pour the cider. When the glass is half full, begin to bring it upright while continuing to pour. This helps agitate the cider and begins the release of the aroma. As you finish bringing the glass upright, slow your pour and admire it. Watch the bottle! If there are settled particles of yeast and proteins, stop your pour short to prevent the gunk racing from the bottle.

If your bottle has more cider than your glass will hold, pour the remaining cider into another glass without turning the bottle back upright. Doing so will stir the schmutz into the remaining cider, making it cloudy and bitter.

The Taste

Now you're ready to engage in the finest tradition in the land—the sampling. Follow these steps for the perfect taste:

1. As you raise the glass for the first time, close your eyes, breathe out, and then breathe in deeply through your nose. Take a moment and let the aroma play against your brain.
2. Take a deep sip and note the carbonation and the taste sensations you feel. Is the cider prickly? Sweet? Is there a hint of hay and straw, or a rusted red apple?
3. Swallow. As you clear your mouth, take note of the feelings you have. Does your mouth feel the dry puckering of dark, tealike tannins? Is there an acidity that sparkles? Sugar that stays on your lips?
4. Finally, breathe out and amaze yourself as you realize there's a whole set of aromas to experience. Bet you've never done that consciously before, have you?

That is the way you taste a cider properly! It may seem like a lot of work for a simple act that you've done a few hundred thousand times before. Think of it as the drinking embodiment of the Buddhist principle of mindfulness, of being aware in the moment.

A Proper Vocabulary

You may be a little intimidated by a few of the terms you've just encountered about what you can taste and smell in your cider. A lot of people, when they first start to evaluate a beverage they make, may get hung up on the idea that they don't have a good palate. This is complete nonsense. What is missing is not the palate, it's the vocabulary. There are a number of ways to solve that, but first focus on what you do know—the things you've tasted before.

As it turns out, aroma and flavor are the most powerful evokers of memory. A single smell can pull a reminiscence buried twenty or thirty years in the past. When you taste your cider, try and put the experience in terms of pictures of things from your past. If you taste it and say, "This tastes like the apple pie that mom used to make every Thanksgiving," then that's a great start. When you say those words to someone else, she may not get the exact flavor in her head, but it'll be more evocative than if you say, "It tastes spicy."

Once you can start picturing things in your head, you can start refining them. What makes the cider taste like your mom's apple pie? Is there a particular apple character? Cinnamon? Any clove, allspice, or ginger? If so, what you can now say is, "This tastes like a rich apple pie with a little of that sweet spicy syrup that forms around the chunks of apple. It's warm with an earthy cinnamon that's not hot, and it finishes with a little peppery ginger kick before the carbonation scrubs the taste clean."

Reading wine reviews, you'll notice that the reviewers seem to all pull from the same list of terms, and that's because they do! Several universities and tasting panels—for everything from wine, cheese, beer, maple syrup, and cider—have put together word lists organized by sensation. All of these lists work to focus your palate. Say your cider tastes fruity—now think harder. Is it like a stone fruit? If so, is it more like an apricot or a peach or even a plum? Is the cider floral? Now is it more like a rose? Wildflowers? Jasmine?

Common Flavors and Causes

There are a staggering number of things that you can smell and taste in your cider, as well as reasons they end up there. Here are a few and what causes them:

▼ COMMON CIDER FLAVORS AND AROMAS

Name	Description	Cause
Acetaldehyde	Green apple Jolly Rancher candy	Insufficient yeast activity, or premature racking of the cider away from the yeast
Alcohol	Burning sensation of ethanol	Mostly detectable in very strong ciders or ciders with a fair amount of sugar that ferments away

Name	Description	Cause
Butter/butterscotch	A slick flavor or strong, buttery aroma	Natural byproduct of fermentation, usually cleaned up by the yeast unless they die out or are removed early
Flowery	Smell of roses and wildflowers	Typically a yeast character, also prevalent when honey is used; overuse of potassium sorbate can also cause this
Fruit	Smells like cherries, apples, pears, berries, etc.	These are ester compounds, a natural part of fermentation that you'll want to manipulate
Funk	The smell of a wet farm, wet hay mixed with cold mud	Wild yeasts or a component of the juice
Oxidized	Flavor and aroma of stale, wet cardboard, or maybe a port-like aroma of sugary raisins	Over time, oxygen will gradually morph the cider in ways that aren't always pleasant
Puckering astringency	Like a strong cup of tea	Tannin from the apples or additions for adjustment; too much tannin can make the cider undrinkable
Smoky	Phenols	Unless exposed to something burning, smoke usually indicates an infection of some sort
Solvent	Hot or like nail polish	Produced by stressed yeast, not enough yeast or nutrient, or a hot fermentation
Sour	Tartness	Clean, acidic flavors are produced by the apples or additions of appropriate acid to balance. Acid in the presence of "funk" can indicate an infection.
Spicy	Phenols	Natural product of fermentation; if the character is too strong, it was produced by an overactive fermentation
Vegetal	Flavor of rotten vegetables	Sometimes an infection or a yeast producing too much sulfur
Vinegar	Vinegary/acidic smell	Acetobacter in the cider, fermenting and changing the ethanol to acetic acid

Other People's Opinions

At some point, you need that critical, unblinking eye of judgment to really know how you've done. This is as true with cider as any other endeavor. Since cider straddles the world of beer and winemaking, it should be no surprise that both sides of the fence lay claim to being able to judge the stuff.

The Beer Judge Certification Program (BJCP) has worked for a number of years to raise the profile of cider within the beer world. To that end, they've put together a set of guidelines for two main classes and nine subclasses of cider and perry (any fermented beverage made from pears).

They even have a wonderful score sheet that is presented on the following page. This sheet is designed to allow a judge in a blind tasting panel to record everything he notices about your cider.

How can you get your cider judged? You just need to find a competition somewhere near you. The BJCP website (*www.bjcp.org*) lists a few hundred competitions per year, and each competition draws qualified judges to help evaluate. Simply choose a competition, register your entry, and package your cider in plain brown bottles with no markings. You'll then either drop the bottles off at the competition site, or box them up carefully and send them off (via a non–U.S. Postal Service carrier). Make sure to wrap each bottle in bubble wrap and verify that the box doesn't clink if you shake or drop it.

When the entry arrives at the competition, the organizers record your data and carefully label your entry with an anonymous number. On the day of the competition, the entries are chilled and deposited in front of judges. The judges (at least a pair) will crack open each bottle, pour the cider, read the notes, and proceed to sniff, sip, and write.

The result should be the most honest and critical review of your cider you'll receive. You may win fame and glory with your cider, or you may just end up with some notes telling you what they found and what can be improved. Both of these are pre-eminently valuable.

Additionally, the American Wine Society (*www.americanwinesociety .org*) runs an annual winemaking competition in the fall. While the primary focus of the organization is on winemaking in the classic grape sense, they have competition categories available for apple wines, apple cider, and even the odd apple ice wines.

CIDER SCORESHEET

AHA/BJCP Sanctioned Competition Program

http://www.bjcp.org

http://www.homebrewersassociation.org

Judge Name (print) _____

Judge BJCP ID _____

Judge Email _____
Use Avery label # 5160

Category # _____ **Subcategory (a-f)** _____ **Entry #** _____

Subcategory (spell out) _____

Carbonation Level: ☐ Still   ☐ Petillant   ☐ Sparkling
Sweetness: ☐ Dry   ☐ Medium   ☐ Sweet

Varieties of apple (if declared): _____

Special Ingredients: _____
_____

Bottle Inspection: ☐ (Appropriate size, cap, fill level, label removal, etc.)

Comments _____

BJCP Rank or Status:

☐ Apprentice   ☐ Recognized   ☐ Certified
☐ National   ☐ Master   ☐ Grand Master
☐ Honorary Master   ☐ Honorary GM   ☐ Mead Judge
☐ Provisional Judge   ☐ Rank Pending

Non-BJCP Qualifications:

☐ Professional Cidermaker   ☐ Non-BJCP
☐ Cider Sensory Training   ☐ Other _____

Descriptor Definitions (Mark all that apply):

☐ **Acetaldehyde** – Green apple candy aroma/flavor.

☐ **Acetified (Volatile Acidity, VA)** – Ethyl acetate (solvent, nail polish) or acetic acid (vinegar, harsh in back of throat).

☐ **Acidic** – Sour-tart flavor. Typically from one of several acids: malic, lactic, or citric. Must be in balance.

☐ **Alcoholic** – The warming effect of ethanol/higher alcohols.

☐ **Astringent** – A drying sensation in the mouth similar to chewing on a teabag. Must be in balance if present.

☐ **Bitter** – A sharp taste that is unpleasant at higher levels.

☐ **Diacetyl** – Butter or butterscotch aroma or flavor.

☐ **Farmyard** – Manure-like (cow or pig) or barnyard (horse stall on a warm day).

☐ **Fruity** – The aroma and flavor of fresh fruits that may be appropriate in some styles and not others.

☐ **Metallic** – Tinny, coiny, copper, iron, or blood-like flavor. Cider may turn green (copper) or black (iron).

☐ **Mousy** – Taste evocative of the smell of a rodent's den/cage.

☐ **Oaky** – A taste or aroma due to an extended length of time in a barrel or on wood chips. "Barrel character."

☐ **Oily/Ropy** – A sheen in visual appearance, as an unpleasant viscous character proceeding to a ropy character.

☐ **Oxidized** – Staleness, the aroma/flavor of sherry, raisins, or bruised fruit.

☐ **Phenolic** – Plastic, band-aid, and/or medicinal.

☐ **Spicy/Smoky** – Spice, cloves, smoky, ham.

☐ **Sulfide** – Rotten eggs, from fermentation problems.

☐ **Sulfite** – Burning matches, from excessive/recent sulfiting.

☐ **Sweet** – Basic taste of sugar. Must be in balance if present.

☐ **Thin** – Watery. Lacking body or "stuffing."

☐ **Vegetal** – Cooked, canned, or rotten vegetable aroma and flavor (cabbage, onion, celery, asparagus, etc.)

Appearance (as appropriate for style)   ____ / 6
Color (2), clarity (2), carbonation level (2)

_____
_____
_____

Bouquet/Aroma (as appropriate for style)   ____ /10
Expression of other ingredients as appropriate

_____
_____
_____
_____
_____

Flavor (as appropriate for style)   ____ /24
Balance of acidity, sweetness, alcohol strength, body, carbonation (if appropriate) (14), Other ingredients as appropriate (5), Aftertaste (5)

_____
_____
_____
_____
_____

Overall Impression   ____ /10
Comment on overall drinking pleasure associated with entry, give suggestions for improvement

_____
_____
_____
_____
_____
_____

Total   ____ /50

SCORING GUIDE		
Outstanding	(45 - 50):	World-class example of style.
Excellent	(38 - 44):	Exemplifies style well, requires minor fine-tuning.
Very Good	(30 - 37):	Generally within style parameters, some minor flaws.
Good	(21 - 29):	Misses the mark on style and/or minor flaws.
Fair	(14 - 20):	Off flavors/aromas or major style deficiencies. Unpleasant.
Problematic	(00 - 13):	Major off flavors and aromas dominate. Hard to drink.

	Stylistic Accuracy					
Classic Example	☐	☐	☐	☐	☐	Not to Style
	Technical Merit					
Flawless	☐	☐	☐	☐	☐	Significant Flaws
	Intangibles					
Wonderful	☐	☐	☐	☐	☐	Lifeless

BJCP Cider Scoresheet Copyright © 2013 Beer Judge Certification Program rev. 130219

Please send any comments to Comp_Director@BJCP.org

CHAPTER 10

Additional Fun Ingredients

Now is the time to make the purists run. If they weren't horrified by the notion of supermarket cider, they will be by the time you're done with this chapter. Time to play! In this chapter, you'll learn many of the various ingredients that can completely spin your cider in new and interesting directions. Want to know the secrets behind an ultra-strong cider that will shock people? They're here, with so much more!

Un-Real Cider

To cider purists, like the folks behind the Campaign for Real Ale (CAMRA) real cider campaign, you're committing a grave sin by using nontraditional apple varieties. To those folks, cider is a great delivery mechanism of apple flavors and nothing more. But is that all? Of course not. Cider, like a lot alcoholic beverages, can be tinkered with.

FACT

The Campaign for Real Ale (CAMRA) was founded in 1971, in the United Kingdom, as a consumer group fighting to preserve the then-dying British "real ale" tradition. Over the years, as the campaign has proven successful, they've expanded their reach into other fields, including cider and perry (pear cider). Striving to preserve traditional cider is a very noble goal; however, not everything you make and drink needs to hew to that tradition.

Your goal as you add new flavors should be a cider that ultimately tastes great. The challenge is to maintain restraint in your flavoring so that you don't end up with an overblown mess. Most of the techniques in this chapter are built around the idea of starting small and leaving opportunities to adjust up if you want more flavor.

As always, make sure you use the best ingredient for the job. It would be unfortunate if you decided to save a few dollars and instead wasted all of the money you spent on your juice.

Why Other Ingredients?

Think of every ingredient as offering a new dimension, a new sensation. If you limit yourself to a single set of vectors, then you limit yourself to a relatively narrow set of experiences. Apple is but one taste, and fortunately cider provides a perfect avenue to layer in other flavors. This is your chance to explore what a cider can really be when you free yourself from traditional strictures.

The Approach

How you decide on what flavor additions to add may start with something simple. For example, maybe you have fond memories of your mom's apple pie, or maybe it's a taste in your morning coffee you want to replicate. One approach you can take is to formulate a story around a set of flavors and aromas that you want to explore. This story approach is used by the food industry every day to sell you on a product. You need look no farther than the coffee and tea aisle, filled with names like San Francisco Fog, French Roast, and Sleepytime. Each of those names evokes a simple story or idea to guide your expectations, as do the names of the recipes in this book. Coming up with a story can guide you to a plan that makes sense for you.

ESSENTIAL

Look at other culinary efforts, such as desserts or meals, for traditional combinations. The classic and most popular example is apple pie, but think also of mulled cider or mom's cherry pie, for example.

No matter what flavors you decide to bring to your cider, keep a clear vision in mind and aim for it. Never abandon a fearless curiosity. Are you afraid of messing up? Make a sample batch. Get some extra juice and use it to experiment. Keep it simple! Take your winning experiments and make larger batches. Just remember to scale your additions!

What to Avoid

The first thing to avoid is overkill. If you keep stacking more and more flavors into your cider, your palate gets confused. The flavors compete and the cider tastes muddy. You end up with a cider that doesn't sing. Keep it light. If the flavors you add aren't enough, you can add more, but once you've added too much, you can't go back.

The second thing to avoid for the cider maker is fat. The concern isn't about calories but stability. Fat can kill your cider's head, and it causes a tongue-numbing coating of your taste buds, but the real crime for your cider is that fat can turn rancid. Coconut and chocolate, amongst the most palatable fatty foods, are problematic, but there are ways around the issues, as explained later in this chapter. Just be aware that your Brown Butter Avocado Cider may have some issues lasting in your cellar!

Sugar

Sugar is the most common addition to cider. Even stodgy traditional cider makers add sugar to their ciders if their apples fall short. What does sugar add to your cider, beyond the additional gravity that means a higher alcohol content?

Brewers use sugar to help cut the perceived body, because the simple sugar molecules ferment more easily. Since apple juice contains nothing but simple sugars, it can only help to boost the perception of body. It all depends on the type of sugar you're adding!

There are a number of different sugars, but they all consist of groups of carbon, hydrogen, and oxygen in crystalline form and are comprised of three different single-molecule simple sugars, also known as monosaccharides. You can think of these as yeast super fuel. When you combine them together, what you get are the more complex sugars—disaccharides, trisaccharides, polysaccharides, and starches.

▼ **FUNDAMENTAL SUGAR TYPES**

Name	Type	Formula	Notes
Glucose	Monosaccharide	$C_6H_{12}O_6$	The most fundamental sugar, since virtually every starch you eat gets converted to glucose
Fructose	Monosaccharide	$C_6H_{12}O_6$	Fruit sugar, this is most of what your juice contains
Galactose	Monosaccharide	$C_6H_{12}O_6$	Very rare—you'll probably never see it
Sucrose	Disaccharide	$C_{12}H_{22}O_{11}$	Found in a number of plants, most notably sugarcane and beets
Maltose	Disaccharide	$C_{12}H_{22}O_{11}$	Named for its primary source, barley malt—provides some body
Lactose	Disaccharide	$C_{12}H_{22}O_{11}$	Occurs naturally in milk—provides body without a lot of sweetness

Sugar Varieties

There are lots of different types of sugar. Most of the differences boil down to how much molasses is left with the refined sucrose: The more molasses, the more impurities and flavor. Sources other than corn or beets provide different characters as well. Do yourself a favor and explore the different options available to you. The following list of sugars is just a start:

FACT

Molasses in all of its grades and forms (light, dark, blackstrap) is a castoff of the sugar refinement process. It's what's left over after the sugary cane or beet juice is boiled and spun to create sugar crystals.

- **Cane/beet sugar:** This is the plain, white stuff you buy at the grocery store. Basically pure sucrose, this sugar really just adds alcohol to the cider without much else. Be careful about adding too much lest you end up with cider that tastes like rocket fuel.
- **Brown sugar:** Originally, this is what all sugar was like. Ostensibly, a less-refined sugar that retains moisture from the remaining molasses, common supermarket brown sugars are plain sugar with a little molasses mixed back in. Look for British brown sugars to capture the sweet, smoky, earthy complexity that brown sugar can lend your cider.
- **Turbinado/demerara/raw sugar:** Three names for pretty much the same sort of sugar. These are sugars with lots of impurities and molasses left, but the sugar remains in a crystalline form. Most have a lovely toasted, slightly caramelized flavor.
- **Jaggery/piloncillo/panela:** This is brown sugar made from sugarcane or dates. It has really great caramel and nut flavors. Needs to be broken up or grated before use.
- **Lactose:** A traditional ingredient added to British milk or cream stouts. This disaccharide, commonly found in cow's milk, is not fermentable by regular yeast. This is something to take advantage of—it means you can add natural sweetness and body without fear of residual yeast using it for fuel. Unfortunately, lactose is also one of the least sweet sugars, which means it requires a larger amount to taste sweet.

Using Sugar

You could just dump your sugar into your cider and let it sit on the bottom of the fermenter, but that can cause problems like erupting cider fountains due to CO_2 nucleating on the sugar crystals and rushing out of the carboy or simply falling to the bottom and never dissolving in the cider. Instead, it's best to liquefy it and easily dissolve the resulting syrup in your juice. Once you've made syrup, all you have to do is pour it in and give a quick shake or stir or better yet, place the syrup in an empty fermenter and rack the cider onto it to mix.

Sugar Syrup

Unless you like a big pile of sugar in your cider, or an explosion caused by adding sugar crystal to a fermenting cider, add this syrup to your cider.

INGREDIENTS | YIELDS 1.5 CUPS

1 pound sugar
8 ounces water

1. Add the sugar and water to a saucepan, stir to dissolve, and boil for 10 minutes for regular syrup.
2. To push the color and introduce caramel flavors, continue the boil until the bubbles begin stacking on each other, about 10–15 minutes. Watch it carefully!

ESSENTIAL

To boost your cider by about 1 percent alcohol by volume, you'll want to add about 3 ounces (by weight) of sugar to 1 gallon of juice. That's just shy of a full pound for a 5-gallon batch.

Honey

It wasn't long ago that refined sugar was an expensive rarity. The most widely available sweetener was honey. Today, honey is big business and is shipped around the globe.

In the not-so-distant past, honey came in a little plastic bear. At best, you would see the words "wildflower" or "clover" on your labels. Today, honey comes in a number of varieties all named from the crops the bees harvested it from. Amazingly, each honey provides different flavors and aromas. Even truly regional wildflower honey can provide a variable experience based on the season and available flowers.

Before you get too crazy and shell out big bucks for the fanciest honeys available, be aware that during fermentation a large amount of honey character will blow away in the violent stream of CO_2 produced by fermentation. If you want to use a special honey, like Tupelo honey that tastes of cinnamon and caramel, you'll need to take steps to preserve the honey character. The easiest method: add the honey later after the primary ferment is mostly done, and add a lot of it!

Take Me Back to Tupelo Cyser

This is a special variety of honey wine (also known as mead) called cyser. This recipe calls for pure Tupelo honey, a special honey harvested only in northern Florida and southern Georgia. It is sweet, spicy, and well worth its high price tag. No Tupelo? No problem. Use the best honey you can find.

INGREDIENTS | YIELDS 5 GALLONS

4 gallons fresh, sweet apple juice (3½ gallons chilled)
12 pounds Tupelo honey
1 tablespoon yeast nutrient
2 packets Côte des Blancs yeast

1. In a pot capable of holding at least 2 gallons of liquid, heat ½ gallon juice to 140°F. Do not boil the juice! Mix the honey in and dissolve.
2. In your sanitized fermenter, add the chilled juice. Mix in the prepared honey mixture and yeast nutrient.

3. Add the yeast, close up the fermenter, and follow the Standard Cider-Making Procedure in Chapter 2.
4. Package this as a sparkling cider. You want the bubbles to reinforce the honey and apple nose!

Cyser/Cider

More than just ingredients tie cyser and cider together. Etymologically speaking, both words presumably derive from the same Latin word *sicera*, meaning "strong drink."

Other Syrups

When making cider, don't forget about using other sugary syrups! In the New England tradition of cider, maple syrup is a prime example of a cider addition. The smoky, sweet syrup provides an unusual wood and burnt caramel flavor to the cider, from the long, slow boil that reduces the maple sap. When buying maple syrup for your cider, make sure of two things. First, that it is genuine maple syrup, with no corn syrup or other sweeteners. Second, find the darker Grade B syrup, which contains far more flavor and aroma than Grade A.

Another type of syrup comes from Belgium, and it is a castoff of the sugar/molasses making process. Here in the United States, we call it Candi Syrup, and it comes in multiple colors that all carry a sense of dark fruits, plums, caramel, and chocolates. You can find Candi Syrup at your local homebrew shop.

If you feel like old-school Americana, you can always grab a bottle of corn syrup and add it to your cider. Karo corn syrup even contains a dose of vanilla in it, for an extra flavor surprise.

Acer Cider

This is a smoky, earthy cider, thanks to the addition of maple syrup. It will naturally dry out, so try and aim for a sweet cider blend. Don't fret about adding tannin or acid until you understand the effect of the maple syrup.

INGREDIENTS | YIELDS 1 GALLON

1 gallon fresh, sweet apple juice
1 quart Grade B maple syrup
½ teaspoon yeast nutrient
1 packet Irish stout yeast
2½ teaspoons potassium sorbate (optional)
¾ cup additional maple syrup (optional)

1. In the fermenter, mix the juice, maple syrup, nutrient, and yeast using the Standard Cider-Making Procedure found in Chapter 2.
2. After fermentation ceases, check the flavor of the cider. If you want sweetness, add the optional sorbate and the additional maple syrup. If not, proceed to packaging.
3. If using potassium sorbate and you want a sparkling cider, you'll have to force-carbonate (see Chapter 8) it. Otherwise, bottle as normal. The fizz in this one helps enhance the smoke aroma and flavor.

Acer?

Where does the word *acer* come from? Blame the botanists' fascination with Latin. *Acer* means "sharp" and was applied to the whole family of maple trees due to their sharp, pointy leafs.

ALERT

Once you add the sugar, unless you also add potassium sorbate, fermentation will start again. Remember to provide extra space in your containers for the renewed activity or suffer the mess!

Candy

There are a number of cider addition choices at the candy shop, but for now avoid chocolate bars. Remember: Fat is not good! But look at all those shiny hard candies. Most of them consist of flavorful essential oils suspended in a matrix of sugar crystals. With sufficient time in the cider after fermentation, the sugar will dissolve and the oils will mix in with the cider.

Red Hot Cider

This blush-colored recipe is a shout-out to a classic homebrew mead recipe made with Red Hots cinnamon candies. In this case, you'll use a strong cider as a base to give you a little extra oomph against the fiery boom of the candy.

INGREDIENTS | YIELDS 5 GALLONS

5 gallons fresh, sweet apple juice

3 pounds honey

½ teaspoon yeast nutrient

1 packet Côte des Blanc dry yeast

50 Atomic FireBall candies (or 1 pound Red Hots candies)

2½ teaspoons potassium sorbate

1. Use the Standard Cider-Making Procedure found in Chapter 2.
2. Rack the cider onto the cinnamon candies in a secondary container and wait for them to dissolve (about 2–4 weeks). If you want to preserve the sugar, gently stir in the potassium sorbate at this stage.
3. Lower the temperature on the cider to 36°F to drop any remaining yeast. If you allowed the candies to ferment, add the sorbate now.
4. Bottle this as a still cider. The heat of the cinnamon will be powerful enough without the bump of carbonation.

Chemically Speaking

The characteristic burn of cinnamon comes from cinnamaldehyde, a liquid that composes about 75 percent of the essential oil of cinnamon. In addition to flavoring, it has uses as an insecticide and an antimicrobial.

Coffee

Coffee is not just for breakfast anymore! American coffee has come a long way from the days when Folgers and Maxwell House ruled the American breakfast uncontested. The coffee that you enjoy in the morning is itself the product of fermentation. Most coffee is from the *Coffea arabica* bush. The fruit is picked and soaked for a few days while the flesh ferments away. The beans are then dried, roasted, and bagged for you to grind and brew.

FACT

Ironically, the darker the roast of the bean, the less caffeine the coffee contains. Keep that in mind the next time you need a coffee-fueled pick-me-up!

Like apples, coffee offers a number of varieties and tastes. Different growing regions impart unique flavors and aromas. The coffee roaster further changes these characteristics by the style of roasting performed. The color ranges from green (raw) to cinnamon (the lightest roast) ending at Spanish (nearly black).

Jolting Java Cider

Instinctively, coffee and cider seem to be two great tastes that are potentially awful together. By using whole beans, and a short cold soak, you'll extract the maximum of the sweet, flavorful oils with a minimum of the burnt coffee flavor that would clash with the cider.

INGREDIENTS | YIELDS 5 GALLONS

5 gallons fresh, sweet apple juice

½ teaspoon yeast nutrient

1 packet American ale yeast (White Labs WLP001 California Ale Yeast, Wyeast 1056 American Ale, or Safale US-05)

1 pound whole coffee beans

1 pound lactose (optional)

1. Use the Standard Cider-Making Procedure found in Chapter 2.
2. Rack the cider onto the coffee beans in a secondary container. Let the beans soak for 1–3 days, depending on your taste preferences. The longer you let the beans stay in contact, the stronger, more intense the coffee flavor will be.
3. Lower the temperature on the cider to 36°F to drop any remaining yeast. Rack to a bottling bucket. Boil the lactose in a pint of water to dissolve. Stir the lactose syrup into the cider.
4. Package this as a still cider.

Cream with Your Coffee

Lactose, also known as milk sugar, has a great advantage in home fermentation. It provides a limited amount of sweetness that yeast cannot consume. In this case, it also completes the coffee illusion.

Chocolate

Everyone loves chocolate! But if you threw a candy bar into your cider, you'll end up with a mess and a fatty, flat pint. Like coffee, chocolate is another fermented bean. These beans are encased in a sticky mass in a pod. They are harvested, covered, and allowed to ferment. The fermented beans are dried, roasted, cracked, and then ground into a fatty liquid.

The chocolate liqueur consists of cocoa powder and cocoa butter. You could use pure cocoa powder in your cider, but the powder contributes a harsh taste. A popular technique is to use the roasted and cracked cacao nibs, which are like chocolate chips made from whole cacao beans (available online and in natural food stores). When soaked in alcohol, pure earthy chocolate flavor infuses into your cider.

Cacao and Vanilla Extract

This is the flavor packet for the Cocoa Insanity recipe that follows, but it makes a great addition to just about everything—except your morning coffee.

INGREDIENTS | YIELDS 6 OUNCES

6 ounces vodka
1 vanilla bean, split and scraped
3 ounces cacao nibs (preferably roasted)

1. In a tight-sealing jar, like a Mason jar, mix the vodka and all of the vanilla bean (scrapings and pod). Let mixture soak for 7 days. Pick up and shake every day.
2. Add the cacao nibs, and soak for an additional 4 days. Again, shake the jar every day to encourage extraction.
3. Strain the bean and nibs. Place the strained tincture in the freezer overnight. If you don't have freezer space, let it sit for an additional 1–2 days and then strain.
4. After the overnight freezing, there should be a solid cap of waxy fat along the top. Remove it with a spoon, picking up any strays. Carefully decant the tincture from the settled matter in the jar and use as desired. Store for up to 1 year in an airtight jar.

Defatting

This tincture process has an extra step in it—the freezing and defatting step. By putting the tincture in the freezer for a day, you'll cause the fat from the cacao nibs to solidify at the top. It will also cause any remaining particulate matter to settle out, so carefully pour your defatted tincture into a new container!

Cocoa Insanity

Chocolate makes everything better, but in this recipe, you're getting the earthy tones of chocolate from the nibs. Think apple slices enrobed in dark chocolate.

INGREDIENTS | YIELDS 5 GALLONS

5 gallons fresh, sweet apple juice (avoid any overly bitter juice)

½ teaspoon yeast nutrient

1 packet English ale yeast (Safale S-04 or White Labs WLP007 Dry English Ale Yeast)

3 ounces Cacao and Vanilla Extract (see previous recipe)

1. Use the Standard Cider-Making Procedure found in Chapter 2.
2. Lower the temperature on the cider to 36°F to drop any remaining yeast. Rack to a bottling bucket. Add the Cacao and Vanilla Extract. Adjust the amount to your taste.
3. Package as desired.

Vanilla?

If adding vanilla to something chocolate-flavored surprises you, you're not alone. Many people don't realize that vanillin, the active ingredient in vanilla, is a primary component of chocolate's flavor. In this case, it helps boost your perception of the chocolate.

Other Alcohols

Have some fun with the booze hiding away on your own shelves! Using additional alcohol in a cider may seem a bit counterintuitive. Aren't you going to all this trouble to make your own alcoholic beverage? Other types of alcohol carry enormous flavor, and that's what you're after. For example, like Red Hots candies, cinnamon schnapps can provide an alcoholic boost, as well as that cinnamon punch. Want a raspberry cider but can't find enough good raspberries? Use raspberry schnapps! You can even go old-school and use rum in a cider with a lot of brown sugar for reinforcement. Thanks to marketers, and the rise of the sweet cocktail, just about any flavor is available to you in alcoholic form, including caramel and whipped cream.

Beyond flavors, though, liquor can stop your yeast. Remember that yeast is alcohol tolerant but not alcohol proof. This means, throw in enough booze and you'll kill all the yeast. Why would you want to do that? If the yeast is dead, it can't ferment, and then you have a sweet, alcohol-fortified drink that ages marvelously, like the fine port wines of Portugal.

Fortified wines have a bad rap as "bum wines" (cheap rotgut designed to get you drunk), but a fine port is a thing to behold. In order to make it, all you need to do is closely monitor your fermentation and stop it when the gravity hits the 1.015–1.020 range by adding a heavy dose of hard alcohol. How much? Enough to raise the alcoholic strength of your cider to 18 percent!

In Portugal, they use a clear grape brandy called aguardente to fortify the port. Italian grappa is a similar beverage. For a cider maker, you can use calvados or applejack mixed with stronger, neutral grain spirits (also called pure grain alcohol) to stay true to the ingredients.

Port of Almaty

This is a big drink. This really should be bottled, aged, and enjoyed in small doses over a few years. Don't be scared by the amount of booze you see. It works!

INGREDIENTS | YIELDS 5 GALLONS

1¾ pounds turbinado sugar

1 tablespoon yeast nutrient

3 gallons fresh, sweet apple juice

2 packets Côte des Blancs yeast

1½ liters (151 proof) Everclear pure grain spirit

750 milliliters calvados or applejack

1. Dissolve the sugar in a pint of water, and boil for 15 minutes. Stir, along with the yeast nutrient, into the juice. Ferment and use the Standard Cider-Making Procedure found in Chapter 2.
2. Lower the temperature on the cider to 36°F to drop any remaining yeast. Rack to a bottling bucket. Add the spirits. Mix thoroughly.
3. Package in small bottles, using caps or T-corks. Age for at least 6 months.

The Goal

The amount of spirits for this recipe is calculated assuming you have a cider that has fermented to around 10 percent alcohol by volume; 18 percent is usually considered the safe cutoff point for a fortified wine. If your cider is weaker, adjust the amount of spirit up.

Water

Water may not sound like a "fun" ingredient to add to your cider, but if your idea of fun is being able to drink a low-alcohol, tasty cider all day, then it may just qualify. Even though cider makers usually have to worry about increasing their initial gravity (by adding sugar), there are times when it makes sense to add water (lowering the initial gravity) to your cider. Say your juice comes in scarily high in gravity. A little water can help pull the gravity down. Water can also help you build room in your cider for some of the additions already mentioned in this chapter (sugar, honey, and alcohol) without pushing the total alcohol level of your cider too high.

ESSENTIAL

On the matter of alcohol level: Home fermentation experimenters love to joke about how strong their end products are: "Oh, I made a 14 percent apfelwein that will utterly destroy you." There is a lot of fun to be had that way, but at some point you'll want to have a nice glass of something tasty that won't make you promise to never drink again the next morning.

For beer drinkers, there are wonderfully drinkable beers that come in at 3 percent alcohol by volume. These are the sorts of beers you can drink all day and stay in good stead for the next day. It's not common for cider makers to make a sessionable (lower alcohol) cider, but there's no reason you can't!

The real trick is to calculate how much water you need to add. It all depends on the gravity of your juice. If your cider comes in at 1.050 OG (original gravity) and you want 5 gallons of cider at about 4 percent ABV (alcohol by volume), you'll need to add about 2 gallons of water to 3 gallons of juice to produce a gravity of 1.030. When the yeast finishes fermenting, you'll have a cider that comes in at 3.9 percent.

HOW TO CALCULATE CIDER DILUTION

1. Choose your alcohol level. This example uses 4 percent alcohol by volume. Use this to determine your target original gravity (OG).

$$Target\ OG = \frac{Desired\ ABV}{0.13125}$$

$$Target\ OG = \frac{4.0}{0.13125}$$

$$Target\ OG = 30.5$$

2. Choose how many gallons you want. In this example Target Gallons = 5.
3. Multiply the number of gallons by the Target OG to determine the total amount of sugar you need.

$$Total\ Gravity\ Points = Target\ OG \times Target\ Gallons$$

$$Total\ Gravity\ Points = 30.5 \times 5$$

$$Total\ Gravity\ Points = 152.5$$

4. Take a gravity sample of your juice. Use the number to the right of the decimal point as your Juice Original Gravity. (So if the gravity is 1.050, your gravity is 50.)
5. Divide Total Gravity Points by Juice Original Gravity to determine the amount of juice you need.

$$Juice\ Gallons = \frac{Total\ Gravity\ Points}{Juice\ OG}$$

$$Juice\ Gallons = \frac{152.5}{50}$$

$$Juice\ Gallons = 3.05\ gallons$$

6. To determine the amount of water you need, subtract the juice gallons from the target gallons. Add this much water to your juice and ferment away!

$$Water\ Gallons = Target\ Gallons - Juice\ Gallons$$

$$Water\ Gallons = 5 - 3.05$$

$$Water\ Gallons = 2.95$$

In this example, you'll see the calculations aren't always perfect. Feel free to sacrifice the precise targets in the name of ease. So in this example: 3 gallons of juice mixed with 2 gallons of water will get you close to a cider at 4 percent ABV.

ESSENTIAL

Be mindful of your water when diluting your cider. No matter what, don't use tap water or salt-softened water, and especially don't use tap water poured through a green garden hose. Use water that has been carbon filtered to remove any chlorine. Anything that's good to drink is good to use.

Table Cider

For those nights when you want to have a few ciders without having to worry about getting too sloshed, have a table cider! The term table comes from the Belgian beer industry and its tradition of making tafelbier, which is a low-alcohol beer designed for those who want to moderate their alcoholic intake.

INGREDIENTS | YIELDS 5 GALLONS

3 gallons sweet apple juice (full flavored)
2 gallons filtered water
1 tablespoon yeast nutrient
1 package dried yeast or liquid cider yeast

1. In your fermenter, mix the apple juice, water, and yeast nutrient, then pitch the yeast according to the Standard Cider-Making Procedure (see Chapter 2).
2. Package with sparkling carbonation and serve lightly chilled.

Water/Cider Ratios

The actual volumes of cider and water will depend on your desired gravity and the gravity of your juice. Check the previous section to make those calculations.

CHAPTER 11

Fruit and Vegetable Additions

Sugar and booze are nice additions for your cider, but there are even more options for the intrepid experimental cider maker. What? You didn't think you were done modifying your cider with new and wonderful flavors, did you? What fruit can you add to your cider to make it really sing? What about vegetables—is it a smart idea to add those to a fruity beverage? You'll discover all of this and more, dear reader, in this chapter!

Fruits

It makes sense to add other fruits to your cider. Just about any fruit is full of possibilities and opportunities, and each offers a different set of flavors, aromas, and mouthfeel to your cider. All that it takes is a little gumption on your part and the willingness to experiment. Remember, nothing says you have to make a full batch to figure out how best to use a fruit.

ESSENTIAL

Notice that many of these flavor additions to the cider occur after the primary fermentation is done. In part, this is to allow you to react to the flavor of the batch and, more importantly, to preserve the unique character of your additions.

A key point in using fruit as an addition to your cider is to use more fruit than you think is necessary. It is not abnormal to use 2–4 pounds per 1 gallon of cider. Make sure to add the fruit to your primary fermenter because the yeast will ferment the fruit in short order.

▼ **DIFFERENT FRUITS AND AMOUNTS TO USE PER GALLON OF CIDER**

Type	Pounds Needed (Low to High)	Notes
Apricot	1–3 pounds	Apricot is a really hard flavor to capture; use a lot and be prepared to augment the flavor with flavor extract
Blackberry	½–2 pounds	Tart and tannic, a great adjustment fruit for a flabby cider
Blueberry	1–3 pounds	Blueberries are surprisingly delicate; use smaller berries if you can find them since the flavor is less diluted
Cherry	½–2 pounds	Use less of the sour cherries than sweet varieties like Bing and Rainer
Cranberry	½–2 pounds	Very tart and tannic; start with a small amount and adjust up if you want more
Grape	1–3 pounds	Take a clue from winemakers and find smaller grapes; as with blueberries, the juice will be more concentrated and flavorful
Grapefruit	1–2 pounds	Bring breakfast to your cider; use varieties like the giant pomelo or Ruby Red for a softer grapefruit flavor

Type	Pounds Needed (Low to High)	Notes
Lemon	½–1½ pounds	Varieties like Meyer lemons are softer and less acidic, so you can push them more
Lime	½–1½ pounds	If you want a different profile and can find them, Key limes offer a tangy yet softer flavor than the classic Persian lime
Mango	½–1½ pounds	Earthy, acidic, and a little funky; can make an interestingly sweet, tart cider
Orange	1–2 pounds	The classic citrus—oranges can vary in tartness and sweetness, so try them first; juicing oranges from Florida tend to be more intense
Peach	1–3 pounds	Like apricots, the peach taste is fleeting, so you'll want to load up and be prepared to augment the flavor
Pomegranate	½–2 pounds	Pomegranate has become the hot "healthy" fruit and is loaded with antioxidants that carry health benefits for you and your cider, though it carries a naturally acidic punch
Raspberry	½–2 pounds	Lends a great big punch of color and acid to your cider with black or red raspberries
Strawberry	1–3 pounds	Strawberry is really difficult to capture and hold on to, so use more than you'd think is necessary
Watermelon	½–2 pounds	The picnic classic brought to your cider; watermelon juice is a common refresher available at Hispanic markets

ALERT

Just like apple juice, make sure that any processed fruit you buy is free from the ferment-killing preservatives potassium sorbate and sodium benzoate.

Juice

Some fruits, like oranges and lemons, are easily juiced. Use your favorite juicer/reamer to produce at least ½ liter for each gallon of cider that you plan to make. If the fruit is soft and squishy, you can mash the fruit into a purée and then pass it through a fine mesh sieve to remove seeds and skins. Don't add sulfite to the juice. Instead, give the juice a hard freeze.

When the cider has finished its primary ferment, add your thawed juice and let the ferment resume. You want to wait until the cider ferment has subsided to help preserve the aromas and flavors and keep them from flying off into the atmosphere.

Whole

Other fruits aren't amenable to juicing, but a long soak in an alcoholic solution will dissolve most of the goodies you desire from your fruit. To use whole fruit, wash it well to remove any traces of dirt and pesticides. Cut the fruit into bite-sized chunks and toss the chunks into a freezer bag.

The freezing helps stun any wild yeast and bacteria on the fruit. This does not kill all of the natural-borne critters—many will die—and merely freezing will not sanitize the fruit. Thankfully, the cider's acidity and alcohol will provide decent protection from the remaining bugs.

The other benefit comes from a flaw in the way home freezers freeze foods. Unlike a commercial blast freezer, your home freezer works slowly. When water freezes slowly, the forming ice crystals become longer and sharper. These tiny knives cut through the cell walls of the fruit. It won't matter while everything's frozen, but once the fruit warms and the crystals melt, the pierced cells release all the sugar, flavors, and goodies straight into your cider.

If you don't want to freeze the fruit, you'll have to manually break up the fruit to get the goods into your cider. You can either purée the fruit, or attack it with a good old-fashioned potato masher.

Frozen

If you don't have a local farmers' market, or you can't find ingredients that you want to explore in your area, you can always try the frozen-food aisle in your grocery store—thanks to the wonders of the modern IQF (individually quick frozen) process. Thanks in part to the craze for smoothies, more and more fruits are showing up in the freezer cases, waiting for you.

To use frozen fruit, you can either chuck it in whole or take the time to pulverize in a blender, with a little fresh juice, for a rough slurry. You'll get faster extraction from the slurry, but the work-to-benefit ratio puts it in the questionable value area.

Store-Bought Juice

While diluted juices will work, it's better to find juices that are 100 percent your target fruit. Usually the label will display whether a product is comprised of 100 percent fruit juice or what percentage of actual juice is contained within.

Another choice, for the few juices that get frozen, is to use the concentrate just like you use apple juice concentrate. Just mix the frozen cylinder into the juice base and let the juice be the dilution base instead of water.

Purée

Breaking a fruit down and busting open its cells allow you to maximally extract all the fruity goodness. But juicing a fruit generally removes the skin and seed material, which add earthy, nutty, bitter components to your cider. If you don't want the hassle of dealing with fresh fruit yourself, look for 100 percent fruit purées.

Most homebrew shops will carry a small line of fruit purée (typically Oregon Fruit Products brand) that provides you the opportunity to add cherry, blackberry, or raspberry flavors to your cider. Many folks use these with sugar and water to make fruit wines, but added to a cider they are bold and powerful. Make sure you're getting real fruit purée and not puréed fruit mixed with syrup.

Cooked Fruit—Jams, Jellies, and Sauces

It's not very often you end up using cooked fruit in a cider. But if you absolutely want to add a flavor profile from a jam, jelly, or sauce to your cider, be aware that the pectin in cooked fruit might cause a problem. Most of the cooked fruits or jams and jellies that you'll want to add to cider are naturally pectin rich, which allows them to set after cooking. But because pectin is insoluble in alcohol, it will come out during or after fermentation and cause your cider to become hazy, or it will create wisps or strands in your cider. So don't add jam straight to your cider! To ensure that your cider remains clear, you can add pectinase, a pectic enzyme, available from homebrew shops and stores with extensive canning supplies. Dissolve the jelly you want to add to your cider in a little warm cider, allow it to cool, and then add the pectic enzyme. Add all of this to the cider and let it run.

Extracts

You may notice when you look around a home-brewing store that there's a whole shelf devoted to nothing but flavor extracts in an endless variety: cherry, blueberry, peach, etc. For the most part, it's highly encouraged that you avoid using extracts. Several have strong artificial aromas that are off-putting.

The one exception to this rule is strawberry. That funny little seeded fruit has big flavor problems: It requires an unbelievably large amount to infuse flavor, and the flavor fades quickly. Most commercial strawberries are rather weak in flavor. You can add 3–5 pounds of strawberries to a cider before capturing the strawberry essence only to have it vanish in two months' time. Layering a strawberry extract on top of the fresh strawberries will help boost the flavor, while the real fruit will hide the chemical nature of the extract.

"Fruit" Cider

This is a base recipe for almost any fruit cider that you'll want to make. Consult the fruit list to learn the amount of fruit to try, but don't forget you are the cider maker, so trust your own tastes!

INGREDIENTS | YIELDS 1+ GALLON(S)

1 gallon sweet apple juice
1 teaspoon yeast nutrient
1 package dry yeast or liquid cider yeast
1–4 pounds frozen chunked fruit of your choice

1. In your fermenter, mix the juice and yeast nutrient. Pitch the yeast according to the Standard Cider-Making Procedure (see Chapter 2).

2. After primary fermentation, transfer to a secondary fermenter and add the fruit. Mix thoroughly and wait 1–2 weeks before packaging.
3. Package to a sparkling level of carbonation and serve chilled.

Thawing

Don't worry about thawing your frozen fruit; it will thaw in the juice. The icy fruit will drop the temperature of your cider, so don't be surprised if fermentation is a little slow to take off.

Cider Tropicale

Peach is a notoriously difficult flavor to capture in a cider, so be prepared to use a lot of it. The mango here provides the other bright acidic note, and its pungent earthiness will also ground the cider.

INGREDIENTS | YIELDS 1 GALLON

1 gallon sweet apple juice (balanced sweet)

1 teaspoon yeast nutrient

1 package dried yeast or liquid cider yeast

2 pounds frozen peaches

1 pound frozen mangoes

1. In your fermenter, mix the juice and yeast nutrient. Then pitch the yeast according to the Standard Cider-Making Procedure (see Chapter 2).
2. After primary fermentation, rack to a secondary fermenter and add the peaches and mangoes. Mix thoroughly and wait 2 weeks before packaging.
3. Package to a sparkling level of carbonation and serve chilled.

More Peach!

If the peach flavor still isn't enough for you, consider dosing your cider with some peach schnapps. As a flavoring agent, it retains the power of the peach.

Sour Cherry Cascade

Old-fashioned pie cherries are also known as sour cherries. They carry an intense blast of puckering sourness over the richest earthy cherry flavor you can imagine. A pie, or a cider, made with regular "sweet" cherries just won't have the same richness that sour cherries convey.

INGREDIENTS | YIELDS 5 GALLONS

4½ gallons sweet apple juice (balanced to the acidic)

2 quarts 100 percent sour cherry juice

2 tablespoons yeast nutrient

1 package dried yeast or liquid cider yeast

½ ounce cinnamon extract

1. In your fermenter, mix the apple juice, cherry juice, and yeast nutrient, then pitch the yeast according to the Standard Cider-Making Procedure (see Chapter 2).
2. After the primary fermentation, rack to a secondary fermenter and add the cinnamon extract. Mix thoroughly and wait a few days before packaging.
3. Package to a sparkling level of carbonation and serve chilled.

The Power of Juice
Part of the decline in the sour cherry's popularity is its limited growth area and harvest season. This is where juice comes to the rescue. Most folks will never see a whole sour cherry, but the juice is widely available at Trader Joe's and online purveyors.

Berry Blast

Artificially flavored "berry" things can be found everywhere, but this is the real deal. You can double up on the berry to really push it over the top.

INGREDIENTS | YIELDS 5 GALLONS

4¼ gallons sweet apple juice

1 (49-ounce) can Oregon Fruit Products Red Raspberry Purée Seedless

1 (49-ounce) can Oregon Fruit Products Blackberry Purée Seedless

2 tablespoons yeast nutrient

1 package dried yeast or liquid cider yeast

1. In your fermenter, mix the juice, purées, and yeast nutrient, then pitch the yeast according to the Standard Cider-Making Procedure (see Chapter 2). Make sure to provide 1–2 extra weeks of settling time to clear the extra fruit solids.
2. Package to your carbonation preference (see Chapter 8). Still cider will present more of the sweet flavor; sparkling cider will be brighter, drier, and acidic.

CranCider

Cranberry cocktail is already mostly apple juice anyway, so it's only natural to turn the tables and make a hard cider from it, too. In this recipe, you'll use jellied cranberry salad.

INGREDIENTS | YIELDS 1 GALLON

1 (8-ounce) can cranberry dressing (jellied), or the equivalent of homemade cranberry dressing
1 strip orange peel
1 gallon sweet apple juice
1 teaspoon pectic enzyme powder
1 teaspoon yeast nutrient
1 package dried yeast or liquid cider yeast

1. In a pot, mix the cranberry dressing and orange peel with an equal volume of juice. Heat gently and stir the jelly until it dissolves. Do not boil! Do not simmer! Remove the orange peel and cool the mixture, covered, to room temperature. Add the pectic enzyme.
2. In your fermenter, mix the juice, dissolved cranberry dressing, and yeast nutrient, then pitch the yeast according to the Standard Cider-Making Procedure (see Chapter 2).
3. Package to your carbonation preference. Still cider will present more of the sweet flavor; sparkling cider will be brighter, drier, and acidic.

Strawberry Shortcake

Since strawberries fade fast, you'll want to keep this cider's gravity moderate and not try to make a rocket fuel cider. The lactose will help boost the body to give more heft to the strawberry.

INGREDIENTS | YIELDS 3 GALLONS

3 gallons sweet apple juice (balanced to the acidic)
1 tablespoon yeast nutrient
1 package dried yeast or liquid cider yeast
6 pounds fresh strawberries, cleaned, hulled, halved, and frozen
¾ pound lactose milk sugar
1 cup water
1 ounce strawberry extract (or up to 2 ounces based on your taste preferences)

1. In your fermenter, mix the apple juice and yeast nutrient, then pitch the yeast according to the Standard Cider-Making Procedure (see Chapter 2).
2. After primary fermentation, rack to a secondary fermenter and add the fresh strawberries. In a small saucepan on your stove, boil the lactose sugar in the water for 5 minutes to dissolve into a syrup. Mix thoroughly into the fermenter and wait a few days for fermentation to restart and finish.
3. After the fermentation is complete and the cider is cleared, add the strawberry extract. Taste the cider and adjust the flavor as needed. Remember that the strawberry taste will fade.
4. Package to a sparkling level of carbonation and serve chilled.

Vegetables

Whereas fruit seems a natural addition to cider, not many people think of adding vegetables to their cider. But there are a number of vegetables that are filled with sugar, and that's what you want. For example, a good portion of white sugar is refined from sugar beets.

Look for vegetables that, like beets, contain a fair amount of sugar. Depending on your preference, you may want to avoid watery vegetables like cucumbers. And unless you plan to convert the starch to sugar, avoid starchy vegetables like potatoes. What you ideally want is a vegetable that makes a great juice.

ALERT

The most obvious thing you must watch for when you're choosing vegetables is sulfur. Think any member of the *Allium* genus, including all the onion- and garlic-style vegetables such as onion, garlic, chives, leeks, etc. The sulfur that they impart carries through to the aroma.

A perfect example of a cider-friendly vegetable is the carrot. Carrots contain more sugar than any vegetable apart from the sugar beet. They are warm, slightly acidic, and not nearly as earthy as a beet. If you have access to a home juicer, carrot juice is cheap and easy. If not, check your local grocery store for freshly squeezed carrot juice.

Other vegetables may not provide much sugar, but they can provide other flavors. Cucumber, for example, is an extraordinarily bitter vegetable when you incorporate the peels. However, there's another vegetable that everyone forgets about that can provide everything a flabby apple juice needs and is traditional in cider-friendly regions—rhubarb. Rhubarb is a strange plant that contains a world of tannin and acid. Rhubarb is so naturally astringent and sour that it didn't achieve its modern culinary uses until the advent of plentiful sugar. While most commonly thought of as a pie filling (when combined with sugar and made into a jam), there are plenty of examples of rhubarb being made into wine, mead, and even cider.

ALERT

The leaves of rhubarb contain oxalic acid, which has a nasty toxic effect on the kidneys, effectively shutting them down. For an average person in good health you'd have to consume 43 grams of pure oxalic acid to kill you. This translates to over 10 pounds of leaves, so you're safe.

The rhubarb stalk contains vegetable tannins that provide for astringency. They also contain malic acid, the same acid that occurs naturally in apples. This will help the rhubarb's flavors to blend naturally. Additionally, the red color that will infuse your cider comes from anthocyanin compounds that also act as antioxidants!

Chilis

On the picante side of the fence, there's nothing wrong with backing your sweet cider with a little bit of heat. Look no further than plants from the *Capsicum* genus, which include the chili pepper. Native to the Americas, the chili has become a worldwide staple, prized for the kick it gives your food.

With chilies there are two facts to consider—the heat and the vegetal taste. If you put a bell pepper into a cider, you'll get all that chlorophyll "green" taste with nothing else to show. The habanero, as well as the bhut jolokia (ghost pepper), is massive burn, with little else obvious.

A great middle ground is the chipotle, which is a smoked jalapeno that has just enough heat to be noticeable, with more interesting flavor thanks to the smoking. You can find them dried or canned in adobo (tomato, garlic, vinegar). For cider making, the dried version is a better choice.

Dried chili peppers are also easier to use, since all you have to do to infuse them is soak them in a liquid. You can quite literally "dry chili" your cider in this way, without much worry. The capsaicin (the compound in the pepper responsible for the burn you feel) will leach into the cider. Since it carries a mild antifungal quality, make sure you to wait until primary fermentation is done before adding any chili peppers.

What's Up, Doc?

Carrot juice is a staple for those trying to improve their nutrition. Ginger is a classic pairing with carrot; the peppery sweetness boosts the carrot impressions.

INGREDIENTS | YIELDS 5 GALLONS

4½ gallons sweet apple juice (balanced to the acidic)

2 quarts carrot juice

2 tablespoons yeast nutrient

1 package dried yeast or liquid cider yeast

1 ounce ginger syrup (either buy premade from a cocktail supply store or make your own by boiling 1 cup water with 1 cup sugar and 2 tablespoons grated ginger)

1. In your fermenter, mix the apple juice, carrot juice, and yeast nutrient, then pitch the yeast according to the Standard Cider-Making Procedure (see Chapter 2).
2. After primary fermentation, rack to a secondary fermenter and add the ginger syrup. Mix thoroughly and wait a few days before packaging.
3. Package to a sparkling level of carbonation and serve chilled.

Other Options

If you want inspiration for other carrot cider flavors, look no further than carrot soups. What about dill? What about caraway? Both go great with carrots and may make interesting additions with or without the ginger.

Rhubarb, Rhubarb!

Come for the color, stay for the wonderfully shocking flavor. Because of its intensity, start with a low dose of rhubarb. If you want more, add more.

INGREDIENTS | YIELDS 1 GALLON

1 gallon sweet apple juice (balanced to the sweet)
1 pound rhubarb stalks, cut into 1"-long segments, and frozen
½ teaspoon yeast nutrient
1 package dried yeast or liquid cider yeast
½ cup sugar
½ cup water
½ teaspoon potassium sorbate

1. In your fermenter, mix the apple juice, rhubarb, and yeast nutrient, then pitch the yeast according to the Standard Cider-Making Procedure (see Chapter 2).
2. Boil the sugar in ½ cup of water and mix with the cider and sorbate. This will sweeten the cider and prevent it from refermenting. Package still and serve chilled.

An Alternative Sweetening

If you want this cider to be sparkling and need to bottle, consider skipping the sorbate and sugar and use an artificial sweetener like stevia or sucralose. The yeast can't touch it, so the sweetness will always remain.

Death from Within

There's nothing quite like the heat of a chili-pepper drink, because it runs through your throat before you know what's hit you. Start small and then add intensity if you like!

INGREDIENTS | YIELDS 5 GALLONS

5 gallons sweet apple juice

2 tablespoons yeast nutrient

1 package dried yeast or liquid cider yeast

2 dried chipotles, cut in half and seeds removed

1. In your fermenter, mix the apple juice and yeast nutrient, then pitch the yeast according to the Standard Cider-Making Procedure (see Chapter 2).
2. After primary fermentation, rack to a secondary fermenter and add the chipotles. Mix thoroughly and wait a few days before sampling. When the heat and pepper flavor are to your liking, transfer the cider off the peppers into another container like your bottling bucket. Package to a sparkling level of carbonation and serve chilled.

CHAPTER 12

Herb and Spice Additions

You now know how to use so many different elements in your cider, but there's still the all-important topic of herbs and spices to explore. If someone were to ask you, "what do you taste when you eat apple pie," cinnamon should be one of the first things that pop into your head. In this chapter you'll learn how to add cinnamon, amongst other things, to make an apple pie–flavored cider.

Spices

Next to the sugar and baking supplies in your kitchen cabinets, you probably have a plethora of half-forgotten spices in bottles and canisters. Just like when cooking, your spice rack can alter and punctuate the character of your cider.

You may have noticed the very careful wording—spices. Both spices and herbs provide aromatic oils, but from different parts of the plants. The easiest way to differentiate them is to know that herbs are leaves; spices are everything else—the roots, stems, seeds. Cinnamon, for instance, is a spice because the useful part is the inner bark of a tree from the *Cinnamomum* genus. Vanilla is a spice since it's the dried pod of the vanilla orchid.

Some plants can be both herbs and spices; for instance, coriander. In seed form, you know it as an orange-scented, sweet component of Indian and Mexican cuisine. When allowed to grow, it becomes the leafy green herb known in America as cilantro. The rest of the world refers to it as Chinese parsley or fresh coriander.

A classic spice used in cider making is citrus zest. You can capture the essence of the fruit from the outermost section of the peel, before you get to the white pith. Much of the essential oil of a citrus fruit can be found there.

An important factor in spice quality is its age. While spices can last for a long time, the fresher and higher quality you can find, the better. The oils will smell and taste brighter and fresher, and your cider will reflect that. Also, buy whole spices whenever you can. Whole spices retain more fresh characteristics than preground spices. Compare freshly grated nutmeg (from an actual nut) to its lackluster preground powdered counterpart.

QUESTION

Is spice freshness really that important?
Yes, the difference between fresh and stale spices is profound! Take a spice, and put a quantity out on a sunny windowsill for a week. Crush it and smell. Crush some properly stored fresher spice and smell. Smell the difference?

To find fresh spices, head to your local gourmet or spice store and ask about the ages of the spices. If you don't have one locally, there are several online stores that can help you out. The Spice House (*www.thespicehouse.com*)

is Chicago's go-to answer and mails fresh spices around the world. Wisconsin is home to Penzeys Spices (*www.penzeys.com*), an upscale spice retailer that operates shops in about thirty states.

There are several ways to use spices to flavor your cider. But very importantly, no matter how you choose to add spice, make sure you crush your spices lightly before starting. By crushing the spices, you're increasing the surface area and oils available for extraction.

Here are some ways to add spices to your cider:

- **Dry spicing.** To borrow a term from the brewing world, dry spicing is simply adding lightly crushed spices to the cider after primary fermentation is complete. The spices infuse for a week or two before you pull the cider off. If you use a hop/spice bag, you can pull the bag from the cider.
- **Syrup.** Boiling in water is a way to maximally extract the oils found in your spices. You can extract in plain water, but it's better to use a little sugar to avoid watering down your cider too much. Don't use juice unless you want hazy cider! Syrups work best with "wet" spices like ginger.
- **Tincture.** Heat and water can draw out oils, but you also run the risk of losing some of the more delicate aromatics. A longer cold soak in vodka will extract every iota of flavor.

Spice Syrup

This syrup provides a deep, earthy oomph to any cider. Go wild with whatever spices you want.

INGREDIENTS | YIELDS 1 PINT

1 pint filtered water
1 cup sugar
1 tablespoon spice of your choice, lightly crushed

1. In a medium pot, combine all the ingredients and bring to a boil. Boil for 5 minutes, turn off the heat, cover the pot, and let steep for 10 additional minutes.

2. Pour the still-hot syrup through a fine mesh strainer into a sanitized jar. Seal the jar and allow to cool on the counter before storing in the fridge for up to 1 month.

3. To use, stir a small portion of the syrup into the cider after primary fermentation, taste, and add more as desired. Adding the syrup after primary fermentation will help preserve much of the spice character. Allow the cider to rest for a few days before bottling.

Spice Tincture

A spice tincture is easily one of the best, most flexible, and most consistent ways to guarantee the right flavor and aroma for your cider. You can create these tinctures well ahead of time and dose your cider to taste.

INGREDIENTS | YIELDS 6 OUNCES

6 ounces vodka
1½ teaspoons spice of your choice, lightly crushed

1. In a tight-sealing jar, like a Mason jar, mix the vodka and the spice. Let soak for 14 days. Pick up and shake every day.

2. Carefully decant (or pour) the tincture from the settled matter in the jar. For extra clarity, filter through a coffee filter and use as desired. Store for up to 1 year in an airtight jar.

Apple Pie Cider

This recipe works best when the cider is left lightly sweet with a medium carbonation to volatize the spice aroma.

INGREDIENTS | YIELDS 5 GALLONS

5 gallons sweet apple juice (balanced to the acidic)
1 pound brown sugar
2 tablespoons yeast nutrient
1 package dried yeast or liquid cider yeast
1½ ounces cinnamon extract
1½ ounces cinnamon syrup
½ ounce allspice syrup, or extract
1 ounce ginger syrup (either buy premade from a cocktail supply store or make your own by boiling 1 cup water with 1 cup sugar and 2 tablespoons grated ginger)

1. In your fermenter, mix the apple juice, brown sugar, and yeast nutrient, then pitch the yeast according to the Standard Cider-Making Procedure (see Chapter 2).
2. After primary fermentation, rack to a secondary fermenter and add the extracts and syrups. Mix thoroughly and wait a few days before packaging.
3. Package to a medium level of carbonation and serve chilled.

Syrup and Extract

This recipe calls for both cinnamon extract and syrup in order to capture the full range of cinnamon flavor. The extract provides that bright, searing cinnamon heat and burn that you associate with anything cinnamon flavored. The syrup provides a deep, earthy cinnamon flavor without the big heat. Together the two provide a brilliant spectrum of cinnamon taste.

Herbs

Comprised of the leaves of aromatic plants, herbs are usually best used fresh. Unlike spices, which tend to be exotic in origin, herbs can grow almost everywhere and require a little soil and daily watering to flourish.

Some of the herbs that are used in cider making include the previously mentioned cilantro, plus mint, basil, tarragon, thyme, and basil. Not all herbs are best fresh, though. The classic example is oregano, which, until dried, carries a tarry, resiny flavor over an intensely spicy flavor. When dried, the resin flavor disappears and the spiciness moderates to a pleasant peppery flavor.

You can use the same techniques with herbs that you use for spices, but because of the moist and delicate nature of the herbs, it is best to use an additional method—unsweetened herb tea. Gentle heat works best to extract the herb's flavors. If you keep the liquor below 140°F, you can use fresh juice as your base. Dried herbs work just fine in tea; you need look no further than the countless herbal teas lining the grocery store shelf.

Just as with spices, before you use herbs you need to crush or bruise them lightly. The back of a knife or rolling them between your hands works well. This will help release the oils. Also, like spices, to preserve the aromatics, use your herb tea after the primary fermentation is complete. If added before or during primary fermentation, all of the carbon dioxide produced by the yeast will scrub out the desired herbal components.

Flowers

Although most flowers aren't technically herbs, it makes sense to talk about them here because you have to treat them like herbs by making teas out of them. Like herbs, they have precious aromatic oils locked up in their petals, just waiting for you to liberate them from their waxy confines.

Be gentle with your heat! The delicate oils will vaporize if treated too roughly and not captured by distillation. You may be familiar with some flower-based distillates, such as rosewater–scented desserts used in Middle Eastern cuisine.

Another flower you may know from its culinary use is the hibiscus flower, used in the form of hibiscus tea. Hibiscus flowers are heartier than roses and contain a fair amount of acid compounds for a zippy punch. The flowers also impart a deep, rich, purplish-red color that will stand your cider off dramatically.

Herb Tea

This tea delicately extracts the power of the herbs without losing too many of the aromatics. If you're worried about keeping your cider sanitary, you can briefly boil the tea, but you'll lose potency. Definitely don't boil if you're using juice!

INGREDIENTS | YIELDS 1 PINT

1 pint filtered water or juice
3 tablespoons herb of your choice, lightly bruised

1. In a medium pot, combine all the ingredients and heat to 140°F. Turn off the heat, cover the pot, and let steep for 10 additional minutes.
2. Pour the tea through a fine mesh strainer into a sanitized jar. Seal the jar and allow it to cool on the counter before storing in the fridge for up to 1 week.
3. To use, stir a small portion of the syrup into the cider after primary fermentation, taste, and add more as desired.

TNT Cider

Two great herbs that are natural playmates are thyme and tarragon. They're used in European cuisine and make a wonderfully aromatic and spicy one-two punch with thyme's savory pungency softened by tarragon's sweet licorice flavor.

INGREDIENTS | YIELDS 1 GALLON

1 gallon sweet apple juice (balanced to the sweet)
½ teaspoon yeast nutrient
1 package dried yeast or liquid cider yeast
¼ cup tarragon tea
¼ cup thyme tea

1. In your fermenter, mix the apple juice and yeast nutrient, then pitch the yeast according to the Standard Cider-Making Procedure (see Chapter 2).
2. After primary fermentation, rack to your bottling bucket and add the teas. Mix thoroughly.
3. Package still and serve lightly chilled.

RhodoCider

You could go to all the trouble of making your own rose water tea, but save yourself the heartache of gathering pounds of rose petals and instead search for your nearest Middle Eastern/Jewish market and buy a bottle of rose water.

INGREDIENTS | YIELDS 1 GALLON

1 gallon sweet apple juice (balanced to the sweet)
½ teaspoon yeast nutrient
1 package dried yeast or liquid cider yeast
¼ cup rose water

1. In your fermenter, mix the apple juice and yeast nutrient, then pitch the yeast according to the Standard Cider-Making Procedure (see Chapter 2).
2. After primary fermentation, rack to your bottling bucket and add the rose water. Mix thoroughly.
3. Package to a medium carbonation and serve lightly chilled.

Zinger Cider

This one is a bit of a cheat because it's made with Celestial Seasonings Red Zinger herbal tea that contains flowers, herbs, and spices for a colorful and zippy cider.

INGREDIENTS | YIELDS 1 GALLON

1 gallon sweet apple juice (balanced to the sweet)
½ teaspoon yeast nutrient
1 package dried yeast or liquid cider yeast
1 cup triple-strength Red Zinger or Jamaica hibiscus tea

1. In your fermenter, mix the apple juice and yeast nutrient, then pitch the yeast according to the Standard Cider-Making Procedure (see Chapter 2).
2. After primary fermentation, rack to your bottling bucket and add the tea. Mix thoroughly.
3. Package to a medium carbonation and serve lightly chilled.

Jamaica

Red Zinger is an herbal blend built around hibiscus flowers. In Latin America, hibiscus tea is called Jamaica, and giant packs of Flor de Jamaica can be found cheaply in local Latin markets. It's the hibiscus that gives the distinctive red color and tart, cranberry-like bite.

Making Cider Vinegar

Eventually, all fermentations go sideways, no matter how careful you are. It is part of the natural cycle of a fermented product's life. And for fermented beverages, that end stage is vinegar. The name comes to English from Latin via French. Combining the Old French words *vin* ("wine") and *aigre* ("sour") yields a word that means "sour wine."

Despite the wine association, vinegar can be made from any alcoholic beverage. For instance, malt vinegar is made from unhopped beer, sherry vinegar from sherry, and cider vinegar from cider. In general, vinegar is acetic acid diluted in a flavorful water-based solution. The magic happens when a colony of acetobacter, an acetic acid–producing bacteria genus, is exposed to ethanol and oxygen. Where does the acetobacter come from? It's everywhere around you right now! It's found on flowers and fruits and just about anywhere that humans make alcohol.

ALERT

Acetobacter will happily and greedily eat every last drop of ethanol it can find. Unless you really like vinegar, it is strongly recommended that you make your vinegar in a different location than where you make your cider.

Cure All?

If you read through alternative medicine and diet books, you'll discover a large belief in the power of cider vinegar to heal what ails you. There's nothing new about this belief. Chinese medicine has used cider vinegar for thousands of years. Even the man who gave his name to the oath that doctors take, Hippocrates, prescribed cider vinegar for many of his patients' maladies.

Here in the United States, the modern cider vinegar movement kicked off with the 1958 publication of Dr. DeForest Clinton Jarvis's book, *Folk Medicine: A Vermont Doctor's Guide to Good Health*. In it he prescribed a mixture of honey and cider vinegar to acidify the body, eliminate bad bacteria, and keep things humming.

Among the claims of apple cider vinegar proponents are:

- **Blood sugar regulation.** Some studies have shown that drinking an ounce of cider vinegar at bedtime can reduce the amount of sugar in your bloodstream by the morning.
- **Cancer.** A few lab studies show cider vinegar has an effect on cancer in petri dishes, but so far this doesn't appear to be replicated in human trials.
- **Cholesterol.** It may just be, according to experiments performed on rats, that cider vinegar can lower your bad blood serum cholesterol levels.

- **Hair and skin care.** Regular washing of your face with a mix of 1 part vinegar, 2 parts water supposedly helps balance the pH of your skin for softer, smoother skin. Rinsing your hair with a one-to-one mixture removes buildup and restores shine to your mane.
- **Digestion.** Advocates claim that a regular dose of cider vinegar helps correct conditions in the digestive tract, settles and calms the stomach, and even helps to manage acid reflux.
- **Detoxing and cleansing.** This goes back to the ancient Egyptians. Modern devotees claim that nutrients and enzymes found in cider vinegar clear the lymphatic system and rid the liver of toxin buildup.
- **Diet and weight loss.** Several studies show a possible link between cider vinegar consumption and lowered food intake without a loss of satisfaction. This may be tied to its effects on blood sugar.

While the old saying recommends an apple a day to prevent a medical practitioner's visit, the evidence for the effectiveness of cider vinegar is still lacking scientifically. The good news: Cider vinegar is still tasty and a perfectly wonderful addition to everything.

Natural Cider Vinegar

This recipe will produce a potent and brisk vinegar that's cloudy from the result of the acetic acid fermentation. Don't worry about the floaty bits; they're harmless and may even be healthful (but you can filter them out, if you like).

INGREDIENTS | YIELDS 1 PINT

1 pint cider, any flavor
1 tablespoon premade, nonpasteurized apple cider vinegar, homemade or natural (such as Bragg Organic Apple Cider Vinegar)
1 canning jar with lid
1 cheesecloth, folded over 4 times
1 rubber band

1. Combine the cider and natural vinegar in the canning jar, put on the lid, and shake it up. After thoroughly mixing the vinegar and cider, remove the lid and cover the jar with the folded cheesecloth. Rubber band the cheesecloth to the jar, and swirl it once a day for 3 days.

2. After a month of seemingly no activity, you'll notice a whitish-gray, weblike skin growing over the surface of your cider. That's the "vinegar mother." This gradually thickening puck of goo is actually made of cellulose, the same material found in plant cells. (It's off-putting but completely harmless.) Once the mother has formed, the vinegar will be ready in a month or two.

3. Grab a small sample with a straw, doing as little damage as possible to the mother, and taste it. If it's intensely sour, your job is done. If you like, you can filter the vinegar of the big bits of the mother and seal it up.

4. You can pasteurize the vinegar by bringing it to 155°F in a nonreactive saucepan for 30 minutes. Fill sanitized canning jars with your still-hot vinegar, then lid them up. Pasteurization is optional.

Don't Be Afraid of the Water

Don't buy into the macho aesthetic that harsh is better. Raw, this vinegar will probably be brutally acidic. Dilute it with clean, freshly boiled water to taste. If pasteurizing your vinegar, dilute before you heat the vinegar.

Maple Cider Vinaigrette

Use your vinegar for this supremely easy salad dressing that you can whip up in a few seconds. Pair this with some sharp greens and sliced apples for a salad that is anything but boring.

INGREDIENTS | YIELDS 2 CUPS

1 cup cider, any flavor
¼ cup apple cider vinegar, homemade or natural, with live mother
2 tablespoons maple syrup
1 teaspoon Dijon mustard
1 cup neutral-flavored vegetable oil, such as grapeseed oil

1. Combine all the ingredients, except the oil, in a large bowl. Whisk together.

2. Adding a few drops at a time, whisk in the oil furiously to emulsify. Once the dressing looks creamy, add more oil. Once you've added a

quarter of the oil, add the oil faster and whisk until thoroughly incorporated.

Shaken, Not Stirred

Some chefs today prefer to shake their dressings. You can use a cocktail shaker or jar with a liquid-tight lid. Just add all the ingredients together in a jar and shake until thoroughly combined.

CHAPTER 13

Cider from Scratch

Now that you've made your cider from juice, you no doubt have a romantic notion of orchards filled with row after row of apples, waiting for your magical touch to convert them from mere fleshy globes to bright, bubbling nectar. With a little bit of equipment, you can do just that!

Finding and Selecting Fruit

If you're lucky enough to have an orchard, or live within easy distance of a pick-your-own orchard, then you're set and ready to go. You can almost certainly guarantee that the varieties available to you will mostly be of the usual culinary apple varieties, but no matter! A fresh-picked culinary apple will be better than any grocery store apple (grown who knows where, picked who knows when, and stored in long-term cryogenic storage).

If your idea of harvesting fruit involves the grocery store or farmers' market, do your best to find quality apples that haven't been waxed. If the apples have been waxed, make sure to give them a thorough washing before using or aging.

QUESTION

Why are apples waxed?
According to the Washington State Apple Commission, apples lose their natural coating when washed after picking. To protect the apple from moisture loss and provide a glossy mirror finish, it is thinly coated with a nonpetroleum substance like carnauba wax or shellac. While safe to eat, it doesn't hurt to wash first.

The Forgotten Apple

There's an alternative to the commercial or home orchard—the abandoned orchard. All around the United States, particularly the East Coast, there exist stands of old, neglected apple trees. They are hidden away in the forgotten corners of farms or woods untouched by suburban sprawl. If your region of the world has any history of apple growing, odds are some of the trees haven't yet met the bulldozer or chainsaw.

Why? Humanity may have manipulated many characteristics of the apple tree, but the fundamental nature of the tree itself hasn't changed. Once an orchard is established, you can walk away from it and the trees will still keep going along their merry way for well over a hundred years (barring disease and trauma). Sure, the yield will slow and the results will be less than ideal. Mankind's stewardship does help!

What to Pick

The key with cider is to pick apples at their peak of sugar and ripeness, before the fruit turns mealy. The easy way to tell when your trees are ready for harvesting is when you begin to have some apples fall naturally to the ground after a wind blows the tree. At that point, you can start to find individual apples that are ready for harvesting by reaching up and twisting the apple from the tree. If it twists off cleanly and freely, you're set!

Why not look at the color or the firmness? The problem is that these factors vary from variety to variety. Some styles (particularly pale gold or green) don't undergo dramatic color changes. To make matters worse, some varieties vary their color at ripeness by region and weather! Some apples don't soften until far too late, just before they turn into giant mush piles, which is less than ideal for cider making.

If you want a more scientific determination of your fruit's general ripeness, cut a slice from a target apple. Drip your drugstore's cheapest iodine over the slice (completely separated from the other fruit), and watch the color. If the color stays iodine brown, your fruit is ripe. If the iodine changes to purple or black, your fruit is unripe and still needs some time. You want to keep the test slice away from the rest of your fruit, since iodine has an unpleasant, medicinal flavor to which most people are extremely sensitive.

The Ripening Process

What's happening to a fruit as it ripens? As fruits grow, there's a steady transformation. Some of these you can observe as color and textural changes. For instance, unripe lemons look like hard green limes and only become bright lemon yellow when they ripen.

But behind the scenes (er . . . peel), apples are a climacteric fruit, that is, they continue to ripen after being picked. When a fruit starts growing, its primary components are rigid bundles of proteins and starch. Starch is made of two incredibly complex molecules, amylose and amylopectin. Both of these are complicated chains of glucose, one of the fundamental sugars.

When a fruit ripens, these chains of starch are gradually broken down into smaller molecules. Eventually they are transformed into sugars that you can taste as sweetness. Additionally, proteins and pectin break down to soften the fruit.

Why do fruits transform starch into sugar?
Glucose is a fundamental energy source for animals. It provides raw power to, among other things, the human brain. This provides a genetic advantage to plants producing sugar—glucose-hungry animals, including humans, will eat the now-sweet fruit and then scatter the seeds, spreading its genetic payload.

What causes this ripening? There are number of factors at play, but for apples (and other pomes), the primary culprit is the fairly simple molecule of ethylene gas (C_2H_4). Ripe apples, bananas, and a number of other fruits produce it in quantity. Actually, it's not just the fruit; most of the parts of a plant produce the gas. One of the primary differences for nonclimacteric fruits is that the fruit itself does not produce ethylene.

Ethylene formation is a natural part of the plant's growth cycle. The dropping of leaves, or abscission, usually marks the uptick of production. Ethylene starts with an amino acid called methionine that is gradually transformed via a series of steps into the target gas.

FACT

If you've ever thought, "Hey, this bruised or cut fruit rots much faster than before," you're not wrong. Bruising or cutting ("wounding" in proper parlance) causes a massive release of ethylene gas, which speeds the ripening/rotting process.

Ethylene is naturally released, and when it hits the plant, it acts as a hormone. When ethylene hits a plant's receivers, it triggers a genetic response to start the ripening processes.

If you need to ripen a fruit quickly, put it in a closed paper bag with a ripe apple or banana, and wait a day or two. Both apples and bananas produce a ton of ethylene, which is useful if you have some less-than-ripe apples!

How Much to Pick

A natural question to ask as you're busy at work in the orchard is, "Just how many of these darn things do I have to pick before I'm done?" The answer is a lot! For a gallon of juice, you'll need to pick 16–20 pounds of apples. You will yield about 8–9 pounds of juice from that quantity of apples, which equates to roughly a gallon of juice.

Obviously, this will vary based on the apples, the amount of moisture during the growing season, and other factors. If you're getting your juice from a cider press, you can ask for it by volume, but if you're growing and harvesting on your own, learn the art of flexibility! Have a few extra containers on hand just in case you yield more juice, or be prepared for extra-concentrated flavor if your apples don't yield as much liquid.

What Not to Pick

The first rule of thumb for what not to pick should be obvious, but it needs to be said anyway: Don't use rotten fruit! It's already started the process of fermentation, and not in any sort of good way!

Second, don't use fruit that's overly mushy. There are aging options that you'll have to consider, but overly mushy fruit is too close to rotten to be considered safe.

Third, inspect any fruit that may be lightly bruised. If grinding and pressing is following immediately, you can cut around the damage. On the other hand, any fruit that has an obvious insect infestation should be chucked without second thought.

Don't get lazy and pick apples off the ground, unless the apples are washed and sanitized. It can have deadly consequences! In 1996, one child died and sixty-six people become seriously ill when they drank unpasteurized Odwalla apple juice made from either rotten fruit or fruit gathered from the ground. Dangerous *E. coli* bacteria grew in the juice. Today, Odwalla pasteurizes their juice to prevent a recurrence.

Among apple growers, ground apples are also called falls, windfalls, or groundlings. Why not use an apple that's fallen to the ground? The truth is, you can, and you would probably be just fine most of the time, but it's not your safest option. The *E. coli* species and its variants are some of the most common bacteria, and the most studied. The danger from *E. coli* is mostly to children, the elderly, and those with compromised immune systems. For most folks, infection may give you gastric distress, but if a virulent strain takes hold, it can cause meningitis, peritonitis, and hemolytic-uremic syndrome (a deadly breakdown of the blood and kidneys resulting in serious chronic renal failure or death).

While the exact cause in the Odwalla case was never clearly established, the speculation was that pickers at an orchard gathered ground apples that had been exposed to cow dung. Feces is a prime transmitter of *E. coli*. This picking occurred despite Odwalla's policy against buying falls. At the time, they didn't pasteurize their juice because they wanted to avoid the inevitable destruction of flavor, aroma, and nutrition that happens. Instead, they relied on washing and rinsing the fruit with a bacteria-killing acid. If the fruit were also starting to rot, a mushy apple would provide plenty of protection from the acid rinse. While rare, incidents like this explain why pasteurization is an industry standard practice.

Now that you've been sufficiently scared, be aware that, for centuries, the standard harvesting technique was to knock ripe apples off the tree with a pole or shaker and gather them from the ground. But people have done a lot of things in the past that have sometimes killed them. The decision is yours to make, but prevailing modern wisdom says don't do it. Regardless, make sure you give your apples a thorough inspection, then wash and sanitize before you process them.

Postpicking Processing

Finally, the backbreaking labor is done! Just kidding! Now that you have your apples picked, you must make a choice: Do you get on with grinding and pressing immediately, or do you wait first?

Waiting on Your Apples

Why wait? Old-school cider makers believe that a proper cider apple's ripening is rarely finished by the time the harvest arrives. Instead, tradition dictates a brief month-long hold in cool storage to allow the apples to finish their full ripening process. The idea is to give enough time for ethylene to work its magic on the harvested fruit and convert all of the starch into sugar. Additionally, there is water loss that is occurring during this time that concentrates the flavor.

If you wonder whether or not to age your apples, perform the iodine test described earlier, and observe any changes. If the iodine reacts at all, a short aging stint (2–4 weeks) may be in your interest.

A critical component to aging your apples is very open storage. Think of a box or laundry basket with a loose weave. Containers like paper bags or fruit sacks will trap so much gas that the fruit will flash past ripe straight into rotting. You must let the apples breathe and rest in a dry, cool, cellar-like area (55°F–65°F).

Don't wait too long, though! If you allow the fruit to age for an excessive period, the pectin will strengthen, come out of the cells, and naturally create gel that cider makers call "slimy pulp." Face it; virtually nothing slimy is going to be good! The amateur cider maker largely dependent on culinary apples should note that culinary apples are far more prone to going slimy.

There are two ways to tell when apples are finished aging. In the "grocery store" manual test, the apple should yield slightly to finger pressure. It won't bounce back, but your fingers won't sink easily. The other way is the iodine test. Cut a slice, drip some iodine, and if it's brown, you're ready to grind.

Wash Before You Grind

Regardless of whether you age your apples or not, before you grind them, you need to take care of some business first! More than likely, when your apples came in from picking, they were covered with dirt, dust, and orchard detritus. Before you use them, you need to give them a wash. Washing apples isn't that hard. Simply fill a vessel with cold water, dunk a bunch of apples in the water, scrub them, rinse them, and off they go. Make sure you get rid of any dirt or unsightly matter as it can harbor creatures that can make your cider less than tasty. If you have waxed apples from a grocery store, consider using a tablespoon each of baking soda and lemon juice dissolved in several gallons of water.

A tip about apple washing and speedily finding bad apples: Good apples float in water, bad apples sink. If your apples sink, don't use them! (Pears, on the other hand, always sink.)

Once your apples are washed, give them another dunk in a sanitizer bath. This will serve as your final safeguard toward anything really unsafe crawling into your cider. Readily accessible food-grade sanitizers include bleach with vinegar (1 tablespoon each of bleach and vinegar in 2½ gallons of water), iodophor, Star San, and Saniclean. Using an overly strong solution isn't more effective, and it can negatively impact your cider's flavor! If you use bleach, make sure to give the apples a rinse in clean, not previously used, water.

Let your apples drip dry before grinding. Don't fret about having perfectly dry apples; you just want to minimize the diluting water factor.

Grinding

Now that your apples are clean, you must make them ready for juicing. What does that mean? You're going to have to go a bit beyond just slicing your apples in half. To get a proper apple grind, you must tear your apples up into wee little bits, about the size of a pea (approximately ¼"). You are not trying to create apple sauce or apple butter! If you hear someone talking about "scratting," that's grinding.

Don't forget, cider making from scratch is a lot of manual labor! Now more than ever, you should engage your friends to aid your efforts. Just promise them a selection of cider when it's all done. Maybe have a cider dinner party!

Why do you have to chop your apples up so fine? Unlike the tiny grape, an apple is a fairly large fruit. If you try to bear down on the apple with an incredible amount of force, like a hand-cranked hydraulic jack designed to lift a car, you'll fail miserably. You may get about a third or half of the juice available from an apple before your press gear falls apart.

By grinding your apples down, you bust through the skin and cell walls and increase the surface area relative to the juice-bearing flesh. By exposing more flesh, you make your pressure more effective.

Grinding is a relatively simple task. Set up your grinding gear and feed your apples into it. The apples are chewed up and ground down, and the gushy, wet pulp is collected in a receptacle for pressing. It's very important that you have clean vessels on hand to collect the pulp. Don't be surprised if you have a bunch of juice escaping from your grinder. You'll want to collect that, too. Yes, this is a messy operation and is best done outdoors.

Grind on Down

Your goal is to get your apples chunked into bits roughly ¼" in size. If you're a particularly dedicated sort, you can break out your biggest kitchen knife and go *Psycho* on the fruit. For the slightly less driven, you can take an apple slicer to your apples, throw the slices in a food processor, and give them a tantalizingly brief whirl via your pulse button. Done!

These methods are good if you're working on a small group of apples, but if you have pounds and pounds, or tons, of apples to grind, it's hopeless. The first solution is to beg, plead, and borrow any apple-grinding equipment you can find from an orchard or fellow hobbyist. Offer your labor in exchange for a few runs with their equipment. A professional orchard may ask you to meet a certain minimum buy-in before it will press your apples.

ESSENTIAL

Bringing your own apples to an orchard is a great thing to do to augment the usual sort of juice. Even just bringing a selection of crab apples will boost the character of your juice. If you ask nicely, and call ahead, the orchard itself may even have a few crabs and oddities to toss in the press!

Modern society, in all its wonder, provides a plethora of vendors with solutions ready for those with the money. A standalone apple grinder with rows of stainless steel, apple-destroying teeth will run you in the neighborhood of $200 before taxes and shipping. That may seem like a lot of dough, but if you make more than 10 gallons of cider, the grinder is only adding roughly a dollar per pound. The less-expensive grinders are manually powered, so prepare for an annual workout!

For roughly half the cost of a standalone apple grinder, you can make a homemade one out of a plastic laundry sink and an unused, new garbage disposal. Simply cut away the drain from the sink, and fit the mounting flange for the disposal in the hole. You may have to bend the lip to fit and allow a clean mounting. Mount and wire the disposal per instructions, but instead of sending the debris to the sewer, collect it in a bucket or a mesh bag suspended in the bucket and secured around the outlet.

Cut your apples in half, and feed them into the running disposal. It's best to get a bunch of apples cut first before running the disposal. Keep a wooden dowel on hand to shove the apples in there. Don't use your hands unless you've always wanted the nickname "Stubby"!

ALERT

Don't get ahead of yourself. Perform grinding and pressing together. If you grind too many apples ahead of time, they'll oxidize and rust, ruining the juice's sweet flavor and color.

For the true master DIYer, do yourself a favor and search for Matthias Wandel (*www.woodgears.ca*) online. Matthias is an Ottawa-based tinkerer in the best sense of the word. Matthias assembled a handmade wooden apple grinder for his family's home cider experiments. Every year, they produce 60 gallons of fresh cider using the scratter he built from wood. The grinding drum itself uses stainless steel screws to chew up the apples. Aspects of his design have been copied by other enthusiasts. It's worth exploring the plans that he sells.

A Cold Alternative to Grinding

If you cannot procure a grinder, another option exists if you have a large freezer or are willing to work in partial-batch sizes for a few days. Take your washed and dried apples, cut them in big chunks, and chuck them in the freezer until frozen solid. When you let them thaw, the juice will flow freely from the apple.

Why does this work? Your average household freezer works far more slowly than you'd imagine. When food freezes slowly, the water inside the cells has a chance to form long ice crystals, which, thanks to water's odd properties, take up more room than liquid water. These long ice crystals act like sharp ice knives and penetrate cell walls, busting up the fruit, and letting juice leak everywhere.

If you're using a press, make sure to throw the apple chunks in the press bags before they thaw. If you don't mind a much lower yield, you can avoid a press altogether, and squeeze the freshly thawed apples in the bags.

The purists are now recoiling in horror, and for good reason. The concern is that freezing an apple will damage the aroma and flavor. You know what? They're absolutely right. The good news is that you can adjust for that damage. If you can process or buy a modicum of fresh juice, you can boost your cider and hide most of the damage. You'll never quite reach complete equity with 100 percent fresh ground juice, but it's a good alternative to 100 percent commercial juice.

Bag It

No matter how you choose to grind your apples, you'll need something to hold the juicy pulp together for pressing. In old-fashioned pressing operations, farmers dropped the pulp as it came out of the grinder into open-slatted oak trays lined with cheesecloth. Once full, they wrapped up the pulp and began with a new box.

Today, most people use special strong nylon mesh drawstring bags to hold the pulp. Filled as the apples are ground or loaded after grinding, the nylon bag is sturdy, cheap, and very effective. Alternatively, you can find loose-meshed cloth from the store and drape it over a bowl or cut-down bucket. Cover the cloth with mush and then wrap the mush with the remaining cloth and tie it. Each cloth should hold somewhere in the range of 7–10 pounds. These leaky bags (also known as "cheeses") will serve you well.

Pressing

Now it's time to put some real pressure on. Once properly scratted, your apples need a good hard squeeze to get them flowing. By the time you're done, the pomace (the pressed apple mush) will be pressed into sturdy and surprisingly dry sheets.

The standard means of pressing is to stack the cloth bags ("cheeses") in a wood box or basket with a drain spout. The cheeses have wood slat boards between them to spread the pressure and facilitate draining. After several racks are assembled, pressure is applied to the top via a jack of some sort that is fixed to a yoke over the stack. Some cider makers use a hydraulic jack capable of applying 6 tons of force. Others use a scissor jack, like you might find in your car's trunk (roughly 1–2 tons of force).

If you're feeling industrious, you can start with oak or maple slats, and create your own basket and boards. From there, just mount the basket in a draining pan of some variety. It's super easy to make one. And from there, just attach a jack, and you've got a press. You'll want to have scrap wood or wood blocks on hand to extend the jack's reach as you press the apples further together.

If you're not feeling particularly "wood shoppy," you can cheat and use just about anything that can be made to drain everywhere. For instance, a plastic 5-gallon bucket with holes drilled into it works. The idea is to do as little as possible to impede the free flow of juice from the cheese.

ESSENTIAL

Make sure that whatever comes in contact with the juice is food grade! This means no soft woods like pine. For longevity, make sure you seal your wood with a food-grade sealant. This also applies to any commercial press you buy!

For those not so mechanically inclined, you can find a variety of apple/fruit presses available at local stores or online. Many basket presses use a screw-and-ratchet system to provide the pressing force instead of a jack. It's very effective and self-contained. Make sure you procure pressing racks as well. While you can press one giant cheese without them, as winemakers do, your pressing won't be as efficient. If you're already willing to spend $400 for a well-respected brand of press like a Jaffrey, cough up a few more dollars for the plates!

Press Time

Once you have your cheeses assembled, and your press ready to go, let the juice run free for a few moments without adding any pressure. Once the juice stops flowing, slowly add pressure and let the juice flow. Add pressure in increments, pausing to let the juice run.

If you try and ratchet your press all the way down immediately, you're going to damage the press, the bags, and the fruit. Relax, take your time, and enjoy the connection to the past.

Catch your juice in a food-grade container. Strain it through a fine mesh if you're so inclined to catch any big parts that have escaped the press. You can easily do this when transferring to your fermenter with a fine mesh sieve in a funnel.

Fresh-Pressed Cider

This is it—the ultimate fresh cider, with a full connection to history and tradition. This will take you from apples to fresh juice with a few hours labor and to cider with a couple weeks of patience.

INGREDIENTS | YIELDS 4–6 GALLONS OF CIDER

80–100 pounds apples, fresh or briefly aged
1–5 pounds sugar, optional
Campden metabisulfite tablets, optional (see table in Chapter 5 for amount)
4–6 tablespoons yeast nutrient
1 package active dry yeast or liquid cider yeast

1. Wash the apples thoroughly in cold water, and then give them a quick dunk in a no-rinse sanitizer, like Star San. Prepare the apples for your grinder, cutting them in pieces if needed.

2. Grind your apples into at least a pea-sized chop. Don't try and make apple sauce; that won't juice well. Either grind directly into pressing bags or prepare to scoop into bags. Each bag should hold around 9 pounds. When you've prepared as many bags as your press will hold, stop grinding.
3. Place a bucket under your press. If desired, place a fine mesh strainer over the bucket as well. Stack the cheeses in your press with a press board between each cheese. Let the juice run naturally at first and then slowly add pressure.
4. After the juice stops flowing, pull the cheeses and repeat steps 2 and 3 until all the apples are processed.
5. Measure the gravity, and add sugar to adjust gravity, if desired. Measure the pH and stir in the appropriate amount of metabisulfite and yeast nutrient.
6. Use the Standard Cider-Making Procedure for still cider (see Chapter 2), and wait 24 hours before proceeding if using metabisulfite.

Work Party

As a cider maker, crushing and pressing is the most work you'll do, so take advantage of another helpful hint from the past: Throw a party. Make like Tom Sawyer with a white-washing brush and talk up the fun of the experience. Serving a little of last year's cider isn't a bad idea, either!

Pomace

Now that you've pressed, don't think you're quite done yet! There's still the matter of the pomace (the pressed apple mush) to deal with. Just because you squeezed the living daylights out of it doesn't mean there's no use left to it. In other words, don't throw away your pomace.

The first use of pomace was a traditional beverage called ciderkin. With supplies being scarce, every last drop of goodness had to be extracted from what was on hand. Ciderkin was made by soaking the pomace in an amount of water equal to the juice extracted and pressing it a second time. This second pressing was collected separately and sometimes boosted with a little extra sugar. The amount of flavor extracted depended on the efficiency of your initial pressing, a boon to those with inefficient presses. This practice is still used today, but only by some manufacturers of cheap juice and cider.

Instead of extracting the remaining apple flavor with water, you can go big and use vodka! Some cheap apple brandies do this. You can use this sort of spirit as a replacement for applejack in a number of recipes.

Ciderkin

Need a reward for all your hard, sweaty crushing and pressing labor? Consider a nice cool glass of fresh, sweet ciderkin. If you want more character, consider going easy on your press to allow the pomace to retain more flavor.

INGREDIENTS | YIELDS 2–4 GALLONS OF JUICE

1–4 cheeses of fresh apple pomace
2–4 gallons filtered water
1–3 pounds sugar, optional

1. In a bucket or shallow pan, place the pomace cheeses. Measure the amount of juice extracted from the first pressing, and cover the cheese with that much water. Let the pomace soak for at least 1 hour, but no longer than 4 hours.
2. Place a receptacle under the press, and carefully load the cheeses back into the press, separating with racks. Let the juice run free before adding any pressure, and then slowly add pressure until no more liquid flows.
3. Taste and add sugar to adjust the sweetness. Drink fresh, or if desired, use the ciderkin as a base for any cider recipe in this book. Ciderkin makes a good base for heavily flavored ciders.
4. Finally, before you throw that stuff out, consider using it as mulch or at the very least compost! Just imagine the ultimate recycle as you use the remaining nutrients of this year's crop to fuel next year's harvest.

Fake Out

The wine world equivalent of ciderkin is called "false wine," or a "second-press" wine. Vintners will add sugar to boost the gravity and ferment a fresh table wine out of what would otherwise be waste.

An Alternative Juicing Regimen

Could there be a more efficient way to grind, crush, press, and filter? Since the late 1960s, there's been a revolution in terms of juicing. Proponents of the juicing movement push a cornucopia of benefits from nature's vegetable and fruit pantry. While the health claims themselves may be up for debate, the benefit to the cider maker is the creation of the countertop home centrifugal juicer. The basic design incorporates a rapidly spinning grating blade with a basket that throws the juice in one direction and the pulp in another.

Before his passing, you might have seen fitness expert Jack LaLanne pitching juicers on infomercials for his Power Juicer. The Power Juicer and others like it are centrifugal juicers. The idea is to break up all the fruit and vegetable matter, and turn it into super healthful juice with loads of nutrients, vitamins, and fiber. The question you're no doubt asking yourself is, "Can I spend $100–$150 on one of these juicers and avoid spending many hundreds on a traditional cider press?"

It depends. During tests with a juicer, it was revealed that a medium-sized culinary apple yielded just under a ½ cup of juice. The juice was cloudy and full of fiber and protein. This is not a defect. Instead it is the design of the juicer. Remember, to proponents of juicing, the advantage of a cold "juiced" blend is the additional fiber and vitamins that it provides, which cause this cloudiness.

ESSENTIAL

While a centrifugal juicer will work, it's not recommended that you process a large quantity of apples this way. It will take quite a while and possibly burn out your juicer. It is excellent for making small batches, though!

For cider-making purposes, you can settle the juice prior to fermentation with a spell of cold storage. A quiet overnight rest in a refrigerator at 35°F–40°F does wonders for your cider's clarity. Between the cold and the gravity, a remarkable amount of material—protein, fiber, apple chunks—will fall out of solution. The next day, you just carefully transfer the juice from the settling tank into a new fermenter.

If you take this route, you'll have to make a choice. Do you want to allow/prevent a wild fermentation while the cider is settling? If you want clean, yeast-driven ferment, then add sulfite before you put the juice up for its cold nap. If you want a mild, funky character, go ahead and let it settle unsulfited; the chilly temperatures will keep the wild critters at bay for a day. If you really want to bring the funk, then you'll want to let the cider warm back up to fermentation temperatures for a day or two after clarifying.

No matter what choice you go with, make sure everything that comes into contact with the juice has been sanitized thoroughly! This includes the juicer and the catch basins. Don't forget that the leftover pulp, as fine as it is, has its uses!

Postjuicing Tasks

Congratulations! You have now survived making your very own juice from scratch. From this moment on, your tasks as a cider maker are exactly the same as they've been with your other batches. You can add sulfite and settle your juice, pitch it with yeast, let it ferment, package, and enjoy!

Before you put everything to bed, make sure to wash your grinding and pressing apparatuses really well. The wooden parts in many juicing arrangements will gladly grow apple-juice-fueled mold and funk. Follow your manufacturer's instructions to disassemble your gear, clean it, and then let it thoroughly dry before reassembling it for storage until the next batch of apples is ready to process.

CHAPTER 14

Other Cider Traditions

Is your head spinning yet with all the cider knowledge you've acquired? Don't worry, there's even more to get your head wrapped around! But don't worry; it's easy to deal with. So far you've learned a lot of techniques, but all from a modern North American point of view. There's much to learn about cider in other countries and even old American traditions.

Cider Around the World As Recognized by Cider Experts

While every country that's ever grown apples has developed a cider tradition, the vast majority of ciders are the same. In fact, if you make the first cider in Chapter 2 or the Cider au Naturel recipe (see Chapter 5), you've created the vast majority of the world's ciders. The primary differences become a matter of the apple varieties and minor adjustments to acidity, bitterness, and sweetness.

Different cider writers and judges recognize different cider styles. Not surprisingly, each group focuses more finely on their home territory's cider traditions. For instance, American cider judges recognize New England cider, while British writers tend to focus on the differences between true West Country ciders and draft ciders. Classical French ciders are all about a special technique called keeving that is covered in Chapter 16. But the vast majority of writers talk about "natural," "real," "draft," and "specialty" ciders. Most of the recipes covered in this book fall into that nebulous realm of specialty ciders.

If you were to taste each cider-making culture's self-identified cider types, you would find that no two regions' ciders of the same name are going to taste the same. The region, the apples, and the sun all have an influence, and they will give you different worlds of flavor to aim for.

FACT

The French have a special term for the influence of a region on the agriculture. It is *terroir*, which boils down to the "sense of the land." The belief is that the composition of the soil, the moisture, and the sunlight all will affect the flavor of grapes and the resulting wine. It may have started with wine, but people now talk of the terroir of a great number of things.

New England Cider

When you think of New England, classic American images come to mind, particularly those of fall with dramatic bright bursts of leaves ready to drop. In amongst that fall stuff is the sweet juice that you know and love, infused with cinnamon and heated. The long cider tradition in the United States took root in New England.

When the New England cider industry was in full swing, life in America was very different. The difficulties with securing good ingredients didn't just extend to good barley and hops for beer but to good anything. Life was much more hardscrabble, and many new things were created using just what was available and at hand.

New England cider is a perfect example of that. The apples in the region were grown in mean, rocky soil that, thanks to nutrient deficiencies, generated acidic, strongly bitter apples with a low amount of perceived sugar. To compensate, growers used the things they had on hand, like molasses and brown sugar. Even things like raisins were added for richness, tannin, and yeast.

On the molasses front, thanks to the triangle trade, molasses was everywhere. It was already the basis for one of New England's primary exports, rum. Adding molasses to the cider made sense because it would both boost the alcohol levels to compete with strong rum punch and add intensely complex notes of smoke, burnt sugar, and bitterness to the tongue.

You'll see this same sort of hardscrabble ingenuity in what could be considered the New England cider's cousin, the Devon scrumpy. Sadly, today if you want to sample some old-fashioned traditional New England cider, you're flat out of luck. No traditional cideries survived the rise of the mills and Prohibition. Instead, now you are left with a handful of modern interpretations of the style.

Dirty Water New England Cider

Don't let the name put you off. It's named for the Standells' 1966 hit "Dirty Water," which is played after every home Boston Red Sox victory. This is a classic New England cider with a bit of dryness without being overly so. It uses brown sugar instead of molasses because modern brown sugar contains molasses.

INGREDIENTS | YIELDS 5 GALLONS

½ pound raisins
2 pounds dark brown sugar, preferably a British brand, like Billington's
5 gallons apple juice, balanced to the acidic
1 packet Lalvin EC-1118 dried wine yeast
2 tablespoons yeast nutrient

1. Combine the raisins and brown sugar in a pot with 3 cups of cold water. Bring to a boil and stir to dissolve. Add the boiled syrup and raisin mixture to your sanitized fermenter.
2. Use the Standard Cider-Making Procedure for still cider described in Chapter 2.
3. Condition the cider for a minimum of 3 months before enjoying.

Scrumpy

Scrumpy—just the name seems to imply that something's wrong. Scrumpy is a type of cider most often associated with Devon, in England, and even in the United Kingdom, it's a bit of a debate as to how to define scrumpy. Is it a rough, immature, down-market farmhand's drink that is likely to do you in? Or should it be treated as the finest of fine brews?

Even the name's origin is a bit of a tossup. Did it come from *scrimp*, for old withered apples given to laborers? Is that related to the word *scrump*, used to describe the act of gleaning or stealing leftover apples from the orchard?

There are a few things that seem consistent. Scrumpy is, traditionally, a natural cider with no added sugar. The alcohol level starts around 6 percent and can reach up into the clouds. Regardless of the alcohol by volume, it is always still, and usually dry, with a hard tannin edge.

It has the nickname of "windfall wine" because one of the tricks to boosting the alcohol was to try and naturally concentrate the juice by letting the apples sit on the trees and wither a bit. After all, only the water evaporates, and the sugar isn't going to move anywhere. The slight withering leads to a stronger juice and therefore a stronger cider.

Traditionally, scrumpy is not a refined product; it's hazy, maybe even a little chunky. The rough-and-tumble definition may fall right in line with the examples of New England cider as a cider made with the mindset of "We have apples, we have other stuff, let's make something to get us drunk!"

Rough and Tumble Scrumpy

Meat can be part of this cider if you so choose. In the olden days, meat would serve as the yeast nutrient and clarifying agent.

INGREDIENTS | YIELDS 2 GALLONS

½ pound raisins
¼ pound raw, chopped steak
2 gallons apple juice
1 packet dried ale yeast

1. Combine the raisins, meat, and juice in your sanitized fermenter.
2. Use the Standard Cider-Making Procedure for still cider described in Chapter 2.
3. Condition the cider for a minimum of 6 months before enjoying.

Basque Sidra

In the Pyrenees Mountains, straddling a chunk of the border between France and Spain, there exists a proud and fiercely independent region called Basque Country, home to the Basque people and their culture.

Cider making dates back to at least A.D. 1000. *Sagardo* is the Euskara, or Basque language, word for "apple wine." It is traditionally made as a natural cider, with no additional yeast, around 5–6 percent alcohol by volume, and packaged completely still. Basque sidra, Spanish apple cider, is interesting to home cider makers for two reasons: the manner of serving, and the use of malolactic fermentation.

Sidra begins like any other natural cider, with apples that are scratted, pressed, and left to ferment. This wild ferment will usually invite some other critters to the game besides your friendly neighborhood yeasts. These will include the acid-producing bacteria, so the cider may go through the whole pellicle (see Chapter 15), sick, clear, funky, and acidic phases before being ready for the next steps.

Traditional fermentation occurs in large oak or chestnut barrels, and from these (or similar barrels) the cider is served. Since the cider is not carbonated in any way, Basque cider makers needed to find a way to stimulate the release of the drink's aromatic compounds. This release is normally provided by the carbonation. Instead, they pour the beer with dramatic and aggressively turbulent pours. Usually the cider, in the little cider shops, is poured from the barrel in a thin stream to a waiting glass six or more feet away. All of the roiling ends up producing a momentarily frothy glass with a big release of esters and phenols for the drinker to enjoy. If you don't want to practice long-distance pouring, a vigorous pour between two glasses should provide adequate aeration.

Because many of the apples native to the Basque area fall into the sharp or sweet range of flavors, a Basque cider stopped after completing primary fermentation will be extraordinarily tart. Most of the acid, even with the presence of lactic acid bacteria, will be malic acid. The human palate registers malic acid more harshly than some other acids, like lactic. This is where malolactic fermentation comes into play.

Malolactic Fermentation

Malolactic fermentation is well studied due to its heavy use in winemaking. Turns out that grapes are a pretty good source of malic acid as well. Makers of chardonnay wines, in particular, use malolactic fermentation to soften their wine. By converting the malic acid to lactic, the drinker perceives a richer and rounder wine with a lightly cutting acidity.

If you have engaged your natural critters to do the fermentation work and have gotten a formation of lactic-producing bacteria, then you're in luck. Many species of *Lactobacillus* can covert malic acid into lactic acid.

Don't bottle until you're certain that the fermentation is complete. As long as the process is still going, CO_2 is being produced and can cause bottles to explode!

If you didn't go the all-natural route, or simply want better control over your flavor, you can buy a malolactic fermentation (MLF) culture from your local home-brewing or winemaking shop during the late winter. Some stores will even carry a freeze-dried MLF culture year-round. You would simply pitch this culture into the cider after primary fermentation is done and let the cider sit for a few months. During this time the cider will become cloudy and maybe smell a little like butter. Once the cider is clear again, you're ready to package.

If your cider still smells buttery after MLF is done, and the cider is clear, you can try clearing the aroma by adding some fresh yeast and a little bit of sugar. The yeast will ferment the sugar, engage in a clean-up process, and hopefully clear out the remaining diacetyl (a natural byproduct of fermentation that has a buttery flavor and smell).

Basque in Glory

If you cannot get your hands on fresh-pressed juice, you can try leaving the cider exposed to the air for 12 hours before closing the fermenter or adding pure commercial yeast and Lactobacillus cultures together. Those options won't be as interesting, complex, or as likely to succeed completely as the fresh-pressed option, though.

INGREDIENTS | YIELDS 5 GALLONS

5 gallons apple juice, balanced to the acidic, fresh-pressed only
1 tablespoon yeast nutrient
1 packet malolactic fermentation culture (MLF, optional)

1. Use the Standard Cider-Making Procedure for a still cider described in Chapter 2.
2. If *Lactobacillus* cultures haven't taken hold in the cider, add the MLF culture to start reducing the malic acid.
3. Condition the cider for a minimum of 4 months before enjoying.

German and Eastern European Ciders and Apfelwein

The Germans do have a cider tradition hidden among all their wine, beer, and schnapps. In stark contrast to the British and French insistence on proper bittersharp cider apples, the Germans are perfectly happy to use the commonly available culinary apples. To a British cider maker, this is the equivalent of telling a German brewer that using corn and rice makes perfectly great beer!

Regardless, drinkers around the German state of Hesse (or Hessia) love their apfelwein, and they sit in the summer beer gardens drinking from little diamond-etched glasses called *gerriptes*. It can be served straight or mixed with sparkling water or even sparkling lemonade (a lemon-lime soda, like Sprite). This is not unusual in Germany where they serve a mixture of beer and lemonade as a common summertime beverage.

FACT

If the name "Hessen" seems familiar, you've probably remembered an elementary school lesson about the American Revolution and the British use of German mercenaries to supplement their own forces. The British called all those mercenaries Hessians, the name of a man from Hessen, regardless of where they actually came from.

You'd expect a cider based on nothing but culinary apples to be sort of "meh," but the German apfelweins pack a sour punch. This is actually why they cut the cider with water. The resulting beverage is said to be *sauer gespritzter*, or sour injected. The reason the apfelwein ends up sour is that culinary apples are largely sweet and tart without much bitterness. When the sugar is fermented away, the acid remains without anything to give it balance.

Usually, German apfelwein will fall in the 6–7 percent alcohol by volume range as a naturally fermented product, but it is not uncommon to see some apfelweins end up in the 10–12 percent range. Usually, these come in wine bottles and are still, while the softer stuff is often carbonated. The lower-strength versions tend to be almost water white, while the stronger versions begin to verge toward gold, but they'll never be dark.

The odd thing about apfelwein is that until recently it had a rather low profile among American cider enthusiasts. This is odd, because thanks to the Germans' use of culinary apples, one could argue that apfelwein is the easiest type of cider to make. Just grab some juice, chuck it in a carboy, and go. In fact, you've already done this with your first cider.

Apfelwein became popular with a lot of beginning cider makers thanks to Homebrewtalk.com moderator Ed Wort and his easy-as-pie apfelwein recipe.

AppleJacked Apfelwein

This is absolutely one of the easiest ways to make some potent rocket fuel! This differs from the Internet-sensation apfelwein by using apple concentrate to boost the apple character. Be really careful about your fermentation temperature with this. Ferment too warm, and you'll create a headache in a glass.

INGREDIENTS | YIELDS 5 GALLONS

5 gallons apple juice
1 pound table sugar
1 (12-ounce) can frozen apple juice concentrate
1 tablespoon yeast nutrient
1 packet Côte des Blancs yeast

1. Use the Standard Cider-Making Procedure for still cider described in Chapter 2.
2. Condition the cider for a minimum of 4 months before enjoying.

Sugars

Feel free to substitute whatever sugar you want in place of the table sugar. If you want to get closer to the original apfelwein recipe, sub in another pound of sugar in place of the concentrate.

CHAPTER 15

Experimental Cider

Getting bored of apple this, apple that? The great news is that cider provides an excellent working base for a host of other flavors and techniques. You'll be surprised at how easy it is to turn out a cider with immense flavor combinations that outshine the commercial products. Have you ever had a cider with oak or one that showcases hops, the bitter partner of beer? After this chapter, you'll be able to make these and more!

Why Experiment with Cider?

The word *experimental* conjures up images of white lab coats, beakers, and thick eyeglasses with tape. The good news is that for cider making, you don't need any of that. What you do need is a stout heart and fearlessness about getting something wrong.

The benefit of playing with your cider is the possibility of creating a new flavor that makes your jaw drop. If you don't feel like taking a huge risk, many of the techniques discussed in this chapter can be applied to a smaller batch. In fact, it is highly encouraged that you split your cider up into smaller parts and experiment with those. You might as well take advantage of fall's harvest and expand your flavor stash!

Got Wood?

Before the late 1800s, there were no durable, neutral, stainless steel kegs or cheap, easy glass and plastic bottles to hold your cider. Back then you could bottle it in expensive stoneware bottles or even champagne-style bottles, but by far the popular choice was a wooden barrel.

Whether the barrel was a barn's open top and ladle arrangement, a vessel for aging, or something fancier akin to a beer barrel used for pub service, most ciders spent a fair amount of time in contact with wood.

The use of wood shouldn't be a big surprise; wineries use endless racks and warehouses full of barrels to age their wines. Unlike wineries, which use a lot of fresh oak, most cider or beer would have ended up in barrels that had been used repeatedly or lined with a tarry mass of resin. Either way, not much oaky character would have worked into the cider, but oak can add great flavors and mouthfeel to your cider and is recommended as a way to add tannin to an otherwise lackluster cider.

One problem for cider makers using barrels: Bacteria love living in wood. The endless pores and channels provide a perfect breeding ground and protective home. What this means is that you'll never be able to guarantee that your wood is sanitary. For that reason, any wood additions should be added only after the primary fermentation to grant the cider the bacterial protection that a low pH and ethanol offer during primary fermentation.

Barrels and Alternatives

Unless you're working with a lot of cider, a full-sized barrel (53–60 gallons) requires more juice than the average home cider maker can wrangle. Thankfully, the recent rise of microdistillers has expanded your options. Several of these small distilleries—like Woodinville Whiskey Company in Washington and Texas-based Balcones Distillery—now sell freshly used 5–10 gallon barrels to anyone with the wherewithal to use them. But be warned: They are expensive. Making the smaller barrels is just as labor intensive as making the larger ones.

If you want to sanitize the barrel before use, prepare a metabisulfite solution and rinse the barrel with it. Some folks like to rinse the barrel with more of the target spirit to add a little extra character.

ALERT

Under no circumstances should you use burning sulfur sticks on barrels that held hard liquor like whiskey. It can prove to be an explosive situation!

Also available on the market are several oak products designed to aid vintners with "exhausted" oak barrels. Larger options include wooden spiral and honeycombed staves, but these can be hard to find. Smaller, easier-to-use options include "beans" (oak cubes) and chips. If you can find them, choose oak beans over oak chips. The bean's cube shape provides a better ratio of surface area to woody core and has more layers of toasted flavor. They behave more like barrel staves than the more shredded options.

ESSENTIAL

Your local homebrew shop may carry a product called "oak powder," which is effectively oak dust. Don't use this stuff, because it's potent, one-dimensional, and harsh without giving you the good flavors you want from oak. If you're looking for tannins, use powdered grape tannin instead.

When barrels are readied for the wine and spirit market, they are heat-treated to various levels of toasting. As the exposure to fire is increased, the barrel becomes increasingly dark and the toast more intense as the proteins brown and the wood sugars caramelize. Bourbon barrels are actually taken all the way to a charred stage. The char provides the carbon that helps filter and soften the whiskey. Like real barrels, the chips and beans/cubes have levels of toasting to them. For aging purposes, stick with the medium or lower toast to avoid overpowering the apples.

Using Oak Cubes or Chips

Before you use your newly purchased oak cubes or chips, you'll need to prepare them. After all, wood can harbor a number of undesirable elements, not the least of which is the dust on the outside of the cubes. It is harsh on the palate and a safe harbor for bacteria.

To prepare the oak cubes or chips, you can steam or boil them for 15 minutes to remove the harsh outer coating and sanitize the exterior. (Remember, you can never fully sanitize wood due to the vast array of hiding places, but this will get you the freshest, purest oak flavor.)

If you're game for something more, soak your oak in alcohol for a few weeks. A very popular option is bourbon. Another good choice is rum. For a spirit preparation, just dump 2–4 ounces by weight of oak cubes into a glass jar and cover with the spirit of your choice. Seal the jar and shake every day for a week. Let the cubes settle for a few weeks or more. When it is time to use them, measure out the cubes again by weight. Leave the spirit and sediment behind in the jar.

Add the oak to your secondary fermentation, and age to taste, at least 2 weeks. With beans, the best results occur at 2 weeks, with about 2 ounces of beans, minus their soaking liquid. More complex characters can be achieved by aging for a month or more at cold (under 50°F) temperatures. Chips require both less weight (approximately 1 ounce) and time (as short as 3 days), but the complexity suffers.

ALERT

Don't try reusing the cubes; that's just asking for an infection and unpredictable oak character.

If you want to try something wine based, you can soak your oak in the wine of your choice, but to be on the safe side, add some vodka or brandy to the wine to up the alcohol content. Wine's pH and alcohol level will protect it a little, but it's not perfect.

Woods Hole Cider

For a bourbon-barrel version of his cider, use American oak cubes and bourbon instead of French oak cubes and rum.

INGREDIENTS | YIELDS 5 GALLONS

5 gallons fresh, sweet apple juice
1 tablespoon yeast nutrient
2 packets English ale yeast
2 ounces French oak cubes
4 ounces spiced, dark rum

1. In your fermenter, mix the apple juice and nutrient. Use the Standard Cider-Making Procedure described in Chapter 2.
2. Soak the oak cubes in the rum for 2 weeks in a sealed glass jar.
3. After fermentation ceases, add the oak cubes but not the rum itself. Discard or imbibe the rum to see how strong the initial oak flavor is.
4. Package still to allow the oak to open up slowly on the tongue and nose.

Hop to It

Hops are one of the four main ingredients in beer, but, aside from homeopathic sleep aids, they go virtually unused elsewhere. Cider makers have just begun exploring the use of this aromatic, bitter flower.

Hops grow on a bine, which looks a lot like a vine but for one crucial difference. Vines grow in long lines that attach to surfaces via curling tendrils. A bine instead uses short, grabby hairs, like the hooks on Velcro, to adhere to surfaces.

Why use hops in a cider? They provide a few important effects. It is up to you to determine which contributions you want and discover how to balance these sharp, new flavors in your cider.

Hop Contributions

First, no matter how you use your hops, you're going to inherit their innate antimicrobial effect. Back in the 1300s, brewers discovered that beers that used hops, as opposed to just herbs and spices, lasted longer. It would take the rise of modern biological science to understand that compounds in the hops were keeping spoilage organisms at bay. Hops are particularly effective against gram-positive bacteria, like *Lactobacillus*.

Second, hops bring bitterness. The same chemicals that fight bacteria, alpha acids, transform when boiled into iso-alpha acids. These compounds are exceedingly bitter. In beer, this bitterness is what provides the palate break from the sweetness of malt. You may be thinking, "I don't want bitterness in my cider!" But remember, two of the primary categories of cider apples are bittersweet and bittersharp. A little bitterness will actually give your cider some backbone.

Lastly, there are the wonderful flavors and aromas contributed by the hops. There are currently more than seventy different hop varietals available to the home brewer and cider maker, each with a unique flavor, but to prevent you from going mad, they fall into the following flavor families:

HOP FLAVOR FAMILIES

- **Citrus:** Orange and grapefruit flavors have become intrinsically associated with American craft brewing, thanks to the abundance of Cascade and Centennial hops in many classic craft brews. If you've had an American IPA, you'll recognize the freshly ripped orange peel aroma.
- **Earthy floral:** Classic English hops, like Fuggle and Golding, have an earthy, grassy, floral character that is the hallmark of classic English ale.
- **Piney:** Another American hop characteristic. If you smell a hop and feel like you're in a pine forest, this is it.

- **Spicy:** You may have heard the term *noble* hop before. It is a term that applies to select Continental European hops that display a spicy, herbal aroma. They are prized in European lagers.
- **Tropical:** A new category of hop flavor and aroma available through new American hop types like Citra or Australian Galaxy.
- **Winey:** Another new category, with the rise of New Zealand's Nelson Sauvin hops.

Hops come in two different common form factors: whole cone and pellets. Whole-cone hops, which are the whole, dried cone flowers of the female hop plant, look like soft, green, squidgy pine cones and have a sticky, yellow, resiny goodness. They are picked and immediately dried to preserve their character. Pellet hops are the same fresh hops pulverized by a hammer mill. Some folks prefer the whole hops, because they are processed less. However, they store poorly. Others prefer the pellet hops, because they are easier to use and store better.

No matter what type you use, make sure your hops stay in the freezer until you're ready to use them. Warm temperatures and not being sealed properly will cause them to stall and age rapidly, leading to awful cheesy flavors.

FACT

Hops are easy to grow at home. Any homebrew shop can get you the parts and basic information, but be careful of growing hops among any apple or prunus trees or shrubs (plums, peaches, etc.). These plants can harbor pests destructive to hops, so keep them separated.

Getting Bitter

The bitterness that you want from hops comes from a set of compounds called alpha acids. In order to keep their punch in your cider, they have to be boiled. The boiling causes the molecules to isomerize, or rearrange. This iso-alpha compound is intensely bitter and stable and will blend with water. You can boil your hops in a little juice or sugar water for 5–30 minutes. Use no more than ½ ounce of hops. If using juice, remember to use a little pectinase to eliminate any fruit haze. A brewer's rule of thumb—a hop boiled longer will provide more bitterness but it provides less distinctive hop flavor and aroma. Boil for shorter periods of time to preserve the flavor and even less time for the aroma.

Add this bitter tea to the cider prior to primary fermentation. The flavor presentation of the hop changes when passed through the turbulent cycle of fermentation and becomes less vegetative and harsh. If you want more substantial hop aroma, then read on!

Getting Aroma

Another brewer's technique that you can adopt is called "dry hopping." It simply consists of adding a small quantity (½–1 ounce) of hops to the cider after primary fermentation is done and letting them settle for at least a week at cool fermentation temperatures. Your homebrew store will sell a fine mesh bag called a "hop bag" that you can fill with hops and something heavy and neutral like stainless steel nuts or glass marbles. Over the week or two of contact, the hops essential oils will infuse into the cider, bringing a lively hop aroma and flavor without the iso-alpha bitterness. The hops will still contribute a minor amount of bitter tannins from the green matter, but tannin is a desirable trait in most ciders.

Be careful about the amount of time you leave the hops on the cider. This isn't one of those "a little is good, a little more is better" situations. Over time, more green, grassy chlorophyll and tea flavors will leach into the cider and get in the way of your enjoying it.

Hop Varieties

There are many hop varieties to play with, and following are a few key ones. Unless noted, the descriptions refer to the hop by the region where it is classically grown. Hops from a different region (say an American-grown version of a British hop) will taste very different, as flavor expression in hops are very sensitive to specific territories.

Name	Alpha %	Description
Amarillo	6.0%–9.0%	Big, bright grapefruit flavor
Cascade	5.0%–7.0%	Big; orange and grapefruit craft beer hop
Chinook	12%–15%	Old, high, alpha hop that is sharply piney and bitter; use if you want bite
Citra	10%–13%	Mango, pineapple, orange; distinctive
Columbus/Tomahawk/Zeus	14–18%	Clean pine cones and a little dank
East Kent Golding (EKG)	4%–7%	Classic English hop, with deeply earthy, floral aroma
Fuggle	3%–6%	Classic English hop with more spice and wood than EKG
Motueka	6%–8%	New Zealand hop, with a combination of classic, noble spice and mangoes
Nelson Sauvin	12%–14%	New Zealand hop that smells and tastes like the famous sauvignon blanc grapes grown on the island
Northern Brewer	7%–10%	Classic hop transplanted to the United States from Great Britain; noted for smelling of wood and mint
Saaz	2.5%–5.5%	Classic, noble hop from the Zatec township in what was once Bohemia and is now west of the Czech Republic; mildly spicy and restrained, with a classic lager profile
Tettnang Tettnanger	3.0%–6.0%	Spicy and floral, this is one of the prized German noble hops; offers more oomph than Saaz

Hop in My Belly Cider

This cider uses a dry-hopping technique to pick up the aroma characters of the hops. In this recipe, the hop showcased is the mango-pineapple flavors of Citra, but use whatever you want. Use American ale yeast in this to emphasize the hops.

INGREDIENTS | YIELDS 3 GALLONS

3 gallons fresh, sweet apple juice

½ teaspoon yeast nutrient

1 packet American ale yeast

¾ ounce Citra hop pellets

1. In your fermenter, mix the apple juice and nutrient. Use the Standard Cider-Making Procedure described in Chapter 2.
2. After fermentation ceases, rack into a secondary container and add the hops. Store for 2 weeks between 63–66°F for optimum flavor/aroma extraction.
3. Package sparkling to boost the hops.

Freshness Dating

When dry hopping, it's really important to get good quality hops. If the hops are browned or have been stored warm, the flavor will be off, and in the cider that will be extremely noticeable.

Malt-Cider Beer

In Stephen King's *The Dark Tower* series, he describes his heroes in the fictional Mid-World being served a feast with Graff, a strong, dark, apple cider made with hops. Naturally, a bunch of home brewers have jumped up to make their own versions.

However, before you give Stephen King all the credit for apple ale, it helps to know that he's not the first (fictionally in his case) to combine cider and beer into one beverage. While a number of apple sodas and apple-flavored beers still exist on the market, it's been a harder row to hoe for a real apple beer. A few do exist, but as a home brewer you should take advantage of the opportunity to blend a beer and a cider together!

Ideally, the addition of malt will help you achieve a beer that maintains a natural level of sweetness without being harsh or cloying. Since the super-fermentable cider will undercut the malt, you'll want to go easy on the hops, at least until you know what you want.

Malt Cider

This cider is really half cider and half beer. This is a simplified version of the concept, and it will make you a nice, pale "ci-beer." If you have experienced brewers in your midst, they should be able to help you make something even more complex.

INGREDIENTS | YIELDS 5 GALLONS

1 gallon filtered water
1 (3.3-pound) can pale liquid malt extract
½ ounce Fuggle hop pellets
2 teaspoons yeast nutrient
4 gallons fresh, sweet apple juice, chilled
2 packets English ale yeast

1. Bring the water to a boil in a 10-quart pot on your stove. Turn off the heat and stir in the malt extract. Stir until completely dissolved. Bring back to a boil. Add the hops and yeast nutrient, and boil for 60 minutes.
2. Turn off the heat, cover the pot, and place in a sink of cold water to chill to 100°F.
3. Pour the apple juice into the fermenter, and add the warm beer wort (the liquid extracted from the mashing process). Swirl to mix and pitch the yeast. Use the Standard Cider-Making Procedure described in Chapter 2.
4. Package sparkling as this is part beer.

Gluten-Free No More

If you're making cider for those who are gluten intolerant, please note that the malt extract makes this a gluten-rich product!

Getting Wild

A constant refrain homebrewers hear is that they should do their utmost to prevent anything unplanned from happening during fermentation. However, it is entirely possible, and sometimes completely desirable, to let cider ferment naturally on its own. If you want to let nature take its course, can you still produce a quaffable cider?

To start, you need to understand what people mean by "wild yeast," because that is a loaded term. Do people mean *Lactobacillus*, a lactic-acid-producing family of bacteria? What about *Pediococcus*, a very aggressive and funky bacteria? If you were looking to make a cider with wild yeast from the orchard, those strains would be included in the mix. They are found in naturally fermented products such as the Belgian lambic, a dry, slightly sour beer.

However, when you hear experimentally minded fermentationists talking about something being "wild," they seem to center their definitions, and efforts, on the use of strains of *Brettanomyces* yeast. Closely related to everyone's friend, *S. cerevisiae*, "Brett" was isolated by brewing scientists investigating spoilage activity in British beer. Hence the name, which means "British fungus"!

There is a vast supply of wild yeasts available to you, and while the Brett world isn't nearly as commercially diverse as the world of commercial yeast strains for wine and beer. you still have options. But prepare for a bit of a challenge. Brett works more slowly than *S. cerevisiae* and drops a whole new world of flavors. The descriptors include barnyard, smoky, clove, sweat, and goaty. Sounds delicious, no? Hordes of enthusiasts prove that it is to some folks!

AVAILABLE *BRETTANOMYCES* STRAINS

- *B. anomalus*: The same as *B. claussenii* (below).
- *B. bruxellensis*: Common Brett isolated from the Brussels, Belgium, area. It is responsible for strong barnyard aromas. If allowed to ferment too warm, the aromas can change to the nasty medicinal phenols.
- *B. claussenii*: Provides fantastic spicy aromas of cinnamon and sandalwood over piles of juicy pineapple. Very popular in making a 100 percent Brett-fermented cider.
- *B. lambicus*: Cherry pie if the pie were stored in a stable for the night. Pleasant when fermented with proper temperature control and oxygen exposure.

There are more Brett strains available, but those are the big three available from White Labs and Wyeast, two of the leading yeast suppliers for the brewing and winemaking industries. If you want to play with some really strange creations, check out the fine folks at East Coast Yeast and their Bug-Farm cultures.

ALERT

> If you ever want to freak out a winemaker, just tell him that you make cider with *Brettanomyces*. He will run from you like you announced that you're a vampire looking for a meal. Vintners seriously fear the impact of Brett on their wines.

To use, just treat the Brett like you would regular yeast. Make a little starter out of apple juice and grow the culture for a few days before adding to the fermenting cider. The Brett will take a little longer to take hold than normal yeast. Give the cider a few months to develop the truly funky aroma and flavors. It's definitely worth it! To boost the "funk," add a little food for the yeast in the form of sugar or juice from time to time. Maintain your fermentation temps; the yeast may be wild, but it still needs your guidance to avoid bad flavors.

A word on odd behavior—if you use Brett as the only fermentation strain, it will, counterintuitively, produce a less intensely funky cider. Instead, it tastes like a normal ferment with a light amount of oddity.

WildCide

Time to get funky! This cider will take time to develop deep earthy tones. This version is 100 percent Brett fermented, which means it won't be as hardcore as some versions could be. You'll want to devote dedicated plastic gear to this and any cider you produce from wild yeast.

INGREDIENTS | YIELDS 3 GALLONS

3 gallons fresh, sweet apple juice
1 packet *Brettanomyces claussenii*

1. In your fermenter, mix the apple juice and *Brettanomyces* yeast. Use the Standard Cider-Making Procedure described in Chapter 2.
2. After fermentation ceases, rack into a secondary container and allow to age for 2–3 months in a cool environment.
3. Package sparkling to boost the perception of funk.

Pellicle

If you notice a sort of slick, filmy white surface forming on top of your cider, don't worry. It's called a "pellicle," and it is a protein layer that protects the cider from oxygen. Welcome to the wacky world of wild brewing!

Meet Your Meat

Meat has had a traditional role in cider making. Before the chemistry was well understood, fermentation was a bit hit and miss. You'll have noticed by now that virtually every recipe you've seen involves a small amount of yeast nutrient. The reason is your yeast needs the nitrogen and other minerals to happily perform its life's duty. Without it, the yeast will fall flat in the calorie-rich, nutrient-lacking apple juice.

Nitrogen played a role in the field as well. Farmers knew that rich land led to huge yields of tasteless fruit that was overripe and cellared poorly. Perversely, some of the best tasting and storing apples came from hardscrabble orchards that seemed on the constant verge of failure. Modern orchardists have to walk a fine line between overfeeding and underfeeding the trees to hit the sweet spot.

What does all of this have to do with meat? It turns out that in the bad old days of magical thinking, cider makers figured out that by mixing meat into their cider, they could make for a more vigorous fermentation. The slowly decomposing meat gave off plenty of nitrogen for the yeast to use. Old, strong, scrumpy cider recipes called for minced meat to be added with the cider for precisely this reason. These meat-filled scrumpy ciders would be horribly off at first, requiring months to age into a pleasant beverage.

From a modern point of view, that's a pretty horrifying concept, so you won't be taking that route. Instead, how about using a nice piece of bacon?

The one problem with bacon is the immense amount of fat that it contains. You'll just need to make a bacon extract!

Pig and Apples

Bacon is righteously popular meat stuff. Choose good bacon with a strong bacon flavor for this. You won't be using the bacon directly, just an extract of its flavor.

INGREDIENTS | YIELDS 3 GALLONS

3 gallons fresh, sweet apple juice

1½ teaspoons yeast nutrient

1 packet American ale yeast

3 strips bacon, cooked on a rack in a 325°F oven for 40 minutes

4 ounces bourbon

1. In your fermenter, mix the apple juice and nutrient. Use the Standard Cider-Making Procedure described in Chapter 2.
2. Crumble the bacon, mix with the bourbon in a sealed glass jar, and store for 4 days in the fridge. Remove the bacon and place the bourbon in the freezer. The next day, the bacon fat should be frozen to the top. Scoop away the fat and keep the bourbon.
3. After fermentation ceases, rack into a secondary container and add the bourbon.
4. Package still to let the bacon flavor rise naturally.

Why Bourbon?
Bourbon is a perfect match to complement the bacon. It will enhance both the sweetness and the smoke.

CHAPTER 16

Advanced Cider Techniques

Sanitize, juice, pitch, ferment, rack, bottle. You've got the basic process down cold now, but surely there's more to making cider than just that, right? As with any human effort, yes, there are many more things you can do, and this chapter will cover several of them. In this chapter, you'll learn how to infuse your cider with caramel, what to do with frozen apples and cider, and how to make an endless keg of cider.

Caramelization/Syrupification

You now know the importance of not boiling your cider juice. Doing so will mess up the freshness, destroy the delicate flavors, and give your cider a cooked feeling. This is all true, but there are times when you want to push through the "mistake" level and get to the sublimeness of total destruction.

You're going to be creating apple syrup. It flies in the face of all the previous advice, but by slowly boiling fresh apple juice, you'll create wonderful, dense, and rich characters you'd expect from a dessert sauce, not fruit juice. If you've used frozen apple concentrate at this point to back-sweeten your cider, you may wonder how this is different. After all, that concentrate is awfully sticky and syrupy when thawed.

Caramelization is a pyrolytic reaction (one that occurs by heating) of the various sugars found in cider. Pyrolysis is a heat-driven chemical reaction—in this case between your stovetop and the sugars found in your juice. When you heat sugars to their melting points, funny things begin to happen, and hundreds of chemicals are produced with profound flavors.

Because apple juice contains protein as well as high concentrations of fructose (fruit sugar), it will undergo what chemists and cooks know as the Maillard reaction, which is a browning process that (among other things) gives browned foods a rich flavor. Your cider syrup will become darker and more intense than a similar sweet solution of sugar water.

To form a properly caramelized apple syrup takes time, roughly 1 hour over a gentle flame. It's a straightforward process that first involves adding juice to a pan and turning on the heat. As the water is driven out and the proteins begin to brown, you'll notice a change in the aroma. It becomes earthy, spicy, and nutty instead of floral. As the water is driven off, the temperature rises into the 240°F range. Bubbles will begin to stack, and when you stir the mixture (with a silicone spoon), you'll see trails where you stirred. Watch carefully, and when the bubbles begin climbing high, you're done.

The resulting syrup is intense and smells like the most potent caramel apple you've had the pleasure to experience. Added to a fermented cider, it provides a boost of deep, earthy apples and sweetness that will remain shelf stable.

Compare all of those changes to a frozen concentration. Manufacturers of frozen apple juice evaporate and concentrate their juice under a vacuum, which reduces the boiling temperature of water. This means less heat damaging the flavors of the apple juice, preserving them for later reconstitution. Once reconstituted, the addition is bright apples and regular sweetness that may fade with time and yeast.

Cider Caramel Boost

The ultimate apple blast! Take it slow with this. Trying to rush it can result in burnt sugar and messy stovetops.

INGREDIENTS | YIELDS ⅔ CUP

2 pints fresh, sweet apple juice

1. Add the apple juice to a clean, nonstick saucepan. Place over medium heat.
2. Keep the juice at a simmer, and reduce for about 50 minutes.
3. When bubbles begin stacking and the temperature reaches 240°F on a candy thermometer, remove from the heat. Either dilute immediately, or store covered until needed.

How to Use

If you add the caramel straight to your fermented cider, it will just harden and fall to the bottom of the carboy (the large bottle in which you are storing it). Instead, heat up a pint or two of cider or juice and dissolve the caramel into it. Add the caramelized juice to your cider and stir it gently in.

Ice Cider

There are several techniques involved in making ice cider. Since cider making and hard winters often go hand in hand, there's a certain natural fascination with temperatures cold enough to freeze your soul.

Frozen Sweet

The first form of ice cider is a result of laziness, or harvest exhaustion, take your pick. If you leave apples on the tree into winter, the apples shrivel—losing water and naturally concentrating sugars. They freeze, turning into apple-cicles.

Turns out, this isn't a horrifying happenstance. As the apples gradually wither and lose water on the branch, the flavor and sugar concentrate. The low temperatures prevent the orchard yeast from attacking the fruit. When the apples freeze, the tiny ice crystals mostly trap water, but extremely flavorful and sugar-rich juice remains free. This happens because sugar lowers the freezing point of the solution it's dissolved in. The ultra-sugary juice requires colder temperatures to freeze.

The cider maker then takes the frozen apples and presses them. The juice yield is much, much lower than normal. But the juice that flows is ridiculously potent. The flavor is intense enough to cause involuntary jaw spasms. For the scientifically minded, this is called cyroextraction.

Alternatively, and the way you'll want to do this at home, ice cider makers will cold store harvested apples until the deepest, coldest part of winter. They grind and press the apples at normal temperatures, and then allow the fresh juice to freeze naturally. If you let the juice freeze and thaw a little, you should concentrate more of the sugar in a smaller area. You'll want to do this in a bucket outdoors, or in a chest freezer. Allow the juice to freeze for 24 hours, and then scoop out the ice to yield concentrated juice. This method is called cryoconcentration.

Cidre de Glace

Sweet and intense—this is the cider that you pull out for a special postdessert treat. You'll need to start with a lot of juice, as you'll only yield about a quarter of your starting volume. Since it takes time to freeze the cider, the juice must be sulfited to prevent other microbial activity.

INGREDIENTS | YIELDS 1¼ GALLONS

5 gallons fresh, sweet apple juice

10 Campden tablets (potassium metabisulfite), crushed

1 nylon hop bag

¼ teaspoon yeast nutrient

2 packets Côte des Blancs dry yeast

Malic acid, to taste

½ teaspoon potassium sorbate

1. Pour the apple juice into a shatterproof, 5-gallon necked container, such as a Better Bottle carboy or a plastic water-cooler bottle. Stir in the Campden (or equivalent metabisulfite powder). Cover the top with foil and freeze. If you live in a cold, wintery climate with consistent temperatures below freezing, you can stick the juice outside and wait roughly a week. Alternatively, you can put the juice in a chest freezer.
2. Check the carboy daily. You're looking for the juice to be frozen completely.
3. When the juice is frozen solid, remove the foil and tie the hop bag around the mouth of the carboy. Invert the carboy into a sanitized 5-gallon bucket. As the ice warms, thick and sugary concentrated juice drips into the bucket. The first runnings' gravity will be off the chart. Stop the flow periodically and check the gravity of the gathered syrup. After collecting a total of 1–1.5 gallons the observed gravity will fall in the 1.130–1.150 range. When you are comfortable with the gravity or volume collected, stop. Remember, the higher your gravity, the sweeter, stronger, and more intense your cider will be. Don't go below 1.115 on your original gravity. Allow the remaining juice to melt again and either consume fresh or make ciderkin.
4. Transfer the juice to a smaller sanitized fermenter. Rehydrate the yeast in warm water. Mix the nutrient and your "super juice." When the yeast is properly rehydrated, pitch it and ferment cool, 60–64°F, to prevent excess ester production.
5. After 2 months, the yeast will have gone as far as it can. Lower the temperature on the cider to 36°F to drop the remaining yeast. Taste the cider and add malic acid to taste. Gently stir in the potassium sorbate. (Half of a Campden tablet, crushed, is an optional addition to serve as a stunner and antioxidant.)
6. Bottle this as a still cider. Age the cider for at least 8 months before trying it for maximum potency.

Frozen Hard

If you don't want to sweat and fret over freezing juice, you can always let nature do the work for you. This is another one of those old-fashioned "oops" discoveries that also yielded one of America's long-time potent beverages, applejack.

Back in the day, everyone had cider barrels, usually kept outside or in the barn. You can imagine that on a cold New England winter night, the barn becomes a mighty cold place where things freeze. In the morning, ready for a drink, a farmer cracks open the barrel only to discover a thick sheet of ice. Cracking the ice, there was still liquid in the middle. Reaching in, instead of finding his usual refreshing cup of joy, the farmer finds himself with a glass of sweet, intense rocket fuel.

As explained before, sugar makes water harder to freeze, and ethanol does the same. You can take advantage of this and create an iced cider that reaches 10 percent alcohol by volume. All it takes is a bucket or keg and a chest freezer. Take your finished cider, place it in the freezer, and let it sit until it becomes slushy, usually about 6 hours. Then you either scoop out the ice with a sieve (letting the cider drip back in the bucket) or rack the liquid away from the ice.

Eisapfelwein

This produces an intense apfelwein that is less complex, and less concentrated, than the Cidre de Glace. It requires less fiddly work as well. Kegs make this process a lot easier!

INGREDIENTS | YIELDS APPROXIMATELY 3 GALLONS

5 gallons fermented cider
1 (5-gallon) bucket or keg

1. Transfer your cider into a 5-gallon bucket or keg. If you live in a cold, wintery climate with consistent temperatures below freezing, you can stick the juice outside and wait roughly 12–24 hours. Alternatively, you can put the juice in a chest freezer.
2. Check the cider frequently by rocking the vessel back and forth. You are not looking for a solid block of ice, instead you're looking for a slushy consistency. If you overshoot, let the cider warm back up a little and melt some of the ice.
3. When the cider is slushy, if you're using a bucket, open the bucket, and scoop out the ice with a sieve or colander. Let the cider drain before discarding the ice. When the ice is completely removed, transfer the cider to a bottling bucket and package immediately. If you're using a

keg, use CO_2 to push the liquid cider from the slushy keg to an empty, sanitized keg. When the liquid is transferred, close the lid and carbonate as desired.

Germans and Eis

In Germany, there's a long-standing tradition of making a frozen doppelbock beer called eisbock. According to legend, supposedly a lazy brewery worker left a barrel of beer out overnight where it partially froze, and the delicious liquor inside was an amazing discovery.

Applejack

Just as cider was America's drink before the rise of beer, applejack, or apple brandy, was America's hard spirit of choice before the rise of whiskey. Remember, in colonial times, an apple orchard was critical to a successful homestead (and legally required to prove ownership in some areas).

A family would have produced large quantities of cider every fall, and they would have been hard-pressed to drink it all before winter set in. With harsh winters and outdoor storage being the norm, a few barrels of freezing cider should be no surprise.

What colonists discovered was that removing the ice from the barrels concentrated the amount of alcohol in the remaining liquid. Doing this process repeatedly can take your cider into the 20–30 percent alcohol by volume range! It also concentrates the flavors and aromas, and can make for a beverage so intensely aromatic you think you smell apple honey. This is an expansion of the technique you can use to make ice cider.

One word of caution—freeze concentration, or "fractional crystallization," as sciencey types call it, concentrates everything, including the fusel alcohols that can give wicked hangovers. What it will not do, unlike what a number of sources might tell you, is achieve a perfect separation of water and alcohol.

The quality of separation is entirely dependent on the temperature you're performing your freeze at. The closer you are to -30°F, the better, but no matter what, you will always have some alcohol trapped in the ice matrix. And no matter what, there's a maximum concentration you can reach dependent on your freezing temperature.

▼ FREEZING AND MAXIMUM ALCOHOL CONTENT

Temperature	Maximum ABV
0°F / -18°C	14%
-10°F / -23°C	20%
-20°F / -29°C	27%
-30°F / -34°C (and below)	30%

To make your own applejack, you'll want to use a wide-mouthed vessel like a 5-gallon pail, a fine mesh sieve, and a freezer or an outdoor area that's below 0°F for at least a day. You'll have to tend to the pail every few hours to break up the ice and strain the concentrated cider from it.

Remember, this is a concentration process. You gain additional alcoholic strength at the cost of volume. For every doubling of alcoholic strength, you lose half your volume. For instance, for a 5-gallon batch to go from 10 percent alcohol by volume to 20 percent, you'll lose 2½ gallons. To go further, from 20 percent to 30 percent, you'll lose another 1¼ gallons to end up with a total of 1¼ gallons of 30 percent alcohol-by-volume spirit.

QUESTION

Isn't making a concentrated spirit like applejack illegal?
There's been a lot of debate about this over the years in the cider-making community, but it appears that the answer is, "Not necessarily." Recently, the United States Alcohol and Tobacco Tax and Trade Bureau (TTB) has relaxed rules regarding freeze concentration where it is traditional, like in the production of eisbock beer. However, there is not a clear ruling on applejack, so make applejack at your own risk!

Applejack

This is a great way to use up last year's cider, since you want strong, dry cider during the coldest part of winter.

INGREDIENTS | YIELDS 1¼ GALLONS

5 gallons of 10 percent alcohol by volume cider, settled and cleared
Sugar, to taste

1. Add the cider to a sanitized bucket and place in a freezer or outside in the freezing cold.
2. Every few hours, open the bucket and break up the ice. Scoop the ice and allow it to drain before discarding. Add the drained liquid back into the bucket and repeat until no more ice forms.
3. Bottle the applejack, and cork with push corks. Age for as long as you can stand before drinking it.

Keeving

Sweetness is a struggle for the home cider maker. No matter what you do, those pesky little yeast cells just can't wait to pig out on all of the glorious glucose and fructose (sugars). They leave your cider sugar-poor and your palate aching for sweetness. There are a few methods that enable you to back-sweeten the cider, but how did cider makers deal with this problem before the discovery of potassium sorbate?

The earliest cider makers knew that their ciders didn't always ferment out. They sometimes naturally stopped and stayed sweet. The basic problem is apple juice's lack of nutrition for the yeast. This is why many of the recipes in the book advise the addition of a yeast nutrient. The yeast that grows isn't strong enough or plentiful enough to finish the job and settle out, leaving natural sweetness behind.

Take that knowledge and combine it with your desired goal of residual sweetness. The answer should be obvious—remove nutrients. How do you do that? Just take a cue from the traditional cider makers and their method of keeving.

What does keeving entail? It requires a little bit of luck and the right apples. You start with traditional low-nitrogen, high-tannin cider apples. If you're stuck with culinary apples, make sure to dose the must with tannin. Traditionally, these apples are stored at a steady 40°F, and then they are ground into a pulp.

The mush and pulp sit for a period of maceration (softening), usually about a day. During this time, tannin and pectin leach from the pulp into the cider. Vintners perform a similar cold maceration step to extract color, tannin, and flavor from red wine grapes. The cold temperature and lack of a yeast addition keeps the fermentation from starting. In fairly short order the pectin and calcium bind together and create a cemented cap of rapidly oxidizing apple pulp.

This cap, or *chapeau brun*, literally "brown hat," is half the secret of keeving. Not all of the pectin gets trapped in the cap, though; part of it forms a transparent gel that falls to the bottom of the vessel. That falling goo takes protein, nitrogen, and natural yeast with it and leaves a zone of clarified cider in between.

To finish the keeving, you have to carefully transfer the clear, nutrient-deficient cider. If you use a racking cane instead of a bucket with a spigot, be very careful when you push through the chapeau, and disturb it as little as possible.

From this point on, you have a choice—you can either try to let the cider separate again and go for yet another keeve, or just let it run naturally. The remaining yeast will ferment the cider very slowly. Your job now is to monitor the progress of the ferment, then rack and bottle as you see fit.

Solera, or Perpetual Cider

Ever wish you could have a perpetual source of cider? You can ensure that you never run out again by taking a cue from Spanish sherry makers who employ a clever system of aging, called solera.

A true solera system involves multiple barrels that feed each other. As wine (or cider in your case) is removed or evaporates from the oldest barrel, it is refilled with wine from the next oldest. This goes up the chain, until you reach the last and youngest barrel, which is topped up with the freshest wine. Since the barrels are never drained completely, each bottle contains some of the original wine used to establish the solera, at least in theory.

FACT

The word *solera* means a "cross beam," or more archaically, "base." Traditionally, solera barrels are stacked. Bottles are then filled from the barrels at the base of the stack, and refreshed with younger wine from above it. So, you're serving the wine from the base, hence *solera*.

For most home cider makers, it's unlikely that they'll keep enough cider and barrels on hand to run a true solera system. That's okay. You can still receive many of the benefits of solera without the hassle. You just need to procure fresh juice whenever you're ready to package more of your cider.

There are two approaches you can take. First, you can add fresh unfermented juice to the vessel you're pulling your finished cider from, let fermentation kick off in there, and wait for it to finish before pulling any more cider. Second, you can ferment your new juice, then let it settle before adding it to the solera vessel just after filling.

▼ SOLERA ADDITION TYPES

Method	Pros	Cons
Fresh juice	No new yeast	Cider clouds up, have to wait for clearing, eventual autolysis (which can lead to off flavors)
Fermented juice	No clarity issues	You must maintain two vessels, and preplan to have fermented juice ready

Why do this simplified solera? One great reason is the quality of juice available over the year. You can start a batch in the fall with fresh-pressed juice and enjoy those flavors in full. As the year rolls on, you can add more processed juice to the batch and still have some of the flavor of fall in your new cider. Also, you'll be taking advantage of the solera cider's aged mellowness to soften any harsh characters while hiding any aging flaws with the burst of freshness.

Some cider makers don't even bother moving the cider to a new vessel. They serve their cider on draft and after a night of cider imbibing refill the keg the next morning, then wait a few weeks before serving again. With careful management, they stretch their cider experience all year long.

The Perpetual Cider

This basic form of a never-ending solera works best with a clean, simple cider. Start your solera with the best juice you can find.

INGREDIENTS | YIELDS 5 GALLONS

5 gallons fresh, sweet apple cider
1 packet Côte des Blancs dry yeast
Malic acid, as needed
½ ounce French oak cubes, steamed for 15 minutes
1 nylon hop bag
Raw, preservative-free cider juice, as needed

1. Follow the Standard Cider-Making Procedure described in Chapter 2.
2. Adjust the cider for acid level, using the malic acid as needed. Ignore the tannin level. Rack the cider into your serving/storage vessel (bucket, or carboy if bottling a periodic portion). Add the oak to the hop bag and add to the cider.
3. If using a keg, carbonate and serve. If you prefer the fresh cider, add to the keg, chill, and carbonate again to desired levels. Otherwise, move the keg to somewhere in the 60°F range, and ferment for 2 weeks before chilling and carbonating.
4. If bottling, add the juice to the remaining aging cider after you've bottled what you want. Referment for at least a few weeks before bottling more cider.

Why Oak?

Since solera typically ages in oak barrels, the oak here is to replicate, in part, any wood character given to the cider by the wood. However, the cider won't receive the effects of microoxygenation when aged in glass or steel.

The True Solera

This form of solera comes closer to the model employed by the Spanish for sherry. It will require having two or more vessels running at a time.

INGREDIENTS | YIELDS 10 GALLONS (5 GALLONS AVAILABLE AT ANY TIME)

10 gallons fresh, sweet apple cider
2 packets Côte des Blancs dry yeast
Malic acid, as needed
½ ounce French oak cubes, steamed for 15 minutes
1 nylon hop bag
Raw, preservative-free cider juice, as needed

1. Follow the Standard Cider-Making Procedure described in Chapter 2 for both batches, in 5-gallon carboy bottles.
2. Adjust the ciders for acid level using the malic acid as needed. Ignore the tannin level. Rack the cider into your aging vessel. Add the oak to the hop bag, and add to one of the batches of cider. Let age for a minimum of 2 weeks.
3. When desired, package part of the oaked cider. Don't package more than half of it. Top up the oaked cider with the unoaked cider, and add the fresh cider to the unoaked vessel.
4. Repeat every time you draw cider from the oaked vessel.

Méthode Champenoise

For the ultimate blast of carbonation, you'll want to look to the makers of champagne, who created a method to make a smashing, sparkly wine with a minimum of particulate matter remaining. Make your cider as you normally would, less than 10 percent alcohol by volume. Prime it with sugar to achieve 4–5 volumes of carbonation (see Appendix C). Bottle into stout champagne bottles and cap. Make sure you either get American-made champagne bottles that fit regular beer caps or European 29 mm bottle caps for European champagne bottles. Most bottle cappers will have reversible jaws or a bell to fit the larger European bottle necks.

Place your bottles in a box for a month to carbonate. This process works best if you put the bottles into the box, cap side down, and then set the box so that the open end is down and the bottles are cap-side up inside the box. At the end of the month, place the box on its side. Every day, grab each bottle and give it a quick twist back and forth. After you're done, wedge the box up slightly. The goal is that, over a month, the box will end up right-side up and the bottles upside down on their caps.

What you're doing with all this twisting and futzing is what the French call "remauge" and the English world calls "riddling." The process keeps the yeast sediment from settling and sticking to the bottle while moving it down the bottle and into the neck, against the bottle cap. This is critical for the next step of the operation.

Now you're ready to "disgorge," but first put your bottles in the fridge overnight to chill. They need to be very cold. In a cold-resistant vessel, place an inch of acetone and a few large chunks of dry ice. In a few seconds, this will drop to -40°F. Don't stick your hands in it!

Don safety glasses, and gently hold a bottle, cap first, in the ice bath. Count to thirty, pull the bottle, and there should be a thick ice plug against the cap. If it goes into the shoulder, you've gone too far and will need to let the bottle thaw. But assuming you didn't, hand the bottle off to a partner who opens the bottle (facing away from anything breakable!) and lets the carbonation push the ice and yeast from the bottle. Working quickly, add a "dosage" (the French term for a topping liquid) to refill the bottle and cork it. Instead of working with traditional corks, look for the white plastic hammer-in corks that you tap in place with a few smacks from a rubber mallet. Buy wire cages at the same time and tighten them by twisting the part of the hoop that sticks out. If you can find a traditional swivel tool, great; if not, use a pair of pliers.

Traditionally, champagne producers use a mix of brandy and sugar for the dosage. For an über-sparkling cider, why not use calvados or applejack and a little sugar?

ALERT

The warning about safety glasses isn't meant for show. Your bottles will be under a lot of pressure, and the stress of the quick freezing may cause them to shatter. Be smart! Safety glasses exist for a reason!

Once the cages are cinched down, and the bottles secured, give them a quick dunk in a bucket of water to wash away any residual mess from the process. Put the bottles away for 2 weeks to rest from bottle shock. From the description, this may seem like a lot of work, but once you start doing it, you realize there's nothing to it.

Champagne Cider

Make your next dry cider into something insanely special. Yes, this will take more work than chucking it into a PET bottle, but it's worth it! Don't forget to break out the safety glasses!

INGREDIENTS | YIELDS 24 (750 ML) OR 12 (1½ L) CHAMPAGNE BOTTLES

5 gallons dry, fermented cider
Priming sweetener, 4–5 volumes (see Appendix C)
24 or 12 bottle caps
750 ml calvados or applejack
1 cup sugar
1 quart acetone
2 pounds dry ice
24 or 12 plastic champagne corks
24 or 12 champagne wire cages

1. Adjust the cider to your preferred acidity level (see Chapter 7). Go light since the carbonation will add significant carbonic acid.
2. Combine the cider and sugar in a bottling bucket. Bottle it into champagne bottles. Make sure the caps are well fixed. Place the bottles upside down in a box and then turn the box upside down, so the bottles are right-side up. Let it carbonate for a full month.
3. Place the box on its side. Every day for a few weeks, give the bottles a quarter twist back and forth. Over the course of the riddling process, prop the box so that it slowly becomes upright and the bottles are upside down, resting on their caps.
4. Chill the bottles overnight. In a pitcher, mix together the calvados and sugar. Mix the acetone with several chunks of dry ice in a container so the mixture is about 1" deep, and dip a bottle cap down in the mix for 30–60 seconds. Point the bottle in a safe direction and uncap. After the

yeast plug shoots out, add, via syringe or baster, enough calvados mixture to top the bottle up.

5. Insert the cork, and seat with a rubber mallet. Secure a wire cage over the cork. Rinse the bottle in a water bath and put away for 2 weeks. Chill, pop, and enjoy in slender flute champagne glasses.

Acetone?

Acetone—a toxic, flammable solvent commonly found in nail polish remover—certainly stands out as a sketchy ingredient, but when combined with dry ice, it's much more effective than the traditional salt/ice bath. Don't worry about food safety; the acetone will never get near the cider, especially after the bottle rinse.

CHAPTER 17

Growing Your Own

You've done it all now. There's no hill left to climb except to become an apple farmer yourself! Yes, this takes commitment. Thankfully, growing apple trees isn't out of reach for a dedicated hobbyist with space. A word before you start planning your orchard. You must remember that even in today's world of instant gratification, an orchard takes a few years before you starting reaping the benefits of a tree's munificence. This means at least two years of tending, caring, pruning, watering, and so on before you get to pluck the first sweet globe. This chapter will serve as a basic primer on planting and growing your own trees.

Tree Needs

Apple trees have certain needs. Meet those needs and they will flourish, offering you a bountiful crop of fruit. Thwart their needs and you'll be stuck with angry, runty trees that give you paltry returns.

To start, an apple tree requires sunlight, and plenty of it. You need to find a spot in your landscape where the tree can flourish with nothing else hogging up its precious solar power. This also means you'll need to stay on top of trimming any trees that could potentially shade out the apples.

Your soil needs to be a well-draining soil. If there's too much clay, water will collect around the roots drowning the tree. A good loamy soil with just enough clay to aid retention is precisely what you need. The soil also needs to be slightly acidic.

Your apple trees will also need to be pruned with a swift hand. Unpruned apple trees tend to get messy, and the natural growth hampers fruit production.

Choosing Your Trees

Keep a few things in mind when you're choosing your trees. If your primary goal is to make cider with the fruit, then really consider the odder, obscure cider varieties. Choosing a cider variety will definitely help you stick to your cider plan given they are not as much as a temptation to eat straight off the tree.

If you have room for several trees, and want to grow a culinary apple for eating, consider growing a variety with good acid, like a Granny Smith, or even one of the many varieties that are good for both eating and making sweet juice—Baldwin or Gravenstein, for instance. While you're at it, growing a crab apple, like a Wickson, makes good cider sense. With a few well-deployed crabs, you can make bland cider into phenomenal cider.

Pollination and Harvest

Whether you're planting one or multiple trees, a factor to watch out for is pollination. To get a full yield from your trees, you need them to pollinate.

Most varieties of apple trees are "self-sterile," which means that they need to be planted with other compatible varieties in order to cross-pollinate and produce fruit. A common tactic for growers is to plant aggressive pollinators like crab apples.

The other consideration is that different varieties of apple trees bloom at different times of the growing season. You must choose varieties that bloom at the same time in order to cross-pollinate. As you research trees, you'll find information on when they bloom. One system involves numbered "flowering groups" that show compatible groups.

SAMPLE MEMBERS OF FLOWERING GROUPS

1. Group 1 (very early): Aromatic Russet, Gravenstein (triploid—see below), Vista Bella
2. Group 2 (early): Bismarck, Idared, McIntosh
3. Group 3 (early midseason): Cox's Orange Pippin, Granny Smith, Jonathan
4. Group 4 (midseason): Ashmead's Kernel, Gala, Golden Delicious
5. Group 5 (late midseason): Coronation, Northern Spy, Royal Jubilee
6. Group 6 (late): Court Pendu Plat, Edward VII, Laxton's Royalty
7. Group 7 (very late): Crawley Beauty

The good news is that some trees are self-pollinating. For instance, Golden Delicious and Granny Smith are both "self-fertile." They don't need other trees to successfully bear fruit, but if you cross-pollinate them with other varieties, they produce an even greater yield.

Most apple trees are diploids, meaning they, like human beings, have two sets of chromosomes. A few trees are triploid, which means that they have three sets of chromosomes, and these trees will not cross-pollinate with a diploid, or their own variety. Make sure you keep an eye out for this, lest you end up with bad genes everywhere!

Zoning Out

One of the big immutable factors in growing any plant is the nature of the weather where you live. Try as you might, you will not get a saguaro cactus to grow in Minnesota, and a maple tree will not flourish in Florida. To help guide your selection process, you need to know your USDA hardiness zone.

In this age of the Internet, you can check what zone you are in thanks to the federal government's interactive website (*http://planthardiness.ars.usda .gov/*). The hardiness zones are based on an area's average annual extreme minimum temperature. The idea is that it would be foolhardy to plant an orange tree in an area that will freeze the oranges and destroy the trees.

On the other end of the spectrum, the American Horticultural Society (AHS) offers a Plant Heat-Zone Map (*www.ahs.org/gardening-resources/ gardening-maps/heat-zone-map*) that helps gardeners plan for protecting plants from the withering and rotting effect of the heat. Great nurseries, online and local, will help you plan what to grow on the basis of your USDA and AHS zones. The advantage of a local nursery is that it's located in your area and has firsthand experience with the oddities of your microclimate that may not be captured by a large national map.

ESSENTIAL

Want to grow trees in your yard but live somewhere hot? A great resource is Kuffel Creek Apple Nursery's e-book *Growing Apples in the City*. (Visit *www.kuffelcreek.com* to purchase.)

Apple trees generally grow best and with the least concern in zones 5, 6, and 7. Zones 3 and 4 require extra work to protect the trees during harsh winters. The warmer zones—8, 9, 10, and even 11—require extra care during the summer to keep plants from becoming cinders.

One reason zone maps are so important to apple growers is the notion of "chill hours"—hours spent below a temperature threshold (45°F) after the plant has blossomed. Apples require the most hours chilling out in order to bear good-tasting fruit.

One theory behind chilling requirements is that trees require a certain amount of stress to trigger the blossoming process during the spring. The thought is this: If a tree begins naturally blossoming after 600 chilling hours (hours spent between 32°–45°F) in a region that averages 800 hours, its blossoms will freeze, preventing fruiting. It's also good for the farmer if the tree blooms in a short period of time, because it compresses the farming tasks, pollinating, pruning, harvesting, and so on into concise blocks of time.

The Magic of Grafting

Left to their own devices, trees have rapidly changing genetic traits. Each apple contains a new tree with a mix of desirable and undesirable characteristics. With their life savings on the line, farmers will do just about anything to control their crop outcomes and avoid losing their shirts. This is where grafting comes into play, because it enables the creation of exact clones of a variety. This monoculture style of farming, where a single variety is grown for a number of years, is great from a commercial farming point of view.

FACT

All commercial apples are clones sharing the same genetic structure. This means the Roxbury Russet you grow has the exact same DNA as the original Roxbury Russet from colonial times. It also means that every apple tree of a variety is susceptible to the exact same diseases, one of the downsides of monoculture farming.

Almost every commercial apple tree is a combination of two plants: a rootstock and a scion. The scion is the sexy part. It's the part that forms leaves, bears fruit, and forms the vast majority of what everyone thinks is the tree. Way down, though, if you look carefully, you'll find the markings of Dr. Frankenstein magic: grafting.

Grafting works because the vascular systems of the rootstock and the scion can be stitched together. In human terms, this is the equivalent of joining your upper torso to your best friend's lower torso. Done right, the graft is taped up and the plant heals with sap, water, and nutrients running over the new connections. The tree is now set to make exactly the same fruit as the scion. The only sign of the surgery is usually a thicker piece of trunk at the join.

It's obvious that the choice of the scion makes a difference to the eventual plant, but what about the poor, humble rootstock? Turns out that the thing delivering water and nutrients to the rest of the plant is unbelievably important and another point of control for farmers.

Agricultural research stations have produced a number of uniquely identified rootstock sources from trees under their care. Each rootstock has different traits, including cold and disease resistances. They also impact the final size of the tree by providing a limited amount of nutrition. When you go to buy trees, you'll see them labeled as "dwarf," "semi-dwarf," etc. With proper growth and pruning, for instance, a dwarf tree will produce a large amount of fruit while never exceeding three feet in height.

Tree Forms

Depending on the time of year you choose to start your apple grove, you'll have several forms of trees to choose from. The greatest variety and best plants will be sold in the winter and early spring. You can buy apple trees out of season, but choices will be limited and you may be unhappy with the quality of the tree.

There are four primary forms that you'll find in North America:

- **Bare root:** This is a big stick with a giant root ball at one end. The tree comes with a big root ball and a few branches. It is an easy start to growing your own. Look for these in September in order to get the varieties you want.
- **Bench graft:** A young one-year-old tree that looks like nothing more than a foot-long stick. It's not a very encouraging sign, but you'll be able to get this going in no time.
- **Potted:** This is the form of tree you'll find at your local big-box store and commercial nursery. They're easy to plant, but the trees usually require a fair amount of pruning to come to proper fruition. Variety choice is also usually limited due to the extra work in growing a tree to this stage.
- **Whip:** A two-year-old tree. Much like the bench graft, it looks similar to a 3-foot stick, and it is arguably the way to go to get your hands on the best variety with reliable growth. Many nurseries require orders of multiples.

Planting

Now that you've got your trees, it's time to get them in the ground! Find that nice, sunny spot in your soon-to-be-orchard, and mark out the position of your tree. Depending on the size of the rootstock, you may need to leave as much as 12' between trees, but odds are good that you have dwarf or semi-dwarf stock and therefore can place the trees close together. Regardless of the stock, you'll want to make sure that grass is cleared away a few feet from each tree. You don't want the grass competing with the tree for resources.

A new style of planting calls for trees being planted to have as little as 18" separation. As the trees grow, you prune them to keep their growth under control. If you don't want to be that aggressive, you can go for a more moderate 3'–5' feet apart.

Plan your holes accordingly and prepare your trees. Bare root or stick trees require a good root soak. Make sure the roots are loose and free of clay. Soak them in a bucket of water for a few hours while you prepare your holes.

Prepare a few big holes that are about a foot wider than the root ball on your trees. Make the hole just deep enough that the graft is 1" or 2" above the surface of the soil. In the center of the hole, make a cone of dirt. This cone will be the root support as you're planting the tree.

Grab your tree and spread the roots out around the cone. If the plant was potted, skip the cone and gently break up the root ball along the bottom. Place the soil back and tamp it down as you go. You want the tree packed into place with no air pockets around the plant. When done, make sure the tree sits with a small ring of soil around the stem to hold water for a bit. If your soil needs it, this is a good time to add some natural fertilizer. Don't overdo it; you want the tree to be stressed for fruiting! After each tree is done, give it a gallon of water. Really soak the tree down.

Once you've gotten the trees down and soaked, you'll want to cover the area with a layer of mulch and bark. Together they work to prevent water evaporation and suppress weed and grass growth around the base of the tree. They also help regulate the temperature around the roots. You'll want to take a cup of latex paint, thin it down with a cup of water, and paint the trunk of the tree, avoiding any areas sprouting. If you paint over sprouts, you'll prevent them from growing, so carefully wipe them clean if you accidentally paint them.

Support

Young trees need plenty of support to keep a stray wind from knocking them down. Your supports can be as simple as a hammered stake in the ground that you tie the tree to with nursery tape or twist ties. For bigger trees, you may have to go with larger posts and wire contraptions. These supports will be needed until the trees have completely established themselves.

If your trees are dwarf sized, they will probably need permanent support since their root systems will be shallow and weaker. You can stick with wood, or use a metal pole, piece of copper, or PVC plastic pipe. Drive the poles into the ground and keep the trees tied in at least two spots to the support with soft plant ties that you can find at the nursery. The extra support will keep the trees well rooted and vigorous.

Ongoing Care

Now that the tree is in the ground, you're responsible for it. It will probably take a year or two before you see fruit, so be patient and document the growth of your orchard to remind yourself of the changes you're seeing.

Water/Fertilizer

Apple trees need water, but a plant can only produce so much energy. The more water and fertilizer you give it, the more branches and leaves the tree will make instead of fruit. Also, first-year trees are incredibly susceptible to drowning in too much water. After that first big gulp of water, you'll want to wait to feed it more water until it's put on a coat of leaves. After that, a good soaking twice a week is sufficient to keep your tress bumping along. If you notice curled leaves, check your soil and either lower the amount of water or increase it.

ALERT

If you live somewhere incredibly dry, use your better judgment. Nothing can live without water completely, so if you notice it's too dry, add water.

For fertilizer, skip over the heavy-duty, super chemically stuff. Also avoid manure. All of these options are so intense they can literally burn the plant. Instead, a good compost or fish/blood meal added with your mulch is usually sufficient in the spring. In June, if you're not seeing much love, give another small bump of compost.

Pruning

It takes a good long while for the hobbyist to get over the fear of pruning. Unlike your fingers and toes, plants do not stop growing because you've cut them. In fact, proper pruning controls not only the shape and height of your tree but also encourages growth and fruiting!

There are generally two seasons in which people prune their trees, winter and summer. Each has a different impact. Pruning during the dormant period of winter stimulates growth come spring. Cutting the tree back during the warm summer months helps retard growth.

When you're looking to trim, you need to make a couple of eyeball calculations. If the tree is getting too large, find the central leader (the center stalk) and trim it back to just above a place where a weaker branch is just moving out. This is called a "weak leader," and by cutting at that point you encourage slower growth along that leader than if you just whacked a few inches from the stalk.

Other things to look for are dead branches, branches moving away from horizontal, branches shooting straight up, and suckers rising from the ground. You want to remove all of these. Remember that you want to encourage the growth of relatively flat branches for maximum growth of fruit.

Always make your cuts as close to the tree as you can. In the summer, look for excessive growth that is shading the other branches. Also look for buds growing in inappropriate places, and cut under them (shallow cut) to stop their growth. If the tree's leaf cover is too thick, you'll need to pinch it back as well by removing leaves.

Culling

Early in the growing season, when your first apples appear, you'll feel great joy, but the next step is incredibly hard. Just as pruning helps a tree grow stronger, you'll have to cull young fruit from the trees to allow the other fruit to grow big, strong, and juicy. If you don't cull the fruit, you're likely to end up with a whole lot of golf-ball-sized fruit that tastes terrible.

For each cluster of proto-fruit, choose one or two to keep and discard the rest to your compost pile to make more compost to make more apples. It is the plant circle of life!

Disease and Pests

Sadly, there are things in the world that will attack your trees and make them sick. Your job as your trees' caretaker is to figure out what's wrong and how to correct it. Here are a few of the more common things, but this is a bare scratching of the surface:

DISEASES

- **Apple scab:** A fungal infection that causes blotches on the leaves and scales on the fruit. Unfortunately, unless you've chosen scab-resistant varieties, the only way to treat it is with hardcore fungicides.
- **Fireblight:** This is the most common of apple diseases. It is a bacterium that affects the whole pome family. You'll notice it immediately, because leaves will wilt, curl, and discolor, like they've been burned. The tree will emit ugly, sappy ooze. The primary treatment is to cut off infected branches with cleaned and sanitized clippers. (Spray with alcohol between cuts!) You may also notice tumors growing on the tree. Scrape them off and discard all the infected material far from your trees.
- **Flyspeck/sooty blotch:** A fungal infection that causes the apples to bear a black spotty coating. Not a huge issue for home growers and cider makers, but it can affect storage properties, and you'll want to clean it before scratting. To help control it, check how well your branches are pruned to insure good airflow.

COMMON PESTS AND TREATMENT OPTIONS

- **Aphids:** If you see ants, you may want to start checking the underside of your leaves. These little buggers suck the life straight out of a tree without any thought to your needs. You can try washing them off or releasing ladybugs to avoid chemical warfare.

- **Borers:** These are beetle larva that usually attack only newly planted trees. You'll have to get in the tree and dig out the tunnels they create in order to kill them by piercing with a knife or wire.
- **Maggots:** If you have problems with these pests, the chemical-free solution is to wrap your apples up in zip-top plastic bags. Cut the corners off the two far corners and zip the bag down along the stem above the apple.
- **Nematodes:** Insidious little buggers that live in the soil and can damage the roots. You can have your soil tested and then treat it. Usually treatment involves exposing the infested soil to sunlight to kill off the worms and sanitizing your gear.
- **Rodents:** Squirrels and rabbits love our plants. Rodents of all varieties will eat the tender bark and fruit. Protect the trees with a chicken wire cage and try and distract pesky squirrels with easy-to-reach food sources.

CHAPTER 18

Cider Cocktails

Why not enjoy your cider mixed into new libations? Modern bartenders are discovering the joy of cider and apple brandies as mixing companions for their latest cocktails. This chapter will give you a few classic cocktails to give your cider a whole new swing. One note: When a drink calls for ice, use a crushed style of ice for the chilling. These recipes depend on the increased surface area of crushed ice to both rapidly freeze and properly dilute the drink. Now let's mix up your cider.

Historic Cocktails

Remember that before the time of modern conveniences, life was pretty scrappy. Every conceivable ingredient you desired wasn't always available, no matter your money or position. With a hard life, people made do with what they had on hand and made a number of decent traditions that still stick today.

For further reading, you should use Google Books to look up older food and drink traditions. There is an amazing wealth of old wisdom available online courtesy of book scanning projects. Some of them will no doubt frighten you, but I bet if you offered a bag Super XXXTreme Spicy Chips to those folks, they'd be a little frightened at the glowing unnaturalness of it.

Wassail

Also known as mulled cider, this is one cider mixer that you've probably had. Medieval wassails were made with beer and mead, so hard cider isn't a stretch!

INGREDIENTS | YIELDS 2 QUARTS

2 quarts hard cider
1 stick cinnamon
5 whole cloves
1 knuckle-sized piece ginger, peeled and sliced into coins
Peel of 1 orange, avoid the pith
8 ounces dark rum (optional)

1. In a saucepan, slowly heat the cider, spices, and orange peel until warmed through.
2. Remove from the heat and place in a bowl. Stir in the rum, if using, as a last-minute addition.
3. Ladle into small heat-proof cups and serve.

Keep Your Drinks Hot

Cold wassail is just no good. If you don't have a Sterno-warmed punch bowl, keep your drink warm by placing a metal bowl in a slow cooker on low heat.

Stone Fence

The Stone Fence is one of America's first cocktails and arguably one of the strongest and easiest to drink. Just watch out! Drink too many and you may feel the next day like you crashed into a classically built stone farm fence.

INGREDIENTS | YIELDS 1 PINT

2 ounces dark rum, applejack, rye whiskey, or bourbon
14 ounces hard cider

1. Add the rum or spirit of your choice to a glass with a small amount of ice.
2. Top with the hard cider. Stir to combine and enjoy.

American Rum?

If you're used to thinking of rum as a fun-time tropical spirit, it may seem odd to mix it with cider in an old-timey American drink. However, back in colonial America, rum was one of New England's major exports. In what historians refer to as a triangle trade, New Englanders bought molasses from tropical sugarcane farms. The farms grew the cane with slave labor from Africa. Traders bought the slaves from Africa with rum produced in New England.

Cider Flip

Flips are a whole class of colonial cocktails lost to time. Quite possibly because very few people have a flaming hot poker available anymore!

INGREDIENTS | SERVES 1

2 eggs
2 teaspoons sugar
1 ounce rum
1 ounce brandy or applejack
12 ounces cider

1. In a metal mug or bowl, whisk together the eggs and sugar until lemony yellow and frothy. Add the spirits and continue to mix well.
2. For traditional service, heat a metal poker to red hot. Stir the cider into the mug/bowl and plunge the poker into the liquid, allowing it to steam and foam. The drink should be lukewarm.

3. For modern service, add ½ cup of cider to the beaten egg and sugar mixture and place the mixture over a double boiler. Stir constantly until the mixture is hot, but not simmering. Take off the heat, add the remaining cider and spirits, and whisk to combine.

Not Egg!

Our modern fear of salmonella has all but eliminated the once-universal use of eggs and egg whites to give a drink a silky texture. The odds of getting sick from a Flip after heating are miniscule, but if you're worried, use eggs pasteurized in shell.

Traditional Cider Drinks

As time has gone on and life has improved, mankind has not stood still in its pursuit of cider drink technology. No, indeed, while you weren't watching, a slew of drinks have become traditions in their own right. Some have even become outlawed. Although you have to wonder at the fainting spells an old-fashioned potent cocktail would induce in those that have banned the snakebite!

These drinks are all designed to be served at the pub or biergarten, so the focus here is on simplicity. Oh and don't dismiss the Shandy or Radler because they're designed to be lower in alcohol. These are both supremely fantastic drinks for a hot summer day when there's a lot of work to be done.

Black Velvet

This is one of the best-known cider cocktails. It is at once fruity, apple-driven, dark, and roasty.

INGREDIENTS | SERVES 1

½ pint cider
½ pint Irish dry stout, such as Guinness

Pour the cider and stout into a glass and mix briefly.

To Float or Not?

Debate rages over whether the Black Velvet should be floated like a Half and Half. To float this cocktail, pour the cider into a glass. Pour the stout slowly over a spoon held upside down just above the surface of the cider.

Snakebite/Diesel

This is an infamous drink in the United Kingdom, with some pubs and bars refusing to serve it because it has the reputation of causing people to become mean drunks in a hurry. The British call a Snakebite with added black currant liqueur a Diesel.

INGREDIENTS | SERVES 1

½ pint strong cider (e.g., K)
½ pint European lager (e.g., Stella Artois)
Dash black currant liqueur, or Ribena black currant soft drink (optional)

Pour the cider, lager, and black currant liqueur (if using) into a glass and mix completely.

Do Snakebites Make People Mean?

The myth of the Snakebite's effect has grown to the point of being taken as fact, but why is it perceived this way? You can blame the actual alcohol itself, not any mystical properties of lager and cider. Both the cider and lagers used to make a Snakebite are far stronger than the typical English beer, so they naturally get people drunk quicker.

Cider and Ginger Shandy

In the United Kingdom, a Shandy is typically a beer mixed with a nonalcoholic soda or soft drink. In this drink, the spicy kick of the ginger beer makes the drink pop and reminds one of a spiced cider.

INGREDIENTS | SERVES 1

½ pint dry cider
½ pint ginger beer/ginger ale

Pour the cider and ginger beer into a glass and mix completely.

Ginger Beer Versus Ginger Ale

Traditional ginger beer is a dark golden, carbonated beverage brewed with ginger, sugar, lemon, and a mix of yeast and bacteria called ginger beer plant. Ginger ale as we know it was invented in Canada as a "dry" ginger ale that is paler and milder than ginger beer.

Cider Radler

Like the British Shandy, the Germans drink a summertime concoction of beer and lemon soda they call a Radler (bicyclist) after the bike riders who ordered them as postriding restoratives.

INGREDIENTS | SERVES 1

½ pint cider
½ pint lemon-lime soda

Pour the cider and soda into a glass and mix completely.

Lemonade

If you ask a German bartender the recipe for a Radler, he'll mention beer mixed with "lemonade." Welcome to a confusing cultural quirk where what Europeans refer to as lemonade is called lemon-lime soda in the United States.

Cider and Booze

As you've already seen in the other recipe sections, cider is no stranger to getting a little assist from the hard stuff. For instance, booze provides the stone for the Stone Wall. But in the previous drinks, the cider was still the main show. These cocktails call for a much larger presence of the spirit giving more balance to the drink. Racheting up the booze can help expose a number of different flavors and aromas that normally would go unnoticed.

Don't forget though, these cocktails are strong stuff. Be careful and show moderation!

Ivan Appleseed Martini

Forget that neon green sour apple martini stuff. This is a real apple martini with nothing neon or unnatural.

INGREDIENTS | YIELDS 1 DOUBLE COCKTAIL

1½ ounces 100-proof vodka
1½ ounces cider, sweet preferred
Drizzle apple caramel (optional)

1. Fill a cocktail glass with ice and water to chill.
2. In a cocktail shaker, mix the vodka and cider. Shake for 1 minute to make ice cold.
3. Empty the cocktail glass and drizzle with apple caramel if using. Strain the martini into the glass and enjoy!

Whoa Nelly!

This recipe calls for 100-proof vodka, the bigger, meaner Russian cousin you usually don't have. Use the strong stuff in this recipe to make up for the relative "soft" nature of the cider.

Balmoral Autumn

A drink stiff enough for a prince and genteel enough for a queen. The mix of the smoky Scotch pairs with the cinnamon to make one think of fall.

INGREDIENTS | YIELDS 1 TALL DRINK

1½ ounces Scotch whiskey
1 cinnamon stick
6 ounces cider, sweet preferred

1. Fill a tall glass with crushed ice. Pour the Scotch over it and stir with the cinnamon stick.
2. Add the cider and stir gently to incorporate. Garnish with the cinnamon.

Blended

This recipe calls for Scotch whiskey. While you can use a blended Scotch, like Johnnie Walker, a single-malt Scotch whiskey is preferred. Sample different single malts to see what you like. Maybe you'll like a heavy peat malt whiskey with tones of sea salt from Islay, off the coast of Scotland, or the sweeter, lighter Scotches of Speyside, a famous whiskey-producing region in Scotland.

The Nor'easter

This is a New England spin on the Dark 'n' Stormy cocktail of Bermuda fame—only now with cider and ginger liqueur.

INGREDIENTS | YIELDS 1 HIGHBALL DRINK

5 ounces sparkling cider
½ ounce ginger liqueur (Domaine de Canton, or homemade)
1½ ounces Gosling's Black Seal rum

1. Fill a highball glass with crushed ice. Pour the cider over it and add the ginger liqueur and stir.
2. Pour the rum on top of the cider. Using a straw, give one gentle stir around the glass to start the rum "storming" to the bottom of the glass. Enjoy!

Dark 'n' Stormy

This recipe is based on the Dark 'n' Stormy of Bermuda, which is Gosling's very dark Black Seal rum floated over a hearty dose of ginger beer with a slice of lime. Gosling's owns the trademark on the Dark 'n' Stormy. If you haven't tried an actual Dark 'n' Stormy, buy some ginger beer and use that in lieu of the cider and ginger liqueur.

The Baked Apple

Add some fire to your cider with a blast of spicy cinnamon schnapps. Think of this as a fast way to make mulled cider!

INGREDIENTS | YIELDS 13 OUNCES

1½ ounces cinnamon schnapps
12 ounces sparkling cider
Red food coloring, to taste (optional)

Pour the schnapps and cider into a glass. Stir and add a few drops of food coloring until you reach the red-hot color you desire.

Make Your Own!

Can't find schnapps you like? Look online for instructions on how to make your own cinnamon schnapps at home.

Kir Normand, or Cidre Royal

Kir is a classic French cocktail that is traditionally a mix of Crème de Cassis (a sweet, dark red liqueur made from black currants) and a white Burgundy wine. The black currant liqueur spices up an otherwise serviceable wine. Like all things classic, variations galore have appeared, including cider variations. If you add calvados (an apple brandy from France), you're making a Cidre Royal.

INGREDIENTS | SERVES 1

½ ounce Crème de Cassis
Splash calvados (optional)
3 ounces Norman sparkling cider

Pour the cassis and optional calvados into a wine glass (or champagne flute for a sparkling presentation). Fill the glass with the Normandy cider. Do not stir.

Crème de Cassis

This thick, black-currant-infused liqueur has been around since the 1840s. The bright, intense acidic character balances out the sugar found in any liqueur and can jump-start anything bland. Almost all of the world's production and consumption of cassis is centered in France.

Applejack Cocktails

As befits America's first spirit, there are a few cocktails that take advantage of Applejack's potency. But really when we get down to it, there is one rock-star cocktail—the Jack Rose. To truly appreciate the power of the Jack Rose though, you need to make one more thing at home and that's your own grenadine. It doesn't take very long and once you do it, you'll never buy a bottle of red syrupy ick from the store again.

Grenadine

Yes, you can buy grenadine in the store, but that mass market stuff is less than stellar. Take 10 minutes and make some at home. Use this when making a Jack Rose (see following recipe).

INGREDIENTS | YIELDS 1 PINT

2 cups 100 percent pomegranate juice (fresh or bottled)
2 cups sugar
4 tablespoons pomegranate molasses
1 teaspoon orange blossom water (optional)
½ shot vodka (optional as a preservative)

1. In a saucepan on the stovetop, heat the pomegranate juice over low heat, and when warm, stir in the sugar until it dissolves.
2. Remove the now-thick syrup and stir in the molasses and other ingredients. Store in a bottle or jar for a month without the vodka or longer with.

Pomegranate Molasses
The result of boiling pomegranate juice until it is syrupy is that it carries a bright red color and a sharper acidic tang than is found in fresh pomegranates. Find it online or in your local well-stocked store.

Jack Rose

A cocktail of America's illicit booze times, the Jack Rose emerged to fame when Hemingway included it in The Sun Also Rises. *This cocktail is to applejack as the martini is to gin.*

INGREDIENTS | SERVES 1

1 shot applejack
½ shot lemon juice
¼ shot grenadine

1. Chill a cocktail glass. Combine all the ingredients in a shaker with ice and vigorously shake until ice cold.
2. Strain into the chilled cocktail glass and garnish with an apple slice and cherry.

The Double Pomade

Inspired by the classic French liqueur called Pommeau, this is a cocktail version of that nearly 40-proof beverage.

INGREDIENTS | SERVES 1

1½ ounces applejack (or brandy, including calvados)
3 ounces cider (a lightly spiced, gingery cider works well)

1. Chill an old-fashioned cocktail glass. Combine all the ingredients in a shaker with crushed ice and vigorously shake until ice cold.
2. Pour into the chilled glass and enjoy.

Pommeau

Pommeau is a traditional Norman liqueur that is a blend of sweet apple juice with calvados, to about 17–20 percent alcohol by volume, that is then typically barrel aged before being bottled and served as a predinner cocktail. The calvados serves to prevent the fresh juice from fermenting. The same technique is used with port to arrest the wine fermentation while sweet.

CHAPTER 19

Cooking with Cider

If you watch any cooking shows or read cookbooks, you'll notice the frequent use of wine in cooking. Why do chefs use wine? They're looking for the addition of fruit, acid, sugar, and alcohol to help break down ingredients and boost flavors. However, wine has downsides: It can be expensive, and unless you know the wine well, it's easy to make a bad choice. If you do pick a wine with the right combination of fruit and acid, your cooking can still go bad based on the amount of oak and grape tannins in the wine. Cider makes a fantastic alternative to wine as it contains many of the flavor characters that chefs want from wine, but none of the harshness. While cider can contain tannins, the amount is usually much less than wine. Since cider tends to the delicate, it's best not to overcook it or you will lose the flavors that make it so sublime.

Appetizer

No good meal should start without a little nosh to stimulate the appetite. So why not start with the Swiss Army Knife of appetizers—fondue. Cider and cheese are a wonderful combination and fondue just lends itself to whatever you want to eat. Like vegetables? Dip some vegetables! Like bread? Bread loves cheese! Dip meat! Dip anything. Get completely meta and dip apples and cheese! (And drink cider too!)

ESSENTIAL

Like wine, don't choose your cooking cider by cost. Choose a cider you would enjoy drinking, but not one that's pricey and artisanal. Remember, many delicate characters will get cooked off. Sadly, unpleasant characters tend to be hearty and stick around!

Cider Cheese Fondue

Choose good English Cheddar for this fondue to keep things traditional. With just a little bit of prep work, you can have a bowl of cheesy goodness ready for a dip of bread, apples, pretzels, or anything else you like.

INGREDIENTS | YIELDS 3 CUPS

1½ cups hard cider
¾ cup chicken broth
1 teaspoon mustard powder
1 tablespoon Worcestershire sauce
½ teaspoon white pepper
¼ teaspoon cayenne pepper
¾ pounds sharp Cheddar cheese, grated (English is best)
¼ pound Gruyère or Emmentaler cheese, grated
3 tablespoons cornstarch
Salt, to taste

1. Bring the cider, broth, mustard powder, Worcestershire sauce, and peppers to a boil. Reduce heat and simmer for 5 minutes.

2. In a large bowl, toss the cheeses with the cornstarch. (This helps prevent the cheese from becoming grainy.)
3. Working with small handfuls, stir the cheese into the cider with a silicone spatula. When melted and smooth, introduce the next handful. When done, taste for salt and adjust. Keep warm and serve!

Liquid Fondue

If you don't have a fondue pot hanging around your house, try this instead to keep your fondue warm and gooey. Take your trusty slow cooker and fill it a quarter full of hot water. Put your fondue in a metal bowl that fits over but doesn't fall into the cooker. Turn the cooker on low and place the bowl over the warm water.

Sauces

If cider is sauce for the mind, then it should be no surprise that those bright acidic and sweet flavors would play well in a sauce. Look at your other cookbooks and see how many sauces call for both sugar and acid. Instead of adding lemon juice or wine, why not use your homemade cider?

Apple Bacon Onion Jam

This recipe takes several hours, a heavy pot, and blender, but it makes everything taste better with the classic flavors of apple cider and vinegar. Use this jam on anything—burgers, eggs, toast, ice cream, a spoon, your finger, and so on.

INGREDIENTS | YIELDS 1½ CUPS

½ pound thick-cut bacon, chopped into 1" pieces

1 medium sweet onion, cut in half and sliced in ¼"-thick slices

4 tablespoons brown sugar

1 cup low-sodium chicken broth

12 ounces cider

4 ounces cider vinegar

2 teaspoons paprika

1 tablespoon Sriracha chili sauce

1. In a heavy Dutch oven, heat the bacon over medium heat and slowly cook till almost crisp, about 10 minutes. Remove the bacon and drain the fat from the pan, reserving 2 tablespoons of the fat.
2. Add back the reserved fat and the bacon. Add the onion and sweat over medium-low heat until the onions are soft, limp, and beginning to brown deeply. This will take about 1 hour. Make sure to stir regularly.
3. When the onions are good and sticky, add the brown sugar and stir over high heat. Add the broth and bring to a boil, scraping the bottom to dissolve the fond (the stuff stuck to the bottom of the Dutch oven). Boil until the liquid is almost gone. Add half the cider and repeat.
4. Add the remaining cider and other ingredients and stir to combine thoroughly. Either transfer the mixture to a powerful blender and carefully blend or use an immersion blender and blend smooth.
5. Return the pot to medium-low heat and reduce until the remaining mixture is thick and well browned. Adjust the seasoning and store cold.

Spare no Expense!

Buy high-quality, thick bacon. Skimping on this step will result in an inferior jam and waste a lot of your time making it!

Cider Glaze

This glaze is perfect for coating just about any meat with the tart sweetness of apples!

INGREDIENTS | YIELDS 2 CUPS

1 cup tart cider
1 cup brown sugar
¼ cup cider vinegar
Salt, to taste

1. In a saucepot, bring the cider and brown sugar to a boil. Reduce heat and simmer for 15 minutes.
2. When the bubbles begin stacking on each other, whisk in the vinegar and salt. Let cool slightly before using as a glaze.

"Dijon" Herbal Cider Honey Mustard

Dijon mustard is made with a special white wine in France. Why not use your cider to make mustard as well? Choose a tart cider for this recipe. Make this a few days ahead to let everything properly hydrate and meld.

INGREDIENTS | YIELDS 2 CUPS

1½ cups tart cider
½ cup apple cider vinegar
½ teaspoon white pepper
½ teaspoon dried thyme, lightly crushed
4 tablespoons honey
2 (2-ounce) tins dry mustard powder
Salt, to taste

1. Bring the cider, vinegar, pepper, and thyme to a boil. Reduce heat and simmer for 5 minutes. Cool slightly. Whisk in the honey.
2. In a separate pot, place the mustard powder and slowly introduce the hot cider mixture. Whisk as you pour to prevent lumps.
3. Continue whisking while heating the pot over medium-low heat until the mustard is thick and luscious. Add salt, to taste. Store refrigerated and tightly covered.

Mustard Cider BBQ Sauce

This sauce is inspired by the mustard-based BBQ sauces of the Carolinas. This isn't quite a true Carolina sauce, but it does a piece of pork proud!

INGREDIENTS | YIELDS 1 CUP SAUCE

1 tablespoon unsalted butter
¼ onion, minced or grated
⅓ cup dark brown sugar
¼ cup cider vinegar
¼ cup cider
¼ cup yellow mustard
1 teaspoon Colman's Mustard powder
2 teaspoons Sriracha chili sauce
Salt and pepper, to taste

1. Melt the butter in a small saucepan and add the onion. Cook over medium heat until the onion is translucent and soft, about 10 minutes.
2. In a separate bowl, mix together the remaining ingredients until smooth and then mix into the onions.
3. Cook for 20 minutes. Cool and serve over a cider-braised pork shoulder.

Open a Window!

Hot vinegar is potent! Open a window as you cook this sauce unless you feel like being driven from your house.

Entrées

Cider makes for some great meals. You'll notice that most of these dishes take advantage of cider's aqueous nature by poaching or braising. These techniques give plenty of time for the cider's flavors to infuse your dish. Even better, the dishes range from the down-home charm of an oven-cooked "BBQ" pork butt to an elegant perfectly poached salmon with an intense cider glaze. Remember to keep some extra cider on hand—what else do you think you'd drink with your dinner?

Cider-"Smoked" Oven BBQ Pork Butt

Don't have a smoker but love BBQ pork? This will tide over those cravings you may have. This recipe takes a while to make, so make sure you time it right to have dinner at a reasonable time.

INGREDIENTS | SERVES 6–8

2 tablespoons kosher salt

2 tablespoons dark brown sugar

2 tablespoons chile powder

2 teaspoons dried thyme, crushed in your hands

2 teaspoons black pepper

2 teaspoons cumin

1 teaspoon paprika

4–5 pound pork shoulder roast (pork butt), trimmed of the fat cap

1 teaspoon liquid smoke

¾ cup cider

1. Preheat oven to 220°F.
2. In a small bowl, mix together the salt, sugar, and dry spices and sprinkle all over the pork roast. Press into the roast really well.
3. Place roast in a Dutch oven and add the liquid smoke and cider to the pot. Don't splash the roast.
4. Roast in the oven for 12–13 hours.
5. Remove the roast to a cutting board. Pull out any bones and then chop/shred the meat with forks. Mix with your favorite BBQ sauce and serve on buns.

BBQ?

This isn't proper BBQ, but not everyone has access to a smoker! The liquid smoke and the cider give that sweet, smoky flavor you associate with good BBQ, so try this recipe out and serve it on the cheapest buns you can find for proper effect. Pair this up with the Mustard Cider BBQ Sauce (see recipe in this chapter) and some coleslaw for a good Southern-style dinner!

Smothered Pork Chops

Smothered anything is a classic of Southern cooking. This version replaces some of the usual water or chicken broth with cider to boost the flavor.

INGREDIENTS | SERVES 4

1 tablespoon vegetable oil

4 large pork chops, center cut, 1" thick

3 tablespoons butter

1 large onion, cut into long, thin strips

1 teaspoon dried thyme, crushed in your hands

1 teaspoon black pepper

1 teaspoon salt

1 teaspoon paprika

3 tablespoons all-purpose flour

1 cup chicken broth

1 cup cider

1 tablespoon cider vinegar

1. In a large Dutch oven, heat the oil on high heat until shimmering, about 3–5 minutes. Add the pork chops and sear until crusty on both sides, about 4 minutes per side. Remove the chops from the pan.
2. Turn the heat down to medium. Add the butter and melt. Add the onion strips and stir until softened and just turning translucent, about 15 minutes. Scrape the bottom of all the porky bits.
3. Add the spices and the flour, stirring to soak up all the liquid. Cook for 2 minutes, stirring constantly.
4. Whisk in the broth and cider until smooth. Add the chops back into the liquid. Bring to a boil and cover tightly. Simmer for 75 minutes.
5. Remove the chops to a warmed plate and bring the remaining liquid to a boil. Reduce until thick, about 5 minutes. Stir in the vinegar and serve immediately over the chops.

Chicken and Mushroom Fricassee

There is nothing like a little cider to keep your chicken moist and add flavor to your sauce. This is one of those meals you can start and walk away from.

INGREDIENTS | SERVES 4

2 ounces bacon or pancetta, cut into small dice
1 (4–5 pound) whole roasting chicken, cut into quarters
2 tablespoons olive oil
1 small onion, sliced
2 cups thickly sliced mushrooms
4 teaspoons flour
1 teaspoon thyme
1 teaspoon oregano
½ teaspoon sage
2 cups chicken broth
2 cups cider

1. Heat a heavy Dutch oven over medium-high heat. Add the bacon and cook until just crispy and the fat renders out. Remove the bacon. Turn the heat to high and brown the chicken parts in the bacon fat until crispy brown, about 4 minutes per side. Remove the chicken.
2. Add the oil and the onion and cook until just starting to wilt (about 10 minutes) and then add the mushrooms. Let the mushrooms cook until

they have released their liquid and the liquid has evaporated, about 15 minutes. Add the flour and herbs and stir to coat the onions and mushrooms. Cook for 1 minute to remove the raw flavor.

3. Whisk in the broth and cider and bring to a boil. Add the chicken back to the cider, cover partially, and cook on low heat for 1 hour. Remove the chicken and bring the pot to a boil to reduce the gravy a little more. Serve the chicken with a generous amount of gravy and don't forget to serve the mushrooms and onions over the chicken.

Poached Salmon with Cider Sauce

This is a great, simple dish that plays the sweet-and-sour tang of cider off the rich lusciousness of a salmon fillet. Wild salmon is best, but even farm-raised salmon tastes extravagant with this method.

INGREDIENTS | SERVES 2

2 center-cut salmon fillets, skin on, 1" thick
Salt and pepper, to taste
1 tablespoon olive oil
9 ounces cider
1 tablespoon unsalted butter
1 tablespoon chopped Italian flat parsley

1. Pat the salmon dry with paper towels. With the edge of a sharp knife, scrape any scales remaining from the skin. Make shallow cuts at an angle into the skin. Make shallow cuts at the opposite angle, leaving diagonal segments in the skin. Don't break through to the meat. Liberally add salt and pepper to the skin side.

2. In a nonstick skillet, heat the olive oil over high heat to shimmering, about 3–5 minutes. Add the prepared fillets, skin side down. Salt the top. Cook for 5 minutes or until you see the salmon cooked a third of the way up the side.

3. Add cider to cover ⅔ of the fillets, cover the skillet with a lid, and turn the heat to low. Poach for 10 minutes or until the salmon is just cooked through.

4. Remove the fillets from the cider and set aside. Turn the heat up to high and reduce the cider to ⅓ cup.

5. Remove from the heat and stir in the butter to emulsify the sauce. Once the butter is incorporated, stir in the parsley.
6. Remove the skin from the fillets and serve on a heated plate with a generous helping of the sauce.

Skin On!

The skin is crucial to the dish as it protects the salmon and enriches the sauce. Don't go skinless!

Vegetables

Vegetables don't have to be the forgotten lonely child of the dinner plate. Treated right, these sides could easily satisfy as well as any main course. Not surprisingly, these vegetable recipes also have a strong connection to New England, America's original cider homeland. They carry a rustic, warming, comforting vibe that is deeply soulful.

Cider Ambrosia

Ambrosia is a name given to this because it's the best mashed root purée you've ever had. If you've never had a parsnip, don't worry; think of it as an oddly fragrant carrot.

INGREDIENTS | SERVES 4–6

4 russet baking potatoes, peeled, and sliced into ⅓" slices
2 parsnips, peeled and sliced into ¼" slices
2 carrots, peeled and sliced into ¼" slices
12 ounces cider
Water, as needed
½ cup heavy cream
½ stick unsalted butter
Pinch nutmeg
Salt and white pepper, to taste

1. Place the vegetables in a pot and cover with cider and enough additional cold water to cover by 1" inch. Bring to a boil and then reduce to a simmer. Simmer for 15 minutes or until fork tender.

2. Drain the vegetables into a large bowl. Add the cream, butter, and nutmeg, and mash until it reaches the desired consistency. Add salt and white pepper to taste, and serve.

Slices

Most mash recipes call for a precise dice of your vegetables. A few years back the folks at *Cook's Illustrated* demonstrated that slices were just as effective and cooked faster with less hassle on the cutting board.

Slow-Cooked "Baked" Beans

Beans provide a deeply satisfying bite of warmth when made just right. This recipe requires a quick overnight soak and all day cooking in your favorite slow cooker.

INGREDIENTS | SERVES 6

3 cups dried pinto beans, rinsed and picked clean of stones
6 ounces salt pork, frozen, and sliced thin
1 large yellow onion, quartered with the root intact
2 teaspoons mustard powder
3–6 cups apple cider
⅓ cup dark molasses
1 tablespoon unsalted butter
Salt, to taste

1. Place the beans in a pot and cover with cold water by several inches. After 6 hours, drain the beans and cover with more cool water. After 6 hours drain the beans.
2. Cover the bottom of your slow cooker with a layer of the salt pork and then onion wedges. The root should help the onions stay together.
3. In a medium bowl, toss the drained beans with the mustard powder and add to the slow cooker. Scatter the remaining salt pork on top of the beans.
4. Pour enough cider over the beans to cover by ½". Pour the molasses on top of the beans.

5. Using aluminum foil, line the top rim of the slow cooker to make a gasket for the lid. Place the lid down and seal it well. Cook for 6 hours on high heat, and then cook for at least 2 more hours on low heat.

6. When the beans are tender, stir in the butter and salt to taste and enjoy.

Beans and Salt

You'll notice that there is no addition of regular salt until the very end of the cooking time. This is because the salt pork provides plenty of salt, plus too much salt early in the cooking process will make your beans tough by chemically altering the skin.

Dessert

What's dinner without a dessert? A poor ending to the day indeed! Big shocker that apples would lend themselves so well to a sweet treat. You'll start with a spin on the fall classic of caramel-coated apples, hit a winter warmth of freshly made applesauce and finally, hit a high elegant note with a poached apple that's to die for. Consider saving a little postdinner room for a nice digestif, maybe an applejack or an eis cider?

Chunky Applesauce

Your childhood favorite made rustic style. Once you know how easy applesauce is and how much better it can be when you make it, you'll question buying it ever again.

INGREDIENTS | YIELDS 1 QUART

3 pounds apples (any variety)
1 lemon, juiced
½ stick cinnamon
¼ cup brown sugar
1 cup cider
Pinch salt

1. Combine all the ingredients in a heavy pot and bring to a gentle boil. Lower the heat, cover, and simmer for 20 minutes.

2. When the apples are tender, pull the pot from the heat. Remove the cinnamon stick and mash the apples with your favorite mashing implement. If you want super-smooth applesauce, use a food mill to purée the sauce.

Sugar

One of the great advantages of making your own applesauce is that you can control the amount, and variety, of sugar in your applesauce. If this sauce isn't sweet enough for you, stir in a little more sugar. If you want more flavors, try adding some ginger or thyme to the applesauce.

Cider-Poached Apples

Think of this as the New England version of the classic French dessert of pears poached in wine.

INGREDIENTS | SERVES 4

2 cups cider
1 cup brown sugar
½ stick cinnamon
⅛ teaspoon powdered ginger
Pinch salt
2 apples, peeled, halved, and cored
½ cup heavy whipping cream
½ teaspoon vanilla extract
1 tablespoon powdered sugar
¼ cup pecans, chopped

1. Combine the cider, sugar, cinnamon, ginger, and salt in a nonstick saucepan and bring to a boil. Boil until the cider becomes syrupy—about 20 minutes.
2. Add the apples to the syrup and simmer for 10–15 minutes or until the apples yield to a paring knife with gentle pressure. Transfer the apples and syrup to a bowl and cool in the refrigerator.
3. Just before service, in a small bowl, combine the cream, vanilla, and sugar. Whisk for 5 minutes or until you get the cream to just hold soft peaks.

4. In a dry pan over low heat, toss the pecans for 5 minutes until lightly toasted and fragrant.
5. To serve, drizzle a plate with a small amount of the poaching syrup. Place an apple, cored-side up, on the plate and top with the cream. Sprinkle pecans over the cream and serve.

Peeling Apples

Wait until the last minute to peel and core the apples. You want to minimize the amount of time the flesh is in contact with oxygen. This will help minimize browning. If you must do it ahead of time, toss the peeled, cored apples with a small amount of lemon juice.

CHAPTER 20

What to Ferment Next

By now, you should be a cider-making whiz! Fermentation is your friend, and you fear no wee beasties. Now is the time to stretch your wings and apply your newfound skills to other fermentable beverages! With just a few adjustments to your process, you'll be able to make your own grape wine, other fruit wine, mead, and beer. This know-how is guaranteed to increase your popularity fourfold!

Wine—Fruit of the Vine

Quite possibly, the easiest next step is to make the move to wine. Cider above 7 percent alcohol by volume is considered a fruit wine. It makes sense since all that's needed to make a fruit wine is sugary fruit juice and yeast.

The obvious target of your winemaking projects is *Vitis vinifera*, or the wine grape. The wine grape has an ancient history going back to Neolithic mankind. Domestication and the eventual change of the grape occurred in the modern countries of Armenia and Turkey around 5,500 years ago.

Grape wine featured heavily in early recorded human culture, with mentions in early stories like *The Epic of Gilgamesh*. Thanks to the wine-centered cultures of both the Romans and then the Catholic Church, wine culture became the default "upper crust" beverage of the Western world. But don't let that intimidate you. The factors are exactly the same—the amount of sugar, the amount of acid found in the juice, and the amount of tannin from the skin and other treatments.

FACT

How can some stores sell a bottle of wine for around $3? Part of it has been a grape glut in California, driving grape prices down. Also, a good amount of that cheap wine is made with old-fashioned table grapes, like Thompson seedless grapes.

There are hundreds of types of wine grapes. Keep it simple and find grapes that are on the names of wines you like—cabernet, chardonnay, merlot, etc. Don't completely ignore the table grapes on the market—you can make acceptable table wines out of those, but just like culinary apple ciders, they won't pack the same punch as a true wine grape. Also like a culinary apple cider, you can boost the character with judicious additions of acid and tannin.

ESSENTIAL

Don't let wine snobbery deter your plans and force you into a French/Italian model of winemaking. Many cultures, like the Basques, have a fresh wine tradition. Many a good meal features just-finished wine poured out at long communal tables filled with garlicky fried chicken and other specialties. The good food and the good company make up for any defects in the wine.

▼ AVERAGE SUGAR IN GRAPES

Variety	Type	Brix	Specific Gravity
Cabernet Sauvignon	Red wine	25B	1.105
Chardonnay	White wine	22B	1.092
Merlot	Red wine	23B	1.097
Sauvignon Blanc	White wine	23B	1.097
Thompson seedless	Table	17B	1.070

A challenge for cider makers looking to make wine is that the average starting gravity of grape juice is very high, and the must has very low nutrient levels. To avoid stressing your yeast and producing less-than-savory flavors and aromas like hydrogen sulfide H_2S (the smell of rotten eggs), you'll need to invest in yeast nutrients.

You have several options to procure wine grapes. If you live anywhere near a grape-growing region, check with your local homebrew shop and see if they get fresh wine grapes. Some vineyards will even sell grapes to you directly. But there is one caveat—grape buys usually happen in lots big enough to make 6–7 gallons of wine, which means about 100 pounds of grapes.

Depending on the weather, the region, and the varietals, vineyards start picking as early as mid-August and don't stop until October. As the grapes are picked, you'll need to be ready to pick them up, crush them, and ferment them immediately. Most homebrew shops will have a way to get your grapes crushed and destemmed. If you're making a red wine, you'll let the juice and skins ferment together and then press the juice from the skins like you press apples. In fact, you can even use the same press! If you're making white wine, you'll press the grapes immediately and ferment just the juice.

A more amenable option for most vintners is vacuum-reduced and packed juice. Available at homebrew shops, these wine kits contain a partially reduced fresh wine must. These Mylar-bagged kits contain everything you need to make a wine. The results from these kits are amazing and consistent.

The last of the wine grape options involves canned wine must concentrate. This is the old-school version of the box kits, and they have a very thick, syrupy consistency and a fair amount of browning, consistent with abuse and oxidation. These make interesting flavor additions, but please don't use them for making wine!

QUESTION

How much will making my own wine cost?
Don't let the price of proper wine grapes or the wine kits deter you. The cost of a kit currently runs somewhere between $70–$110, and fresh grapes are $100–$140. Keep in mind that this is for 6 gallons of wine, or 30 wine bottles' worth! This means your average cost per bottle will be $2.33 to $4.66. And you will blow the corks off similarly priced wine you'll find on the market!

If you do buy commercial grape juice, the same rules apply here as for commercial apple juice—avoid juices with preservatives. The less processed your juice, the better!

Many of the things you've learned about cider making cross over to winemaking. Those dried wine yeasts you've been using? Winemaking is what they've been bred for. And the fermenting equipment discussed in Chapter 5 is absolutely perfect for winemaking, although red wine does need a bigger fermenter to start with. You will also need to give your wine more time to ferment and age than your cider. Sulfites are also a bigger deal in winemaking. You use oak beans and chips exactly the same. You use tartaric acid, instead of malic or citric acid, but the principle is the same. Racking is also more important in winemaking since grape wines throw a lot of sediment. Make sure to rack your wine and keep it topped up for the best flavor.

Basic Wine

This is the basic procedure for producing wine from juice. There are lots of variations and different techniques for extracting flavors, but that would take a whole other book to cover!

INGREDIENTS | YIELDS 6 GALLONS

6 gallons grape juice

Yeast nutrient, dose according to package instructions

1 packet dry wine yeast

2 tablespoons yeast rehydration nutrient

Tartaric acid, to taste

5 Campden tablets (potassium or sodium metabisulfite), or ¼ teaspoon sulfite powder

Fining agent (gelatin or bentonite) (follow package instructions for amounts)

30 (750 ml) wine bottles and corks

1. Sanitize the carboy and mix the juice and nutrient, if needed. (Many vacuum-packed musts come preloaded with nutrients.)
2. Rehydrate the yeast in warm water with a rehydration nutrient for 15 minutes, covered. When frothy, pitch into your wine and cap with an airlock.
3. Ferment for 1–2 weeks at or around 65°F.
4. Rack to another carboy to allow the wine to clear. Let settle. Check the gravity every week. When the gravity has stopped dropping, add tartaric acid to taste. Add the Campden tablets. Stir the wine aggressively, until you've driven all the carbon dioxide from the solution and it stops foaming. Add fining agent according to the package's instructions, and allow the wine to settle for 14–28 days.
5. Sanitize your bottles, corks, and racking cane. Gently siphon the wine into the bottles, cork, and age for 1 week upright before laying the bottles on their sides. Wait at least 1–6 months before serving.

Oxygen Exposure

Wine is incredibly susceptible to oxidation, mold, and acetobacter. All three depend on oxygen to grow and survive. It is critical that you limit the amount of oxygen exposure after fermentation and fining by keeping your aging wine topped up. This means refilling your carboy to just below the airlock when needed. You can use freshly boiled water or other wine, including commercial.

Wine Not of the Vine

Wine doesn't just have to be made from grapes. The process is much the same as making regular wine or cider. You start with ripe fruit, liberate the juice, ferment, and bottle. Virtually anything with sugar content can be turned into a wine of sorts.

One caveat that you need to keep in mind while choosing your fruits: You want acidity in your brew, but not too much! For instance, pure citrus juice, like lemon and orange, is acidic enough to damage and kill yeast. If you do get them to ferment out, you'll usually be left with something incredibly sour and bitter. You can dilute the juice to ferment, and then back-sweeten to eliminate the sourness.

Don't be afraid to pour on the sugar, either. Chapitilization (the process of adding sugar to unfermented fruit or juice in order to increase the alcohol content after fermentation) plays a huge part in the production of fruit wine. Most culinary fruits haven't been selected, grown, and picked with wine production in mind. Therefore, most of them don't have the intense sugar content necessary. Dissolve your sugar in the juice by stirring viciously, or stir in a syrup.

Everything else about fruit wine fermentation is exactly the same! Control the temps. Give it enough time. Rack it over to settle. Then bottle.

Lemon Wine

Want to make lemonade that's a real kick in the pants? Try this lemon wine that will make you scoff at the stuff available at your grocery store. This comes in at roughly 10 percent alcohol by volume. If you have kegs on hand, try this carbonated like champagne!

INGREDIENTS | YIELDS 5 GALLONS

2 liters lemon juice, freshly squeezed (about 35 lemons)

8 pounds sugar

4½ gallons filtered water

1 packet dry white wine yeast

Yeast rehydration nutrient, dosed according to package instructions

2½ teaspoons sorbistat K (potassium sorbate)

4–8 ounces sugar syrup, or corn syrup

1. Sanitize the carboy and mix the juice and sugar to dissolve. You may find it easier to dissolve the sugar in some water first. Top the juice/sugar mixture with enough water to bring to 5 gallons.
2. Rehydrate your yeast in warm water with a rehydration nutrient for 15 minutes, covered. When frothy, pitch into your juice and cap with an airlock.
3. Ferment for 1–2 weeks at or around 65°F.
4. Rack to another carboy and allow to clear and settle.
5. When ready to bottle or keg, transfer the very sour wine into a bottling bucket. Add the sorbistat and stir thoroughly. Add the sweetener, stir thoroughly, and taste. Adjust the sweetness as needed. Package and chill.

Corn Syrup?

The corn syrup in this recipe is suggested as a quick alternative to making your own very thick sugar syrup. But in reality, use your favorite sweet syrup, such as agave nectar or maple syrup. Just adjust the amounts to taste.

Mead—Honey Wine of the Vikings

Mead, or honey wine, conjures up images of thirsty, pillaging warriors, greedily guzzling a potent fuel for their battle lust. It is quite possibly the oldest alcoholic beverage consumed by humanity. Wine, cider, and beer all take human intervention to make effectively—you have to crush and transform the fruit or grain to make ready for fermentation. Mead just takes honey and water.

The first meads were probably an accidental discovery of natural fermentation. Perhaps a hollow log is filled with honey dripping from a hive or comb, gets hit with some rain water, and then yeast floats by on the breeze and settles in the honey water. After a few weeks, a thirsty caveman stumbles by, discovers the pool of odd-looking water, and voilà! Mead.

For thousands of years, honey was mankind's primary sugar source. Readily available and liquid, it shows up regularly in religious worship as a mystical healing force. Honey also stores well, lasting hundreds or thousands of years with little ill effect, all thanks to an incredibly high sugar content and an infusion of hydrogen peroxide from the bees.

Honey

Use only the best honey you can find. Farmers' markets, roadside stands, and online apiarist sites provide excellent value in bulk. Flavored meads make good use of cheaper bulk honey.

ALERT

Be careful! Recent reports suggest that cheap Chinese honey coming into the marketplace is contaminated or adulterated with chemicals that may be harmful to you or your yeast.

The honey found in your cupboard is bound to be a wildflower or clover variety. Like grapes, honey comes in endless varieties affected by the flowers that feed the colony. They range from the ubiquitous and delightfully scented orange blossom to the exotic sourwood. Each variety tastes and smells completely different. Using the same base recipe, you'll get unique experiences.

Mead—Varieties and Terminology

One of the primary distinguishing features of mead is the amount of sugar left over when fermentation is complete. Vintners call this wine's "residual sweetness." In mead making, sweet, or sack, meads are par for the course. A strong sweetness reduces the drinkability of the wine, so many mead makers aim for a medium or dry level of finish. Sweet wines serve as a great base for additional flavors.

Making Mead

Mead takes some patience on your part! It is not unheard of for a mead to take several years to mature, but most can be ready in under a year. Weaker meads (hydromels) can be ready in a few months.

To make mead, heat up a small quantity of water (1 gallon) and dissolve the honey. Add the thinned honey to cold water in a fermenter and pitch wine yeast. A new technique for encouraging optimal yeast health calls for adding small doses of yeast nutrient to the must twice daily for the first 4 days. Supplements are needed since honey, despite its amazing properties, lacks the needed minerals for a healthy fermentation.

After a month, the mead should be ready for transfer to a secondary container. Add acid, fruit, or spice teas to taste and allow to age for another month or two. A few days before bottling/kegging, add clarifying agents. Once bottled, the mead ages from 3 months to 30 years, or until you can't stand it and have to imbibe!

FACT

Some believe the term *honeymoon* comes from the old European practice of providing a month's larder of mead to newlyweds to promote fertility and happiness. Sadly, linguists discount this origin.

Mead Yeast

Unless you're brewing a hydromel, avoid beer yeasts. They lack the ability to survive mead's high gravities, low pH, and native hydrogen peroxide. For this task, you will require the sterner stuff of wine yeast. This book's meads are prepared with Red Star Côte des Blancs, a white wine yeast. Other mead makers swear by the bold, fruit-accentuating nature of Lalvin 71B-1122 yeast. Don't forget to resuscitate your dry yeast in a warm water bath for 10–15 minutes before pitching.

Bruce's Traditional Honey Highlight Mead

Developed and perfected over twenty years of brewing, Bruce Brode's recipe showcases the unique character of your honey and is a great base for adding fruit, spices, or anything your imagination can whip up.

INGREDIENTS | YIELDS 5 GALLONS

3½ gallons water
18 pounds honey (any variety)

1 packet Red Star Côtes des Blancs yeast

2 teaspoons yeast nutrient

Optional Ingredients

2 teaspoons acid blend (a commercial product that consists of a blend of citric, malic, and tartaric acids)

5 teaspoons bentonite

5 teaspoons Sparkolloid (a fining agent for clarifying wine)

1. Sanitize a fermenter. Chill 2½ gallons of water. In a large stockpot, heat the remaining 1 gallon water to a simmer. Turn off the heat and add the honey. Stir to dissolve completely.

2. Revive the yeast in a bowl of lukewarm water.

3. Add the chilled water to the fermenter. Stir in the honey water and ¼ teaspoon of yeast nutrient. Mix thoroughly. Pitch the yeast and allow a primary fermentation for 1 month with temperatures in the 65°F–75°F range. For the next 4 days, add ¼ teaspoon of nutrient in the morning and in the evening.

4. After 1 month or completion of primary fermentation, rack to a secondary container. Allow to age until clear and your samples taste as desired (3–12 months). If needed, add acid blend in small doses until perfect.

5. Before packaging your mead, combine the bentonite (if using, add amount specified by the package) with water and blend for 5 minutes. Add to the mead and allow it to settle overnight. Combine the Sparkolloid (if using) and water (amounts specified by the package) and blend for 5 minutes. Add to the mead and allow it to settle overnight. Rack the finished product carefully into a keg or bottle bucket. Package without sugar for a traditional still mead and enjoy!

Sweet, Medium, Dry

As specified, this recipe will make sweet mead, perfect for dessert or a cold night. If you desire a drier product, simply reduce the amount of honey. For medium mead that has some residual sweetness and honey character, use approximately 15 pounds. To go bone dry and achieve a white-wine-like mead, use 10–12 pounds.

Beer

Beer has always been America's other drink of choice, but it wasn't until the arrival of German and other central European immigrants that modern beer as we know it took off. Before that beer was something of a hit-and-miss proposition in terms of quality, and American beers had a reputation for being harsh, hazy, and not that pleasant.

ALERT

Just a reminder: Traditionally beer is made with barley and wheat, both of which contain heavy amounts of gluten! If you suffer from gluten intolerance or are eating a gluten-free diet, you'll want to try a gluten-free beer recipe.

Today, the quality of brewing ingredients available to brewers, large and small, is unprecedented. Stepping into a homebrew shop, you can find countless different grains, sugars, hops, and yeasts. One place where brewers have an advantage is easy access to topnotch ingredients. Unlike trying to find quality cider ingredients, quality beer ingredients are widely available online and locally.

FACT

It may seem strange, but making beer at home was the norm until the 1800s. Many families brewed their own beer, and you were considered a rude host if you couldn't provide a glass of beer.

There are a few easy lessons to learn for beer brewing:

- Sanitation is critical. You cannot depend on the acidity and strength of your must to defend from infection. Pay extra-close attention to your sanitizing procedures, and ask your local homebrew shop what to use, why, and how.
- Since you must boil your beer must (the freshly pressed fruit juice, or wort, the liquid extracted from the mashing process), you'll need to

worry about cooling the beer down before you can add it to the fermenter with the yeast.

- Fermentation temps are more critical. Beer yeasts used in too warm conditions create undesirable flavors and aromas that can ruin an otherwise good effort.

Here's the good part, you already know the hard stuff—the basics of sanitation, fermentation, and packaging. But there are a number of additional techniques and steps to follow that you'll have to pick up.

- You boil the wort for 60 minutes typically. To do this with the beginner-style batches, you'll need a pot and a stove capable of boiling of 2 gallons of water.
- While the beer is boiling, you'll add hops to the kettle at strategic times. In beer recipes, hop addition timing is always specified in a backward fashion. The time you see (e.g., 60 minutes) indicates that the hops are to be added with that much time remaining in the boil. In other words, if you see a hop addition specified for 60 minutes, you'll want to add them so they are boiled for 1 hour.
- In order to cool the wort to the 60°F–70°F range, you'll need something to dissipate the heat. Advanced brewers use special chilling gadgets, but for your first batches you'll want to take advantage of water's incredible thermal capacity by using very cold water to top up to your target volume.

Beer Ingredients

If beer marketing has managed to soak into your head, you're aware that beer is made of water, barley, hops, and sugar. Each has a different purpose and use in the brewing process and comes in a wide range of forms and types. For the beginning brewer, there are a few key things you'll need to know about malt, hops, and your friendly microbe, yeast.

Malt

To make malt, you first take barley (sometimes wheat) and soak it in a little bit of water. Wait for it to start sprouting, then dry it with hot air. To use malt, you only have to go and buy it. There are over 100 different malt varieties, each with distinct flavors.

Malt Extract

This is what all beginners should use their first time out of the gate. Malt extract is produced by steeping (mashing) malt like you would if you were making a beer completely from scratch. Then, just like other concentrate manufacturers, the maltster (one who makes or deals in malt) boils the wort under a vacuum, to remove water without harshly cooking, until it results in a syrup called liquid malt extract (LME). Alternatively, maltsters can take their worts and spray them with a fine mist in a hot stream of air that drives off the moisture, leaving only a powder called dried malt extract (DME). Both make excellent bases for your beers, but they are not interchangeable on a 1:1 basis because DME is stronger than LME.

Water

Your water must be filtered of all chlorine. Most municipal tap water contains either chlorine or chloramine to keep the water safe to drink until you pour it. To filter your water, use an activated charcoal filter like what you find in your fridge or a water filtration pitcher. For now, avoid reverse osmosis or distilled water. You can also buy plain "drinking water" to substitute.

Hops

Hops are the bitter flower of a fast-growing, temperate climate bine. Brewers use hops to impart a bitter flavor to counteract the sweetness of barley. To extract bitterness, the hops are boiled, and the bitter compounds (called alpha acids) are isomerized and dissolved into the wort. The longer they boil, the more bitterness they impart. Hops are also used to infuse the beer with wide-ranging aromas and flavors. These notes can include the classic European "noble" spice, the brash American pine and citrus, and the earthy British grass and flowers.

Yeast

Like cider, beer needs yeast, and you treat it no differently than the yeasts you've been using for cider. Actually, for a good number of the included cider recipes, you've had beer yeasts, mostly British, recommended to you.

Yeast is arguably more important to the beer-brewing process because of the sheer variety available. Each strain imparts a different set of flavors and aromas. It will take you time to learn what you like, but that's part of the fun!

Plainweiser Pub Ale

This recipe is the most basic beer you can make, and it all starts with malt extract, which is essentially dehydrated beer. In just 4 weeks, you can be drinking your first beery creation.

INGREDIENTS | YIELDS 54 (12-OUNCE) BOTTLES

5 pounds pale liquid malt extract (LME, Pilsner preferred)
¼ ounce Hallertauer Tradition pellet hops (6.0% Alpha Acid), boiled for 60 minutes
¼ ounce Czech Saaz pellet hops (3.5% Alpha Acid) boiled for 5 minutes
Wyeast 1007 German Ale yeast

1. Heat 8 quarts of filtered water to boiling. Turn off the heat. Have 4 gallons of filtered water chilling in the fridge or freezer.
2. Remove the kettle from the heat and stir in the extract. Stir thoroughly, making sure that all the extract is dissolved and the pot bottom is free of any residue. Return to the boil.
3. Once at a boil, begin timing your boil and add the Hallertauer Tradition hops. After 55 minutes have passed, add the Saaz hops; 5 minutes later, turn off the heat.
4. Vigorously stir the pot to create a whirlpool effect, place the lid on, and wait 10 minutes. Chill the beer to 90°F–100°F with a chiller or place the pot in a sink full of ice and barely running cold water.
5. Pour the lukewarm wort into a sanitized fermenter and add chilled water to bring to the desired volume (5.5 gallons typically). Seal the bucket or insert a sanitized stopper in the carboy and shake the beer for 10 minutes to mix.
6. Open the fermenter and grab a hydrometer sample to record the original gravity. Add the yeast to the fermenter and allow the beer to ferment for 1–2 weeks at 66°F.
7. Clean and sanitize 54 (12-ounce) bottles. Prepare a sugar solution of ¾ cup (approximately 4½ ounces by weight) priming (corn) sugar and ¾

cup filtered water. Boil for 10–15 minutes, then add to sanitized bottling bucket.

8. Rack beer onto sugar solution to mix thoroughly.
9. Fill each bottle to approximately 1½–2 fingers width from the top and cap. Store bottles for 2 weeks at 70°F–79°F. Chill one bottle for an hour and check the carbonation level. Wait 1 more week if carbonation is not as desired.

Make Friends!

Inevitably, everyone asks for a carbon copy of the industrial lagers they know. The big breweries invest millions of dollars, and hours, to ensure they can make beers that consistently taste bland. This recipe will get a beginner something similar, but with much better taste!

STATS: Style: Blonde Ale; Brew Type: Extract; For 5 gallons at 1.037 OG, 2.6SRM, 8 IBUs, 3.7% alcohol by volume; 60-minute boil

Glossary

autolysis
The rupturing of yeast cell walls caused by a lack of glycogen. Has a bad flavor impact.

bletting
A process that goes beyond ripening, the start of the decaying process, that is required by some fruits in order to destroy harsh chemicals and unlock the sweet goods inside.

brut
A French term for "dry."

crash
To force a ferment to stop fermenting by lowering the temperature to near freezing. Can either be performed rapidly for immediate clearing or slowly to allow the yeast cells time to clean up as they settle out.

cutting
A viable branch of a tree that can be grafted for cloning purposes.

dry
A cider that finishes with very light residual sweetness.

fine
To add compounds that will force haze-causing particles to settle out.

flocculate
Clumping behavior of yeast as it approaches the end of fermentation. These clumps settle out and become part of the trub (the layer of yeast that appears at the bottom of the fermenter).

grafting
Merging two plants together. Typically done to join hardy apple rootstock to cuttings of fruit-bearing trees that you want to clone.

gravity
A measure of the density of the liquid. For cider, most of the density comes from sugar that the yeast will convert to ethanol.

keeving
An old method of reducing the available nutrients in a cider to leave it naturally sweet.

lees
The leftover yeast that has settled to the bottom of the fermenter. See also *trub*.

must
In the wine and cider world, this is the unfermented juice in its natural sweet state.

packaging
A term for placing the cider in a container for preconsumption storage. It may be a bottle, a keg, a bladder, etc.

pectin
A natural gelling agent found in apples that forms gelatinous globs when exposed to sugar and acid in the presence of heat. Great if you're making jelly or jam, bad if you're making cider.

pellicle
Protein layer that forms to protect cider from oxygen. Appears as a slick, filmy white layer.

pétillant
Cider that has been carbonated to a lightly prickling state. The carbonation is subtle without being over the top.

pitching
Adding yeast to the cider.

racking
Gently transferring liquid (e.g., cider) from one vessel to another.

root stock
A base part of a tree that includes the root ball. Will have one or more scions grafted to it. The rootstock controls factors like the overall height of the tree and its cold/drought tolerance.

russet
A spotty condition found in some apple varieties. Usually found on older heirloom types since modern consumers do not favor the spotted apples.

scion
The part of a grafted tree that carries the desired fruit characteristics.

scratting
To grind up the apples.

sharp
A flavor descriptor for the presence of acid.

sparkling
Effervescent carbonation that tickles the tongue and nose like champagne.

sport
A part of a plant that shows trait differences from the other parts of the plant. For example, the apples on one branch taste and appear completely different from other branches. Some rootstocks come with multiple sports attached to allow a grower to consolidate their trees.

still
No to very little carbonation in the cider.

tannin
A complex polyphenol molecule that imparts bitterness and astringency to the cider. Tannin is important to a well-balanced drink.

tight
A wine term to indicate that a wine has a lot of acid. Considered a good thing for beverages you want to age.

trub
The residue left over at the bottom of your fermenter. This is the beer equivalent of lees.

Additional Resources

Further Reading

For those who want to get really serious about cider making, there are a number of books out there that can teach you tons about the process of growing trees and making cider completely from your own apples.

Cider Hard and Sweet by Ben Watson. This is a fundamental guide to cider making, from a New England perspective.

Cider: Making, Using & Enjoying Sweet & Hard Cider by Annie Proulx and Lew Nichols. Now in its third edition. This book focuses on the process of selecting and growing real cider apple varieties and how to use them. As a bonus, Annie Proulx is the award-winning author of *The Shipping News* and "Brokeback Mountain," so the prose is excellent.

Craft Cider Making by Andrew Lea. If you want the British perspective on cider, then look no further than Andrew Lea's book. It started as an online project to capture his PhD experiences, working for the now-closed Long Ashton Research Station Cider Programme. Now in book form, it's an excellent read with lots of tips and some chemistry!

Making Craft Cider: A Ciderist's Guide by Simon McKie. Providing another British take on cider making. This is a very short book with a balance of chemistry and technique.

Internet Resources

The Cider Workshop
www.ciderworkshop.com
A British discussion group with feeds on Facebook, Twitter, and Google.

OrangePippin.com

www.orangepippin.com

This is an amazing, complete, and comprehensive site for the apple enthusiast or grower, as well as a good source for finding apples locally.

Talisman Cider

http://talisman.com/cider/index.html

This is a website run by Dick Dunn from a family farm in Colorado. This page contains their cider information, as well as access to the Cider Digest, an e-mail discussion group regarding cider making in the United States (also home to the Mead Digest).

Ukcider

www.ukcider.co.uk

A wiki by a U.K. cider enthusiast with a ton of information from various sources.

The Wittenham Hill Cider Portal

www.cider.org.uk

This is Andrew Lea's site, an invaluable resource for the cider enthusiast. More information than you can shake a stick at and with a background that you can trust.

Organizations

The American Wine Society

www.americanwinesociety.org

Every year the American Wine Society holds a major amateur wine competition. While the focus is on the grape, there are a few fruit wine categories that include cider and apple wine.

The Beer Judge Certification Program

www.bjcp.org

It may seem odd to look to a nominally beer-focused group for guidance, but in the United States, the BJCP covers most nonwine home fermentation. They offer two cider classes for special cider score sheets, and are implementing a cider judge certification exam.

Campaign for Real Ale (CAMRA)

www.camra.org.uk/cider

CAMRA has expanded their fight for traditional ale and beer in the United Kingdom to include the traditional arts of cider and perry. They also include a Cider & Perry bar at many CAMRA Festivals, including the Great British Beer Festival in London.

Great Lakes Cider and Perry Association

www.greatlakescider.com

Covering Minnesota to upstate New York, they run an annual cider and perry competition in Michigan and help put on cider events around their area.

North American Fruit Exchange NAFEX

www.nafex.org

A group of amateurs dedicated to finding, collecting, and reviving heirloom varieties of fruits to prevent their loss. For a small annual fee you can join the group and enjoy their newsletter *Pomona* and their online forum dedicated to discussing apples and pears and other fruits.

Northwest Cider Association

www.nwcider.com

Producers, distributors, sellers, and fans all organized together to promote the ciders of the Pacific Northwest.

United States Association of Cider Makers (USACM)

Founded in February 2013, USACM aims to be the craft cider maker's equivalent to the Brewer's Association. It remains to be seen how much involvement there will be for amateur cider makers.

Some Cideries to Try

If you don't see a cidery listed here, don't assume it's bad! The landscape is changing rapidly in the world of cider and so are the available products. Be adventurous and give everything a try, even the large cider makers. Even in a less-than-perfect glass of cider is a lesson to be learned. Make sure to check websites for more recent distribution information.

Widely Distributed

Angry Orchard

www.angryorchard.com

From the brewers of Sam Adams comes Angry Orchard, their attempt at launching a national cider brand. In addition to their three traditional flavors, the Orchard makers do special release ciders like ice ciders, etc. According to their website, the ciders are a blend of culinary apples and cider apples.

Crispin/Fox Barrel

www.crispincider.com/www.foxbarrel.com

Two formerly independent cider makers now owned by SAB Miller's 10th and Blake label. Fox Barrel focuses on pear ciders made from pear juice and not concentrate. Meanwhile, Crispin focuses on cider with regular, varietal, and specialty flavored ciders.

Woodchuck Hard Cider

www.woodchuck.com

The largest of America's cider companies. Started in 1990 and made from the products of a winery making apple wines. Since then it's grown immensely large and is now owned by the C&C Group, the Irish group that produces Bulmers and Magners Irish cider.

Regional

Farnum Hill

www.povertylaneorchards.com

Available in most of New England, New York, and New Jersey. The Farnum Hill ciders are world class, and there's a wide variety to try. Make sure you get to try the Kingston Black! It's a rare chance to try that finicky apple!

Julian Hard Cider

www.julianhardcider.biz

Located in North San Diego County in the foothills above the Colorado Desert, Julian, California, is proof positive that apples will grow anywhere. Relatively new, they've been expanding fast.

Tieton Cider Works

www.tietonciderworks.com

Available in the western United States, Texas, and Illinois, Tieton uses culinary and cider apples to produce at least ten different varieties of cider.

Two Rivers Cider Company

www.tworiverscider.com

Available in northern California and Oregon. A long-running concern for modern American cider companies, Two Rivers has a deeply experimental philosophy with their flavors and at least six varieties year-round.

Wandering Aengus Ciderworks

www.wanderingaengus.com

This Oregon cidery maintains two lines of ciders currently. The Wandering Aengus line uses more than thirty different varieties of traditional cider apples to make several different ciders. The Anthem line focuses on using culinary apples as a basis for different flavor experiments. If you want to know how good a cider can be made from regular apples, give these a try.

Festivals

There may be no better way to experience the growing excitement and variety of the cider market than dropping into a cider festival! Imagine different tables pouring thirty, sixty, or more ciders for your tasting pleasure. Take public transport, a cab, or designate a driver! The festival landscape is forever changing, so do a search to see what's available near you.

CiderCon

www.ciderconference.com

Aimed at the cider professional, the CiderCon is a one-day lecture series on cider concerns and includes a tasting event.

Cider Week

www.ciderweek.com

Taking a cue from the food, wine, and beer industries, cider enthusiasts are starting various festivals with local bars, restaurants, and cideries to promote pomey beverages.

Cider Summit

www.cidersummitnw.com

Started in Seattle in 2010, the Cider Summit is expanding to multiple cities to expand the word about cider.

Franklin County CiderDays

www.ciderdays.org

Possibly the oldest cider festival in America, it happens over multiple days in Franklin County, Massachusetts (in western Massachusetts). It offers multiple seminars about cider making, several tastings, and a BJCP-sanctioned cider competition.

Pour the Core

www.pourthecore.com

Out on Long Island at a picturesque winery, and now in Pennsylvania, this festival brings people together to celebrate the apple and hard cider.

Equipment

Build Your Own Press

www.motherearthnews.com/do-it-yourself/build-a-cider-press-zmaz76soztak .aspx

Correll Cider Presses

www.applejournal.com/correll/index.htm

Beautiful handmade wooden stands for sale.

Pleasant Hill Grain

www.pleasanthillgrain.com/fruit_press.aspx

All the cider making gear you could need.

WoodGears.ca

www.woodgears.ca

Matthias Wandel's great DIY site demonstrating how to build a whole apple-grinding operation with some wood and some know-how.

Sources

www.cidersupply.com

A provider of the chemicals necessary to make an almost-guaranteed keeved cider. This includes the difficult to find pectin methyl esterase (PME).

www.moreflavor.com

One of the country's largest providers of gear for the home brewer, vintner, and cidermaker. They're not exclusively a cider maker stop, but they have plenty of experience with whatever you may be trying to ferment.

www.northernbrewer.com / www.midwestsupplies.com

Another of the country's largest online home fermentation retailers. Both sites are located in the Twin Cities in Minnesota. With lots of good apple and cherry groves in the state, the crew has experience with making beverages from a number of different products.

Useful Processes, Tables, and Calculations

If not specified otherwise, gravity is always calculated in Gravity Units:

Gravity Units = (Gravity – 1) × 1,000
For example, 1.050 = 50 gravity points

Alcohol Calculations

At some point, someone is going to ask you "So, [Insert Your Name], how strong is this stuff?" You'll be able to answer them as long as you know what your Original Gravity (O.G.) measurement was prior to fermentation and where the cider finished, aka its Final Gravity (F.G.)

On the other hand, when you're planning your cider, you may say to yourself, "Self, I want a cider that will be 6.99% alcohol by volume." You'll need to know what your O.G. should start at in order to make that much ethanol!

Target Gravity to Reach Alcohol by Volume

$$\text{Target OG Units} = \frac{\text{Desired ABV}}{0.13125}$$

To make a cider that is 6.99% ABV:

$$\text{Target OG Units} = \frac{6.99}{0.13125}$$

Target OG Units = 53.3
So you want your juice to be at an OG of 1.0533

What's My ABV (Alcohol by Volume)?

ABV = (Original Gravity – Finishing Gravity) × 131
ABV = (1.0533 – 1.000) × 131
ABV = 0.0533 × 131
ABV = 6.98 % ABV

What's My ABW (Alcohol by Weight)?

$ABW = ABV \times 0.8$
$ABW = 6.98 \times 0.8$
$ABW = 5.59\% \; ABW$

What's My ABV (Alcohol by Volume)?

$Original\ Amount\ of\ Alcohol = ABV \times Starting\ Volume$
$Addition\ Amount\ of\ Alcohol = ABV \times Addition\ Volume$

$$ABV = \frac{(Original\ Amount\ of\ Alcohol + Addition\ Amount\ of\ Alcohol)}{(Starting\ Volume + Addition\ Volume)} \times 100$$

What's the new ABV of a cider at 6.9% with a 750 ml bottle of 80% spirit added to it? First of all, you need to be consistent with your volume units (metric versus standard), so since 750 ml roughly equals 0.2 gallons, that is what is used here.

$Original\ Amount\ of\ Alcohol = 6.9\% \times 5.0\ gallons = 0.069 \times 5 = 0.35\ gallons$
$Addition\ Amount\ of\ Alcohol = 40\% \times 0.2\ gallons = 0.4 \times 0.2 = 0.08\ gallons$

$$ABV = \frac{(0.35\ gallons + 0.08\ gallons)}{(5.0\ gallons + 0.2\ gallons)} \times 100$$

$$ABV = \frac{(0.43\ gallons)}{5.2\ gallons)} \times 100$$

$ABV = 0.083 \times 100$
$ABV = 8.3\%$

Gravity Calculations (Dilution/Addition)

You know that your cider's gravity can be adjusted both up and down. These easy calculations will show you just how much water or sugar/juice to add to the mix to achieve your new gravity!

What's My New Gravity (Water Edition)?

$$New\ OG\ Units = \frac{(Starting\ Gravity\ Units \times Starting\ Volume)}{(Starting\ Volume + Addition\ Volume)}$$

4 Gallons of Juice at 1.060, diluted with 1 gallon of water

$$New\ OG\ Points = \frac{(60 \times 4)}{(4\ gallons + 1\ gallons)}$$

$$New\ OG\ Points = \frac{240}{5}$$

New OG Points. = 48

Your 5 gallons of diluted cider will now be at 1.048

What's My New Gravity (Juice/Syrup Edition)

$$New\ OG\ Points = \frac{((Starting\ Gravity\ Units \times Starting\ Volume) + (Addition\ Gravity\ Units \times Addition\ Volume2))}{(Starting\ Volume + Addition\ Volume)}$$

4 gallons of Juice at 1.060, adding 1 gallon of reconstituted apple juice at 1.090

$$New\ OG\ Points = \frac{(60 \times 4) + (90 \times 1)}{(4 + 1)}$$

$$New\ OG\ Points = \frac{(240) + (90)}{(5)}$$

$$New\ OG\ Points = \frac{330}{5}$$

New OG Points = 66

Your new gravity is 5 gallons at 1.066

Carbonation

In order to give your cider the proper whiz bang when you crack open a bottle, you'll want to know how much sugar to add or how much carbon dioxide to inject into the keg to reach your desired bubbly status. These charts will help you get there.

Sugar Priming

▼ PRIMING NEEDED FOR CARBONATION (1 GALLON AND 5 GALLONS)

Volumes CO_2	Sugar per 1 gallon (ounces/weight)	Sugar per 5 gallons (ounces/weight)
1.5	0.34	1.7
1.75	0.48	2.4
2.0	0.62	3.1
2.25	0.74	3.7

Volumes CO_2	Sugar per 1 gallon (ounces/weight)	Sugar per 5 gallons (ounces/weight)
2.5	0.88	4.4
2.75	1.02	5.1
3.0	1.14	5.7
3.25	1.28	6.4
3.5	1.42	7.1
3.75	1.56	7.8
4.0	1.7	8.5
4.25	1.84	9.2
4.5	1.98	9.9
4.75	2.12	10.6
5.0	2.26	11.3

CO_2 Injection

▼ PRESSURE SETTINGS TO CARBONATE CIDER (PRESSURE AS PSI, OR POUNDS PER SQUARE INCH)

Carbonation (Volumes CO_2)	Cider Temperature						
Volumes	30°F	35°F	40°F	45°F	50°F	55°F	60°F
1.5	n/a	n/a	1.4	3.1	4.9	6.8	8.7
1.75	0.4	2.2	4.1	6.1	8.1	10.2	12.3
2.0	2.7	4.7	6.8	9.0	11.3	13.6	15.9
2.25	5.0	7.2	9.6	12.0	14.4	16.9	19.5
2.5	7.2	9.7	12.3	14.9	17.6	20.3	23.1
2.75	9.5	12.2	15.0	17.8	20.7	23.6	26.6
3.0	11.8	14.7	17.7	20.7	23.8	27.00	30.2
3.25	14.0	17.2	20.4	23.6	26.9	30.3	33.8
3.5	16.3	19.6	23.0	26.5	30.1	33.7	37.3
3.75	18.5	22.0	25.7	29.4	33.2	37.0	40.8
4.0	20.7	24.5	28.3	32.3	36.2	40.3	44.4
4.25	22.9	27.0	31.0	35.2	39.3	43.6	47.9
4.5	25.2	29.4	33.7	38.0	42.4	46.9	51.4
4.75	27.4	31.8	36.3	40.9	45.5	50.2	54.9
5.0	29.6	34.2	38.9	43.7	48.6	53.4	58.4

To read this table, find your desired volume along the left hand side and the temperature of your cider along the top. Read to the intersection of those two figures, and set your regulator to the psi (pounds per square inch) listed.

Sulfite Dosing

Sulfite can be an important stabilizing addition for cider makers working from fresh juice straight from the orchard. However, in order to know how much sulfite you need to add, you need to know the pH of your juice. It affects how much is needed to properly stun any undesired microbes.

▼   **SULFITE DOSING BY PH PER GALLON**

pH Range	SO$_2$ Target (ppm)	Metabisulfite (grams/tsp)	Campden Tablets
3.0–3.3	50	0.38/0.25	1
3.3–3.5	100	0.75/0.5	2
3.5–3.8	150	1.14/0.75	3

Anything below a pH of 3 requires no sulfite; anything above 3.8 should be acidified before sulfite additions.

¼ teaspoon of potassium metabisulfite contains approximately 1.5 grams of powder.

Unit Conversions

Like an engineer needs to convert between feet and meters, you may need to convert between a few common units like temperature or gravity measurement.

Plato/Brix to Specific Gravity

$$Specific\ Gravity = \frac{1 + Plato}{\left(258.6 - \left(\frac{Plato}{258.2}\right) \times 227.1\right)}$$

Convert Fahrenheit to Celsius and Back

$$Celsius = \frac{(Fahrenheit - 32)}{1.8}$$

$$Fahrenheit = (Celsius \times 1.8) + 32$$

Cider Tracking Sheet

Cider Name: _____ Started: _____

Starting Gravity: _____ Final Gravity: _____ Alcohol By Volume: _____

Target Style: _____

Target Profile: _____

_____

_____

Ingredients (Amount, Variety, Source, Gravity, pH, acidity)

Juice: _____

_____

pH: _____ Sulfited?: Y / N   Amount Added: _____

Yeast: _____

Yeast Nutrient: _____

Other Ingredients (Amount, Variety, Source, Gravity, When Added)

_____

_____

_____

_____

_____

Procedure Notes:

_____

_____

_____

Fermentation:

_____

_____

_____

_____

_____

Date Primary Finished: _____

Conditioning:

_____

_____

_____

Date Packaged: _____ **Packaging Method:** _____

Carbonation: Still / Pétillant / Medium / Sparkling Finish: Dry / Medium / Sweet

Acid Balance: Low / Medium / High Tannin Balance: Low / Medium / High

Adjustments:

_____

Tasting Notes:

Date Tasted: _____ **Temperature:** _____

Notes: (Aroma? Flavor? Finish? Mouthfeel?) _____

_____

_____

_____

Date Tasted: _____ **Temperature:** _____

Notes: (Aroma? Flavor? Finish? Mouthfeel?) _____

_____

_____

_____

Date Tasted: _____ **Temperature:** _____

Notes: (Aroma? Flavor? Finish? Mouthfeel?) _____

_____

_____

_____

Thoughts on Changes: _____

_____

_____

_____

_____

Index